DATA ANALYTICS 2017

The Sixth International Conference on Data Analytics

November 12 - 16, 2017

Barcelona, Spain

DATA ANALYTICS 2017 Editors

Sandjai Bhulai, Vrije Universiteit Amsterdam, the Netherlands

Dimitris Kardaras, Athens University of Economics and Business, Greece

Printed from e-media with permission by:

Curran Associates, Inc.
57 Morehouse Lane
Red Hook, NY 12571

Some format issues inherent in the e-media version may also appear in this print version.

Printed by Curran Associates, Inc. (2017)

International Academy, Research, and Industry Association (IARIA)
412 Derby Way
Wilmington, DE 19810

Phone: (408) 893-6407
Fax: (408) 527-6351

petre@iaria.org

Additional copies of this publication are available from:

Curran Associates, Inc.
57 Morehouse Lane
Red Hook, NY 12571 USA
Phone: 845-758-0400
Fax: 845-758-2633
Email: curran@proceedings.com
Web: www.proceedings.com

Table of Contents

DATA ANALYTICS 2017

Forward

The Sixth International Conference on Data Analytics (DATA ANALYTICS 2017), held between November 12 - 16, 2017, in Barcelona, Spain, continued a series of events related to data analytics, special mechanisms and features of applying principles of data analytics, application oriented analytics, and target-area analytics.

Processing of terabytes to petabytes of data, or incorporating non-structural data and multi-structured data sources and types require advanced analytics and data science mechanisms for both raw and partially-processed information. Despite considerable advancements on high performance, large storage, and high computation power, there are challenges in identifying, clustering, classifying, and interpreting of a large spectrum of information.

The event was very competitive in its selection process and very well perceived by the international scientific and industrial communities. As such, it has attracted excellent contributions and active participation from all over the world. We were very pleased to receive a large amount of top quality contributions.

The conference had the following tracks:

- Fundamentals for data analytics
- Big data
- Target analytics
- Predictive data analytics
- Sentiment/opinion analysis

We take here the opportunity to warmly thank all the members of the DATA ANALYTICS 2017 technical program committee, as well as all the reviewers. The creation of such a high quality conference program would not have been possible without their involvement. We also kindly thank all the authors that dedicated much of their time and effort to contribute to DATA ANALYTICS 2017. We truly believe that, thanks to all these efforts, the final conference program consisted of top quality contributions.

We also gratefully thank the members of the DATA ANALYTICS 2017 organizing committee for their help in handling the logistics and for their work that made this professional meeting a success.

We hope that DATA ANALYTICS 2017 was a successful international forum for the exchange of ideas and results between academia and industry and to promote further progress in the field of data analytics.

We also hope that Barcelona, Spain, provided a pleasant environment during the conference and everyone saved some time to enjoy the unique charm of the city.

DATA ANALYTICS 2017 Chairs

DATA ANALYTICS Steering Committee

Sandjai Bhulai, Vrije Universiteit Amsterdam, the Netherlands
Dimitris K. Kardaras, Athens University of Economics and Business, Greece
Ivana Semanjski, Ghent University, Belgium / University of Zagreb, Croatia
Eiko Yoneki, University of Cambridge, UK
Andrew Rau-Chaplin, Dalhousie University, Canada
Rudolf Berrendorf, Bonn-Rhein-Sieg University, Germany
Les Sztandera, Philadelphia University, USA
Kerstin Lemke-Rust, Hochschule Bonn-Rhein-Sieg, Germany
Prabhat Mahanti, University of New Brunswick, Canada

DATA ANALYTICS Industry/Research Advisory Committee

Alain Crolotte, Teradata Corporation - El Segundo, USA
Tiziana Guzzo, National Research Council/Institute of Research on Population and Social Policies - Rome, Italy
Serge Mankovski, CA Technologies, Spain
Yanchang Zhao, RDataMining.com, Australia
Masahiro Terabe, Mitsubishi Research Institute, Inc., Japan
Thomas Klemas, SimSpace Corporation, USA
George Tambouratzis, Institute for Language and Speech Processing - Athena Research Centre, Greece
Mario Zechner, Know-Center, Austria
Azad Naik, Microsoft, USA

DATA ANALITICS 2017
Committee

DATA ANALYTICS Steering Committee

Sandjai Bhulai, Vrije Universiteit Amsterdam, the Netherlands
Dimitris K. Kardaras, Athens University of Economics and Business, Greece
Ivana Semanjski, Ghent University, Belgium / University of Zagreb, Croatia
Eiko Yoneki, University of Cambridge, UK
Andrew Rau-Chaplin, Dalhousie University, Canada
Rudolf Berrendorf, Bonn-Rhein-Sieg University, Germany
Les Sztandera, Philadelphia University, USA
Kerstin Lemke-Rust, Hochschule Bonn-Rhein-Sieg, Germany
Prabhat Mahanti, University of New Brunswick, Canada

DATA ANALYTICS Industry/Research Advisory Committee

Alain Crolotte, Teradata Corporation - El Segundo, USA
Tiziana Guzzo, National Research Council/Institute of Research on Population and Social Policies - Rome, Italy
Serge Mankovski, CA Technologies, Spain
Yanchang Zhao, RDataMining.com, Australia
Masahiro Terabe, Mitsubishi Research Institute, Inc., Japan
Thomas Klemas, SimSpace Corporation, USA
George Tambouratzis, Institute for Language and Speech Processing - Athena Research Centre, Greece
Mario Zechner, Know-Center, Austria
Azad Naik, Microsoft, USA

DATA ANALYTICS 2017 Technical Program Committee

Mohd Helmy Abd Wahab, Universiti Tun Hussein Onn Malaysia, Malaysia
Rajeev Agrawal, US Army Engineer Research and Development Center, USA
Rudolf Berrendorf, Bonn-Rhein-Sieg University, Germany
Nik Bessis, Edge Hill University, UK
Sanjay Bhansali, Google, Mountain View, USA
Jabran Bhatti, Televic Rail NV, Belgium
Sandjai Bhulai, Vrije Universiteit Amsterdam, The Netherlands
Amar Budhiraja, IIIT-Hyderabad, India
Juan Vicente Capella Hernández, Universitat Politècnica de València, Spain
Miguel Ceriani, Queen Mary University of London, UK
Lijun Chang, University of New South Australia, Australia
Alain Crolotte, Teradata Corporation - El Segundo, USA

Corné de Ruijt, Endouble, Amsterdam, Netherlands
Ma. del Pilar Angeles, Universidad Nacional Autonoma de Mexico, Mexico
Zhi-Hong Deng, Peking University, China
Mohand Djeziri, Aix Marseille University (AMU), France
Atakan Dogan, Anadolu University, Turkey
Suleyman Eken, Kocaeli University, Turkey
Muhammad Fahad, Centre Scientifique et Technique du Batiment CSTB (Sophia-Antipolis), France
Yixiang Fang, University of Hong Kong, Hong Kong
Diego Galar, Luleå University of Technology, Sweden
Wensheng Gan, Harbin Institute of Technology, Shenzhen, China
Amir H. Gandomi, BEACON - An NSF Center for the Study of Evolution in Action | Michigan State University, USA
Catalina García García, Universidad de Granada, Spain
Felix Gessert, University of Hamburg, Germany
Ilias Gialampoukidis, Information Technologies Institute | Centre of Research & Technology - Hellas, Thessaloniki, Greece
William Grosky, University of Michigan, USA
Jerzy Grzymala-Busse, University of Kansas - Lawrence, USA
Ruchir Gupta, IIITDM Jabalpur, India
Tiziana Guzzo, National Research Council/Institute of Research on Population and Social Policies - Rome, Italy
Mohamed Aymen Ben HajKacem, University of Tunis, Tunisia
Houcine Hassan, Universitat Politècnica de València, Spain
Felix Heine, Hannover University of Applied Sciences and Arts, Germany
Carlos Henggeler Antunes, INESCC | University of Coimbra, Portugal
Jean Hennebert, University of Applied Sciences HES-SO, Switzerland
Tzung-Pei Hong, National University of Kaohsiung, Taiwan
LiGuo Huang, Southern Methodist University, USA
Sergio Ilarri, University of Zaragoza, Spain
Olaf Jacob, Neu-Ulm University of Applied Sciences, Germany
Giuseppe Jurman, Fondazione Bruno Kessler (FBK), Trento, Italy
Zhao Kang, Southern Illinois University, USA
Dimitris K. Kardaras, Athens University of Economics and Business, Greece
Sue Kase, U.S. Army Research Laboratory, USA
Quist-Aphetsi Kester, CRITAC | Ghana Technology University College, Ghana
Thomas Klemas, SimSpace Corporation, USA
Chao Lan, University of Wyoming, USA
Kerstin Lemke-Rust, Hochschule Bonn-Rhein-Sieg, Germany
Ye Liang, Oklahoma State University, USA
Dimitrios Liparas, Information Technologies Institute (ITI) - Centre for Research & Technology Hellas (CERTH), Greece
Sungsu Lim, KAIST, Korea
Hongfu Liu, Northeastern University, Boston, USA

Honglei Liu, University of California, Santa Barbara, USA
Weimo Liu, GraphSQL Inc., USA
Xiaomo Liu, Thomson Reuters Research, USA
Zhi Liu, University of North Texas, USA
Corrado Loglisci, Università di Bari, Italy
Prabhat Mahanti, University of New Brunswick, Canada
Arif Mahmood, Qatar University, Doha, Qatar / University of Western Australia, Australia /
Sebastian Maneth, University of Bremen, Germany
Serge Mankovski, CA Technologies, Spain
Juan J. Martinez C., "Gran Mariscal deAyacucho" University, Venezuela
Archil Maysuradze, Lomonosov Moscow State University, Russia
Michele Melchiori, Università degli Studi di Brescia, Italy
Letizia Milli, University of Pisa, Italy
Azad Naik, Microsoft, USA
Maitreya Natu, Tata Research Development and Design Centre, Pune, India
Richi Nayak, Queensland University of Technology, Brisbane, Australia
Jingchao Ni, Pennsylvania State University, USA
Patrick Obrien, Montana State University, USA
Luca Pappalardo, University of Pisa, Italy
André Petermann, University of Leipzig, Germany
Massimiliano Petri, University of Pisa | University Center 'Logistic Systems', Italy
Gianvito Pio, University of Bari Aldo Moro, Italy
Luigi Portinale, Universita' del Piemonte Orientale "A. Avogadro", Italy
Raphael Puget, LIP6 | UPMC, France
Minghui Qiu, Singapore Management University, Singapore
Helena Ramalhinho Lourenço, Universitat Pompeu Fabra, Barcelona, Spain
Zbigniew W. Ras, University of North Carolina, Charlotte, USA / Warsaw University of Technology, Poland / Polish-Japanese Academy of IT, Poland
Andrew Rau-Chaplin, Dalhousie University, Canada
Yenumula B. Reddy, Grambling State University, USA
Manjeet Rege, University of St. Thomas, USA
Alessandro Rozza, Waynaut, Italy
Gunter Saake, Otto-von-Guericke-University Magdeburg, Germany
Donatello Santoro, Università della Basilicata, Italy
Anirban Sarkar, National Institute of Technology, Durgapur, India
Ivana Semanjski, Ghent University, Belgium / University of Zagreb, Croatia
Sujala D. Shetty, Birla Institute of Technology & Science, Pilani, India
Rouzbeh A. Shirvani, Howard University, USA
Leon Shyue-Liang Wang, National University of Kaohsiung, Taiwan
Josep Silva, Universitat Politècnica de València, Spain
Marek Śmieja, Jagiellonian University, Poland
Dora Souliou, National Technical University of Athens, Greece
María Estrella Sousa Vieira, University of Vigo, Spain
Les Sztandera, Philadelphia University, USA

George Tambouratzis, Institute for Language and Speech Processing, Athena, Greece
Mingjie Tang, Hortonworks, USA
Farhan Tauheed, Oracle research labs, Zurich, Switzerland
Marijn ten Thij, Vrije Universiteit Amsterdam, Netherlands
Masahiro Terabe, Mitsubishi Research Institute, Inc., Japan
Juan-Manuel Torres-Moreno, Université d'Avignon et des Pays de Vaucluse, France
Li-Shiang Tsay, North Carolina A&T State University, USA
Chrisa Tsinaraki, EU Joint Research Center - Ispra, Italy
Aditya Tulsyan, Massachusetts Institute of Technology, USA
Murat Osman Unalir, Ege University, Turkey
Roman Vaculin, IBM Research, USA
Genoveva Vargas-Solar, French Council of Scientific Research | LIG-LAFMIA, France
Simon Waddington, King's College London, UK
Haibo Wang, Texas A&M International University, USA
Liqiang Wang, University of Central Florida, USA
Wolfram Wöß, Institute for Application Oriented Knowledge Processing | Johannes Kepler University, Linz, Austria
Feng Yan, University of Nevada, Reno, USA
Eiko Yoneki, University of Cambridge, UK
Fouad Zablith, Olayan School of Business | American University of Beirut, Lebanon
Mario Zechner, Know-Center, Austria
Yanchang Zhao, RDataMining.com, Australia
Yichuan Zhao, Georgia State University, USA
Angen Zheng, University of Pittsburgh, USA
Qiang Zhu, University of Michigan, USA

Copyright Information

For your reference, this is the text governing the copyright release for material published by IARIA.

The copyright release is a transfer of publication rights, which allows IARIA and its partners to drive the dissemination of the published material. This allows IARIA to give articles increased visibility via distribution, inclusion in libraries, and arrangements for submission to indexes.

I, the undersigned, declare that the article is original, and that I represent the authors of this article in the copyright release matters. If this work has been done as work-for-hire, I have obtained all necessary clearances to execute a copyright release. I hereby irrevocably transfer exclusive copyright for this material to IARIA. I give IARIA permission or reproduce the work in any media format such as, but not limited to, print, digital, or electronic. I give IARIA permission to distribute the materials without restriction to any institutions or individuals. I give IARIA permission to submit the work for inclusion in article repositories as IARIA sees fit.

I, the undersigned, declare that to the best of my knowledge, the article is does not contain libelous or otherwise unlawful contents or invading the right of privacy or infringing on a proprietary right.

Following the copyright release, any circulated version of the article must bear the copyright notice and any header and footer information that IARIA applies to the published article.

IARIA grants royalty-free permission to the authors to disseminate the work, under the above provisions, for any academic, commercial, or industrial use. IARIA grants royalty-free permission to any individuals or institutions to make the article available electronically, online, or in print.

IARIA acknowledges that rights to any algorithm, process, procedure, apparatus, or articles of manufacture remain with the authors and their employers.

I, the undersigned, understand that IARIA will not be liable, in contract, tort (including, without limitation, negligence), pre-contract or other representations (other than fraudulent misrepresentations) or otherwise in connection with the publication of my work.

Exception to the above is made for work-for-hire performed while employed by the government. In that case, copyright to the material remains with the said government. The rightful owners (authors and government entity) grant unlimited and unrestricted permission to IARIA, IARIA's contractors, and IARIA's partners to further distribute the work.

Mining Long-term Topics from a Real-time Feed

Marijn ten Thij

Vrije Universiteit Amsterdam,
Faculty of Science,
Amsterdam, The Netherlands
Email: m.c.ten.thij@vu.nl

***Abstract*—In our current society, the availability of data has gone from scarce to abundant: huge volumes of data are generated every second. A significant part of these data are generated on social media platforms, which provide a very volatile flow of information. Leveraging the information that is buried in this fast stream of messages, poses a serious challenge. In this paper, we aim to distinguish all topics that are discussed in real-time in a social media feed by employing clustering and algorithmic techniques. We evaluate our approach by comparing the results to a post-hoc clustering approach.**

***Keywords*–Topic Detection and Tracking; Twitter; Cluster Analysis; Content analysis; First Story Detection.**

I. Introduction

In recent years, social media have revolutionized the way people communicate and interact with each other. This development has transformed the Internet into a more personal and participatory medium, where social networking is the top online activity. The massive amount of data, that is accumulated as a result of these online interactions, discussions, social signals, and other engagements, forms a valuable source of information. In our current work, we focus on the application and leveraging of this information for a particular sector: the horticulture industry.

The horticulture industry is a traditional sector in which growers are focused on production, and in which many traders use their own transactions as the main source of information. Growers and traders, therefore, lack data about consumer trends and how the products are used and appreciated. This results in reactive management with very little anticipation to events in the future. Social media can provide the opportunities to enhance the market orientation of the horticulture industry. For example, tracking how and when the products of the industry are mentioned in a social media feed is an important addition to current techniques used in the horticulture industry to actively listen to customers. The feedback that is thus collected, can be used to understand, react, and provide value to customers.

Since the information from a social media feed is very volatile, it is important that the information is processed in real-time. To cope with this challenge of processing in real-time, we propose an algorithm to find and distinguish the aforementioned mentions in a real-time information feed. To do so, we define a story as the repeated and related mentions of a product in the real-time feed. Furthermore, we use the term topic for the content of these mentions within a story. In this paper, we base our algorithm on data that is scraped from Twitter. However, all parts of the algorithm can be easily modified to fit data scraped from other platforms, e.g., Instagram and Facebook, allowing for wider use of the designed approach. Using our algorithm, we are able to give an overview of what is being discussed in real-time with respect to the horticulture sector. This enables businesses to keep up with their reputation and customer satisfaction.

The lay-out of the paper is as follows. First, we discuss the related research in Section II. Then, we describe the dataset used for testing this filtering approach in Section III. Next, we employ clustering techniques to define a ground truth to test our filtering approach in Section IV, followed by the description of our filtering approach in Section V. The results of the comparison of these two approaches are then discussed in Section VI. Finally, we conclude the paper in Section VII with some discussion and opportunities for future work.

II. Related Research

The detection of emerging topics in a real-time information stream has been extensively studied. A good example is the Topic Detection and Tracking (TDT) research project [1], in which news items are combined in stories, that are tracked through time. Examples of TDT systems are the Europe Media Monitor [2], a platform that links news articles mentioning similar topics over time and across languages; and RTreporter [3] and Hotstream [4], two systems for breaking news detection and tracking in Twitter.

Based on the TDT project, Allan [5] defines five tasks that are part of topic detection and tracking, namely,

- Story Segmentation; dividing the transcript of a news show into individual stories.
- First Story Detection; recognizing the onset of a new topic in the stream of news stories.
- Cluster Detection; grouping all stories as they arrive, based on the topics they discuss.
- Tracking; monitoring the stream of news stories to find additional stories on a topic that was identified using several sample stories.
- Story Link Detection; deciding whether two randomly selected stories discuss the same news topic.

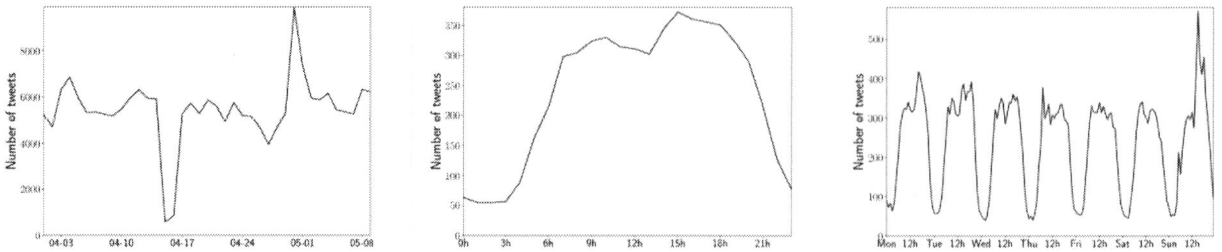

(a) Daily tweet numbers (b) Daily tweet rhythm (c) Weekly tweet rhythm

Figure 1. Overall statistics of the tweets used in this study. Figure 1a shows the daily number of tweets received by our scraper that were tagged as mentioning at least one product. Figures 1b and 1c show the average daily and weekly rhythms.

In our work, we focus on three of the five tasks, namely First Story Detection, Cluster Detection, and Tracking, to a real-time feed of Twitter messages. To perform the aforementioned tasks, which have some overlap, several approaches have been studied in the past. For instance, Weng and Lee [6] used clustering of wavelet-based signals for event detection, and Huang et al. [7] use a concept graph to discover topics by clustering the graph. In this paper, we use a clustering algorithm to find and track topics over time.

Several clustering algorithms have been developed over time, e.g., Affinity Propagation [8], Parameter-free Affinity Propagation [9], Spectral Clustering [10], DBSCAN [11], and Latent Dirichlet Allocation (LDA) [12]. A large body of studies have been devoted to adapting and extending LDA. For instance, Holz and Teresniak [13] employ the term co-occurence to track topics and topic change over time in news documents. Furthermore, Wang and McCallum [14] extend LDA to 'Topics Over Time' to incorporate time on top of term co-occurences. Staying in a similar scope as LDA, Swan and Allan [15] present a technique of topic detection on a corpus of documents based on co-occurences of Natural Language Processing (NLP) features extracted from the documents. In our study, we combine NLP-features of the messages in the information feed with the Affinity Propagation clustering algorithm, since it does not require the number of clusters as input parameter.

III. DATASET

The goal of our work is to develop a system that performs a real-time analysis of messages posted on Twitter, which we implement in *python*. Hence, we set up our own Twitter scraper. We scrape the tweets using the filter stream of the Twitter Application Programming Interface (API) [16]. Since we do not have access to the Twitter Firehose, we do not receive all tweets that we request due to rate limitations by Twitter [17]. Within these restrictions, we set up a stream with the goal to scrape as many Dutch tweets as possible. We use the filter stream with the options **language**, which we set to Dutch, and **track**, where a list of words must be defined. All tweets containing one of these words are caught by the Twitter API. Based on the number of occurences of these words in the dataset described in [18], we define a list of 400 general Dutch words (e.g., *'een, het, ik, niet, maar, die, de, bij, ook'*).

For this study, we do not use all tweets that we scraped in the way mentioned above. Since we are only interested in tweets that could be of value for the horticulture industry, we select a subset of these tweets that cover topics of interest to this industry, using a list of product names provided by our partners from GroentenFruit Huis[1] and Floricode[2]. The terms are split up into two lists: one containing fruits and vegetables, e.g., apple, orange, and mango, and the other containing flowers and plants, e.g., tulip, rose, and lily. We use the tweets that have mentioned at least one of the products on the lists that we obtained from April 1st 2017 12 AM through May 10th 2017 12 AM in Coordinated Universal Time (UTC). During this interval, we have not obtained any tweets from 7 AM on April 15th through April 16th at 6 PM, which is due to the down-time of our scraper. This down-time directly explains the decrease in the number of tweets that can be seen in Figure 1a, which shows the daily number of tweets that are tagged to mention at least one of the products of interest. Since we only consider Dutch tweets, we see a clear circadian rhythm in the number of interesting tweets per hour, both on the daily and weekly scale (shown in Figures 1b and 1c, respectively).

As we want to discover the topics that are being discussed in the real-time stream of messages that we receive, we develop an online algorithm to cluster the incoming tweets on an hourly basis. To test this algorithm, we select two intervals that span a total of two weeks, for which we compare the output of our algorithm for a given set of tweets to the results of a clustering algorithm run on the entire set of tweets at once. Due to the down-time of the scraper and the associated loss of tweets, we choose April 1st to April 15th and April 23th to May 7th as the intervals we process.

IV. CLUSTERING

As we are interested in topics that are discussed with respect to a large quantity of products, we use a post-hoc clustering technique on all tweets mentioning a certain product in an interval to produce a 'ground-truth' or baseline of topics, instead of using labor-intensive human annotated datasets. Since we do not know how many clusters there are going to be, we choose a clustering algorithm that does not need

[1] https://www.groentenfruithuis.nl/

[2] http://www.floricode.com/

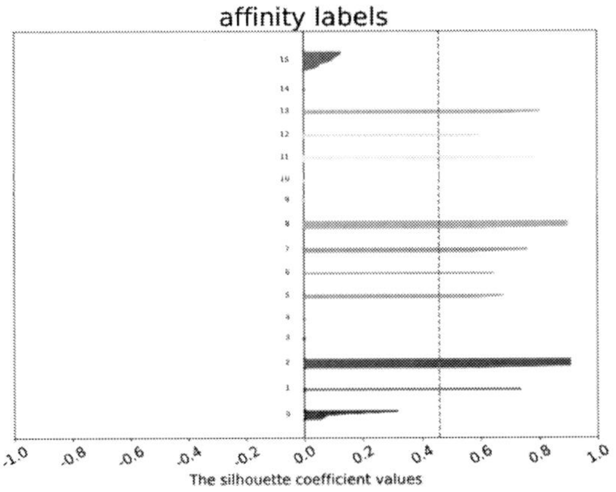

Figure 2. Silhouette scores for clusters of tweets mentioning 'celeriac' that were placed between April 23th and May 7th.

the number of clusters as an input parameter. Furthermore, we want to use an off-the-shelf clustering algorithm that is contained in an existing and actively maintained python module. Therefore, we choose to use Affinity Propagation [8] to produce our baseline, which is contained in the *scikit-learn* [19] module. Furthermore, we employ silhouettes [20] on the clusters formed by Affinity Propagation, to measure their consistency. If a silhouette score of a member of a cluster is close to 1 it is clustered correctly. Silhouette scores close to -1 indicate that the element is similar to different clusters. Clusters that consist of a single element automatically receive the score 0. As an example of this analysis, Figure 2 shows the silhouette scores for the tweets mentioning 'celeriac'. The average silhouette score of all elements is indicated by the red dashed line. The silhouette plot visualizes the silhouette scores per item that has been clustered. Each cluster is represented by a different color and the larger the silhouette is, the more tweets are contained in that cluster.

V. OBTAINING LONG-TERM TOPICS

Although the post-hoc clustering approach works quite well using data from a longer interval, applying the same approach in a real-time fashion is not possible, since this algorithm can only process a complete dataset. Therefore, we develop an approach that can combine the results of hourly clustering, based on the received tweets during that hour.

This approach employs three phases. For the first phase, the tweets mentioning a certain product over the last hour are combined into a corpus. In this step, the tweets are tokenized, stemmed and Part Of Speech (POS) tagged. Then, using an N-dimensional space that represents this constructed corpus per product, the tweets are clustered using Affinity Propagation [8]. After this step, the clusters are represented by the set of tokens contained in their corresponding tweets. Finally, all new clusters are compared to clusters that have been found in previous hours through what we define as a 'stories'. Such a story can be seen as a cluster of clusters over time, and thereby combines the tweets that are similar. The algorithm we use to combine a list of clusters, denoted by C, with the list of current stories, denoted by S, is described in the algorithm displayed in Figure 3. Besides the input of the clusters and stories, the algorithm uses three other parameters. The first two parameters, the similarity threshold and the original threshold, denoted by J_t and J_o, respectively, are used to determine whether a cluster and a story are similar to each other. When a cluster is compared to a story, the comparison is done on two levels. First, the similarity between the tokens of the cluster and the current tokens of the story are calculated. Secondly, the similarity between the cluster tokens and the original story tokens are calculated. Both these similarities are calculated using the Jaccard similarity [21]. The Jaccard similarity between two sets A and B is defined as

Require: list of current stories: S, list of clusters C, similarity threshold: J_t, original similarity threshold: J_o and maximum idle time m_i.

```
for c ∈ C do
    boolean matched = False
    for s ∈ S do
        if s is similar to c: then
            matched = True
            add cluster c to story s
        end if
    end for
    if not matched then
        add c to new story s' and add s' to S
    end if
end for
for s ∈ S do
    update delay: d_s = d_s + 1
    if d = m_i then
        close s and remove s from S.
    end if
end for
return S
```

Figure 3. *Storify* algorithm that assigns the clusters of to the stories.

$$J(A, B) = \frac{|A \cap B|}{|A \cup B|}$$

If both values are not below their respective thresholds, being J_t and J_o, the cluster is added to the story and its tokens become the current story tokens. The reason that we employ two thresholds for the question of similarity is to ensure that the topic of the story does not drift over time from one topic to another. Finally, the maximum idle time, denoted by m_i, is defined as the maximum time that a story remains active without having a cluster added to it. When a story has not obtained an additional cluster for m_i time intervals, then it is closed. We do this to ensure that topics are not dragged on too long, without adding interesting messages to them.

Suppose clustering is done using all incoming tweets during the last hour. As an example of how the algorithm works, consider the following example tweets *"Pick tulips on Dam Square, for free!"*, placed on January 21st 2017 around 9:30 AM, and *"Tulipday on Dam Square great succes, 20.000 free tulips picked."*, placed on January 22nd 2017 around 2:15 PM, which have both been retweeted twice within a few minutes after posting. Then, one of the clusters on January

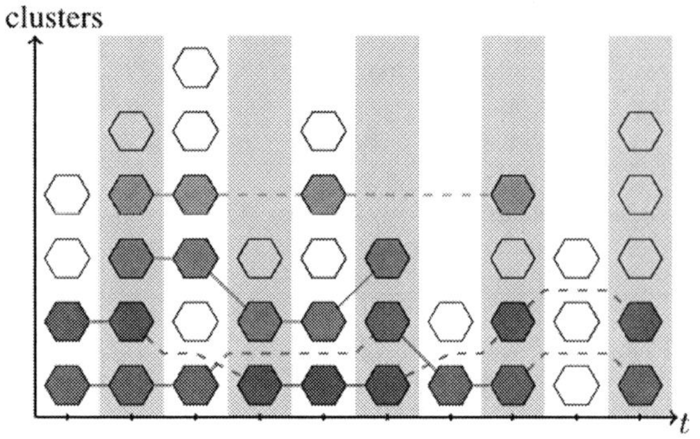

Figure 4. Example of clusters that are linked through time by the storify algorithm.

21st at 10 AM will contain the first tweet and its retweets, containing the following tokens $[pick, tulip, Dam\ Square, free]$. Suppose this cluster triggers a new story, then this story will match with the cluster of the messages places on January 22nd 2017 (the tokens of this cluster are: $[Tulipday, Dam\ Square, succes, tulip, free, pick]$, thus the story and cluster are similar) and if it has not been more than m_i hours ago since the last cluster was added, the new cluster is added to the story.

Figure 4 visualizes an example of our approach to combine clusters through time, which we call the *storify* algorithm. On the y-axis, individual clusters are indicated by black hexagons and the x-axis shows how time progresses. The connections between clusters over time are indicated by filling the clusters in the color of the overal story (e.g., red). If two clusters are combined in the same story in consecutive hours, they are linked by a solid line. If there are a few hours in which a story has been idle, this is indicated by a dashed line.

VI. Performance Measurement

Measuring the performance of the storify algorithm can pose a challenge, because it is difficult to determine a ground-truth for all products considered. Therefore, we employed a post-hoc clustering algorithm on the selected intervals of tweets mentioning a product. Also, we execute the storify algorithm on the same tweets, where we set the parameters $m_i = 48$, $J_t = 0.9$, and $J_o = 0.6$. These parameter values are chosen with the intention to only cluster very similar tweets and to join clusters in a story if they mention similar terms. Futhermore, the max idle time of two days ensures that we do not exclude intervals that arise through the natural circadian rhythm of use Twitter.

Let us first consider the outcomes of both approaches for a single product. Here, we again use silhouettes [20] to visualize the how well the tweets are divided up into stories for our algorithm and clusters for the Affinity Propagation algorithm. Recall that if a silhouette score of a member of a cluster is close to 1 it is clustered correctly. Also, scores close to -1 indicate that the element is similar to different clusters. Figure 5 gives an example of the silhouette scores for tweets mentioning 'chrysanthemum' in the interval April 23th and May 7th. In this figure, we see that the average silhouette score

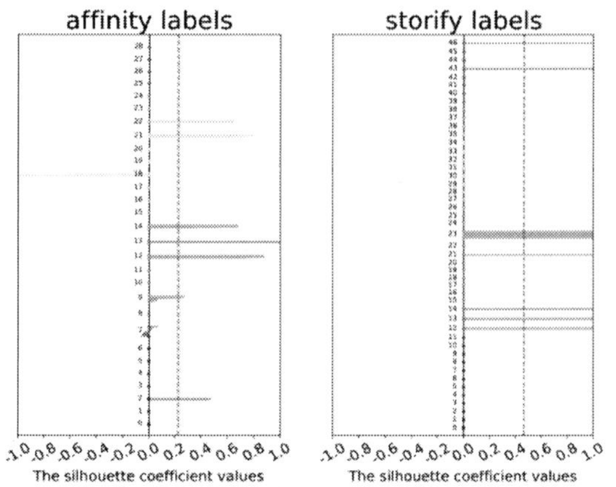

Figure 5. Silhouette scores for clusters and stories of tweets mentioning 'chrysantemum', placed between April 23th and May 7th.

for the storify clustering is larger than the Affinity Propagation clustering. Furthermore, in the Affinity plot, we see that some tweets have a negative silhouette score, whereas in the storify plot all values are positive. Even though the results are not consistent over all products, our approach outperforms the naive total clustering and provides for a better fit of the data for the product 'chrysantemum'.

For a more general comparison of both approaches, we use three metrics used for cluster comparison, namely homogeneity, completeness, and the v-measure. Homogeneity measures if each cluster contains only members of a single class. Completeness measures if all members of a given class are assigned to the same cluster. Finally, the v-measure is defined as the harmonic mean of homogeneity and completeness of the clustering, as defined in [22].

Figure 6 shows the distribution of the three parameters for the described parameter settings. Clearly, the completeness scores are the lowest overall. This can be easily explained, since the storify approach gives more clusters of singular tweets than the Affinity Propagation does. This is a direct result of the usage of the maximum idle time and is, therefore, an expected outcome. In general, these three metrics are all skewed towards 1. Therefore, we can conclude our approach gives similar results as the naive total clustering approach, even though we have not optimized the parameters of our model.

VII. Conclusion and Future Work

Given the results of our analysis thus far, the storify algorithm appears to be very promising for application to a real-time social media feed. Even though we have not yet optimized the parameters of the model, the results compare very well with a direct post-hoc clustering done on all the data. The only difference between the two approaches is that the overall clustering finds fewer clusters containing a single tweet. To assess whether this difference undermines the validity of the algorithm, we plan to extend the analysis of these results not only to the groups in which the tweets are clustered, but also to the time at which these tweets are placed. For this analysis, the metric proposed by Krippendorff [23] seems very promising.

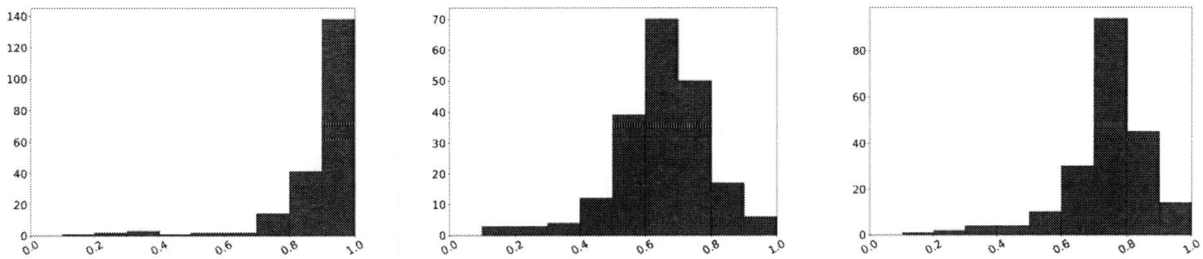

(a) Homogeinity (b) Completeness (c) V-Score

Figure 6. Distribution of homogeneity, completeness, and v-score based on the outcomes over all products, based on tweets placed from April 23th to May 7th.

Using this metric, we can also compare whether or not the time of placement of the tweets that are clustered between approaches, are similar or very different. Furthermore, we use a one-to-one mapping to map clusters to stories. Using a one-to-many mapping gives the opportunity for stories to become overlapping, which is an interesting topic for further study.

At this moment, the algorithm only runs ad-hoc using data acquired in our tool the HortiRadar [24]. Given the promising results and our interest to find topics that are discussed in a real-time feed, we aim to implement the algorithm in the HortiRadar. Using this real-time implementation, we can then show a visualization of the stories identified by the algorithm in the HortiRadar, which makes the identification of stories in a real-time feed a lot easier. Simultaniously, this visualization can be used as a validation of the chosen parameter settings and the clustering mechanism. Once the real-time visualization is up and running, the next step is to use the results of this study for business purposes in the horticulture industry.

ACKNOWLEDGMENTS

This work is funded as part of PPS KV 1406-101 of the Topsector Tuinbouw & Uitgangsmaterialen. The author thanks Sandjai Bhulai and Rahiel Kasim for their feedback and help designing and implementing this approach.

REFERENCES

[1] J. G. Fiscus and G. R. Doddington, *Topic Detection and Tracking Evaluation Overview*. Boston, MA: Springer US, 2002, pp. 17–31.

[2] B. Pouliquen, R. Steinberger, and O. Deguernel, "Story tracking: Linking similar news over time and across languages," in *Proceedings of the Workshop on Multi-source Multilingual Information Extraction and Summarization*, ser. MMIES '08. Stroudsburg, PA, USA: Association for Computational Linguistics, 2008, pp. 49–56.

[3] S. Bhulai, *et al.*, "Trend Visualization on Twitter: What's Hot and What's Not?" *IARIA DATA ANALYTICS*, pp. 43–48, 2012.

[4] S. Phuvipadawat and T. Murata, "Breaking news detection and tracking in twitter," in *2010 IEEE/WIC/ACM International Conference on Web Intelligence and Intelligent Agent Technology*, vol. 3, Aug 2010, pp. 120–123.

[5] J. Allan, *Introduction to Topic Detection and Tracking*. Boston, MA: Springer US, 2002, pp. 1–16.

[6] J. Weng and B.-S. Lee, "Event detection in Twitter," *ICWSM*, vol. 11, pp. 401–408, 2011.

[7] X. Huang, X. Zhang, Y. Ye, S. Deng, and X. Li, "A topic detection approach through hierarchical clustering on concept graph," *Applied Mathematics & Information Sciences*, vol. 7, no. 6, p. 2285, 2013.

[8] B. J. Frey and D. Dueck, "Clustering by passing messages between data points," *Science*, vol. 315, no. 5814, pp. 972–976, 2007.

[9] B. Mukhoty and R. Gupta, "A parameter-free affinity based clustering," *CoRR*, vol. abs/1507.05409, 2015.

[10] J. Shi and J. Malik, "Normalized cuts and image segmentation," *IEEE Transactions on pattern analysis and machine intelligence*, vol. 22, no. 8, pp. 888–905, 2000.

[11] M. Ester, *et al.*, "A density-based algorithm for discovering clusters in large spatial databases with noise." in *Kdd*, vol. 96, no. 34, 1996, pp. 226–231.

[12] D. M. Blei, A. Y. Ng, and M. I. Jordan, "Latent dirichlet allocation," *Journal of machine Learning research*, vol. 3, no. Jan, pp. 993–1022, 2003.

[13] F. Holz and S. Teresniak, "Towards automatic detection and tracking of topic change," *Computational linguistics and intelligent text processing*, pp. 327–339, 2010.

[14] X. Wang and A. McCallum, "Topics over time: A non-markov continuous-time model of topical trends," in *Proceedings of the 12th ACM SIGKDD International Conference on Knowledge Discovery and Data Mining*, ser. KDD '06. New York, NY, USA: ACM, 2006, pp. 424–433.

[15] R. Swan and J. Allan, "Automatic generation of overview timelines," in *Proceedings of the 23rd Annual International ACM SIGIR Conference on Research and Development in Information Retrieval*, ser. SIGIR '00. New York, NY, USA: ACM, 2000, pp. 49–56.

[16] Twitter realtime filtering. Retrieved: September 30, 2017. [Online]. Available: https://developer.twitter.com/en/docs/tweets/filter-realtime/overview

[17] Twitter rate-limits. Retrieved: September 30, 2017. [Online]. Available: https://developer.twitter.com/en/docs/basics/rate-limits

[18] M. ten Thij, S. Bhulai, W. van den Berg, and H. Zwinkels, "Twitter Analytics for the Horticulture Industry," *IARIA DATA ANALYTICS*, pp. 75–79, 2016.

[19] Scikit-learn python module. Retrieved: September 30, 2017. [Online]. Available: http://scikit-learn.org/stable/

[20] P. J. Rousseeuw, "Silhouettes: A graphical aid to the interpretation and validation of cluster analysis," *Journal of Computational and Applied Mathematics*, vol. 20, pp. 53 – 65, 1987.

[21] P. Jaccard, "Distribution of alpine flora in the dranses basin and in some neighboring regions," *Bull. Soc. Vaud. Sci. Nat.*, vol. 37, pp. 241–272, 1901.

[22] A. Rosenberg and J. Hirschberg, "V-measure: A conditional entropy-based external cluster evaluation measure," in *Proceedings of the 2007 Joint Conference on Empirical Methods in Natural Language Processing and Computational Natural Language Learning(EMNLP-CoNLL)*, 2007, pp. 410–420.

[23] K. Krippendorff, "On the reliability of unitizing continuous data," *Sociological Methodology*, vol. 25, pp. 47–76, 1995.

[24] Hortiradar. Retrieved: September 30, 2017. [Online]. Available: https://hortiradar.bigtu.nl/hortiradar/

A Use Case-oriented Framework for the Evaluation of In-Memory IT-Systems

Stephan Ulbricht*, Marek Opuszko*, Johannes Ruhland*, Sven Gehrke*
*Friedrich Schiller University Jena
Department of Business Informations, Jena, Germany
Email: stephan.ulbricht@uni-jena.de, marek.opuszko@uni-jena.de, johannes.ruhland@uni-jena.de, sven.gehrke@uni-jena.de

***Abstract*—After a comeback in recent years, In-memory systems are now among several candidate solutions to solve future IT challenges. Despite the increased interest in the technology, however, there is a hesitant spread. One reason could be the lack of practical application scenarios that decision makers can apply to their business context. The aim of this work is to introduce a framework to support the evaluation of potential In-memory applications. Relevant factors that influence a possible In-memory use were evaluated using the Multi-Attribute Utility Theory approach, accompanied by an expert survey and therefore create a base for the framework. The framework is then used to evaluate 10 complex real-world In-memory use case scenarios. The results show that the presented approach in this work is suitable to both assess possible use cases and determine cases with high potential.**

Keywords–In-Memory IT-Systems; Business Value; Analytic Hierarchy Process (AHP); Multi-Attribute Utility Theory.

I. INTRODUCTION

Enterprises are faced with the challenge of constantly growing data volumes, increasing competition pressure and the permanent need to instantly react to events. This is one of the main reasons why choosing the"'right"' IT-systems has become a major strategic decision for companies. The selection of the appropriate system may determine the success of a company or in other words, the selection of the wrong system might lead to serious business disadvantages [1]. The challenges and possibilities associated with the term Big Data characterizes today's IT landscapes. In this context, In-Memory IT-systems (IMIS) represent a key technology [2]. Despite promising expectations, the technology has not yet been significantly established in the industry. Companies mainly criticize the lack of reproducible use cases [3][4]. Since the beginning of the boom of the technology, a whole series of application scenarios have been propagated. Based on these examples, which were often tailored to specific sectors and fields of application, many companies could not derive their own benefits and lead in-memory techniques to fruition. According to a study by the consulting company Pierre Audoin Consultants [5], many companies see great potential in the technology, yet there are only a few cases where the benefits are exploited. This is interesting in contrast to the expectations placed on the technology to create business value along all steps of the value chain. This accounts for a vertical integration, as well as a horizontal. In addition to these open issues in the corporate sector, there is a clear need for a generalizable reference model to analyze and evaluate in-memory scenarios [6][7] from a scientific perspective. Hence, a universal evaluation tool is needed to determine whether IMIS is beneficial or not suited in a specific scenario and vice versa.

The decision whether to use an IMIS in a company or not is a complex and multi-criteria decision problem. Beside IT requirements numerous other aspects like the relation with, i.e., employees, customers or suppliers have to be considered. Furthermore, possible massive change in the company's infrastructure [8] has to be evaluated. The representation of this complexity requires a corresponding model which covers all these different aspects. In this work, we will therefore introduce a framework which reflects both the industrial as well as the scientific claims. We will create a design science based system, able to identify and evaluate potential IMIS scenarios. Due to the versatility of the IMIS technology and its potential use in different use cases, the scenarios may strongly differ among each other. Some aspects may be specific and unique, meaning only relevant for a certain scenario. These aspects are directly linked to the creation of business value and are therefore called value-creation dependent. On the other hand there will be aspects of a scenario that are not directly linked. These are called value-creation independent. According to their specific characteristics the weightings of the value-creation independent factors are determined by the analytic hierarchy processing and the dependent factors are determined by the direct ranking method. The evaluation and interpretation of the presented framework is based on 10 cross-industrial use cases.

The paper is organized as follows. Section II introduces the research background, the existing literature in the field of IMIS and the overall structure of the framework. Section III presents the research methodology including the analytic hierarchy process (AHP) and the direct ranking method (DRM). In section IV the application of the framework is shown. The final section summarizes the contributions of this work.

II. RESEARCH BACKGROUND

For a better understanding of the evaluation framework it is necessary to gain a deeper understanding of the technical characteristics of IMIS. The idea of using main memory for the storage of data goes back to the 1980's [9] and 1990's [10]. Caused by the high costs and relatively low storage sizes IMIS was basically a niche technology in the past years. With the introduction of the SAP HANA platform [11], the technology experienced some kind of a comeback. Originally, the SAP HANA platform was developed for accelerated and flexible analysis of large data sets. This new generation of IMIS includes a totally different storage concept in comparison to relational databases. The data in In-Memory Systems is mainly stored in a column-based manner [12]. The advantage is a better data compression [13][14], due to the fact that the data of the same type is stored in a column. In the recent years the focus on analytical tasks has been extended to hybrid IT-systems. The idea is to store the operational and analytical data entirely in a main memory database [15][16]. These hybrid systems are referred to as Online Mixed Workload

Processing (OLXP) [17] and Hybrid Transactional/Analytical Processing (HTAP) [18]. Common data storage expansive and time consuming extract, transform, load (ETL) processes from the transactional into the analytical system are no longer necessary [13]. As a result, operational data can be used for analysis without major time delays.

Due to the different characteristics of analytical and operational tasks, problems and difficulties arise for hybrid systems. The column-based storage of data was originally designed for read-oriented and read-only analysis tasks. A higher proportion of write access typically characterizes operational systems, i.e., enterprise resource planning systems. The merging of these two approaches is often associated with complex join procedures [19]. In read-oriented environments, this can reduce the maximum possible performance improvement promised by IMIS.

A. Problem Context and Related Work

The majority of the early publications in the field of IMIS were characterized by the strong focus on rather technical aspects. To a great proportion, only technical features, such as the column-based storage of data [12], data compression [14] or the persistence of volatile storage media [20] were investigated. The dominance of technical investigations still illustrates the strong technologically driven development. Despite it's potential, only few studies about the evaluation of IMIS use cases have been published to date. The first studies in this field have been carried out by Piller and Hagedorn [6][21]. The authors evaluate first case studies in the retail sector. The case studies were evaluated with the aid of various influencing factors. Based on the factors, first application patterns were derived. Another approach to characterize and classify in-memory systems was presented by Winter et al. [22]. They identified stereotypical patterns based on the data volume and the degree of hybrid workload. An alternative approach for the analysis of In-memory applications addresses the business process characteristics of IMIS use cases. Pioneers in this area were vom Brocke et al. [23][24][25]. They developed a value-creation model, which considers first- as well as second-order effects. They conclude that the value-creation is closely related to process change. The evaluation of several IMIS use cases by Bärenfänger et al. [26] confirmed this results. Another approach focused on the cost benefit effects of IMIS. In this context, Meier et al. developed a model for the economical evaluation of IMIS. Like vom Brocke et al. they distinguish into direct and indirect benefits. In their publication, [27] Ulbricht et al. tried to combine the findings of the different approaches. They presented a structured model for the evaluation and analysis of IMIS use cases, taking various factors into account. Despite the different focuses, one thing all approaches have in common. They all consider the characteristics of IMIS use cases from a quite abstract level. The degree of dissemination in individual sectors, however, indicates the different importance of the particular influencing factors. The question arises, why this technology has already been used quite frequently in some sectors and is hardly ever noticed in other areas.

B. Approach

As mentioned before, the evaluation and analysis of IMIS use cases is a complex, multi-criteria decision problem. In order to represent and solve the decision problem the model of the multi-attribute utility theory (MAUT) is used. This model allows to consider both the system requirements as well as the corresponding importance. To determine the total utility U, the additive model (1) of the MAUT [28] is applied. In this model the system requirements are represented as x_i and the significance (importance) as w_i.

$$U = \sum_{i=1}^{n} w_i x_i \quad (1)$$

In order to provide a better complexity handling, we characterize the several influence factors and bring them into a hierarchy in a first step. In the second step, we select suitable methods for the determination of the significance depending on the characteristics of the influence factors. The different characteristics of the factors lead to a trade off between the operability of the methods and the quality of the results. In the final step, we reveal the results of the utility methods and evaluate the overall framework based on 10 case studies. In this part we demonstrate the feasibility of our concept. The creation of the framework follows the concept of the design science research [29]. Both practical and theoretical aspects are considered in the design process. The several steps of the design process are shown in the following sections. The created artifact is represented by a framework. The overall approach is summerized in Figure 1.

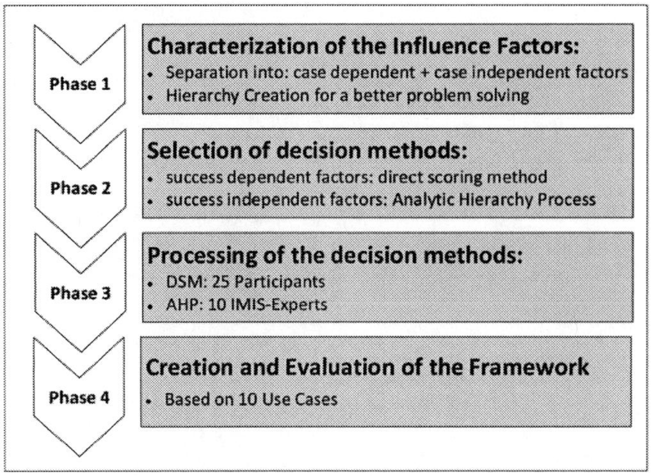

Figure 1. Overview of the Research Methodology

C. Characterization and Categorization of the Influence Factors

In [8], DeLone et al. divided the influencing variables of information systems into success dependent and independent. Analogous to this approach we categorized the influence factors in our framework into value-creation dependent and independent. The whole categorization is presented in the following section. The starting point of the considered influence factors is the IMIS evaluation model from Ulbricht et al. [27]. An overview of the developed framework is given in Figure 2.

1) Value-creation-dependent influence factors: This category includes the factors, which are most relevant for the value-creation of a use case. Due to the strong impact on the business success, they are particularly important for corporate decisions. These factors comprise the internal as well as the external realization conditions, e.g., the capability to realize the results from the IT-system in an appropriate time. Another influence factor is the potential benefit regarding the use of IMIS. This means value-creation through faster data processing or more detailed analysis. In most cases, business value is the most important decision criteria for companies. In this consideration, this point also includes non-monetary benefits and second-level effects like an improved customer satisfaction. In order to achieve independence of the factors, it is important that the potential value generation is considered independent of the other factors. Independence is the prerequisite for the later conducted application of decision methods [30].

2) *Value-creation-independent influence factors:* This category includes factors which are from a solely business perspective of minor importance. This means that these factors have no direct relation to the value-creation. An economically oriented decision maker is in most cases not interested in the underlying data volume or the data structure. On the other hand, these factors play a very important role for the technical evaluation of In-Memory Systems. In order to consider all relevant aspects for the evaluation, company representatives, scientists as well as IMIS vendors are involved in the determination of these factors. In addition to these stakeholder-oriented factors, this

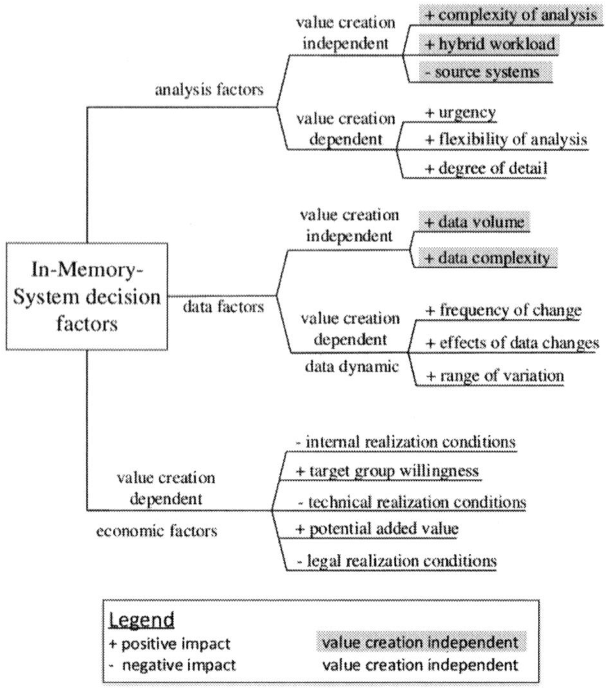

Figure 2. Overview of the analysis and evaluation framework (adapted according to [27])

category also includes technical aspects, which are related to the value-creation. These include, for example, the frequency of change and the range of variation. One of the probably most important advantages of IMIS is the capability of fast data processing. Expert interviews and case studies in this area have shown, however, that the requirements regarding, e.g., the urgency vary significantly between different business areas.

III. Research Methodology

After the basic features of the framework have been described in the previous section, the question arises how the respective relevance regarding the evaluation of IMIS is represented. For this purpose, an additional weighting factor is added to the framework. The respective weights are determined by selected multi-critical decision-making methods. The directly scoring method is used for the value-creation dependent factors. To determine the significance of the value-creation independent factors the AHP method is utilized. The selection criteria and methodology are explained in the following section.

A. Direct Ranking Method

The direct ranking procedure is one of the simplest methods for the determination of the importance of attributes. At the same time, this method produces the least accurate results of the weight determination methods. In practical environments, the direct ranking is frequently used because of its simple and fast applicability. Compared to other procedures, it is not possible to check the consistency or plausibility of the answers. The evaluation is carried out by assigning ordinal scaled preference values. In our framework, we use a range from 1 to 10 for the scale. Due to the normalization of the values, the range of the scale is of minor importance. The weighting of the particular factors is obtained by dividing the individual preferences p_i by the total sum of the preferences. The equation for the determination of the weighting is shown in 2.

$$w_i = \frac{p_i}{\sum_{i=1}^{n} p_i} \tag{2}$$

In spite of the missing methodological variety the direct ranking method suits well for the usage in corporate environments due to its simple applicability. For these reasons, this method was selected for the determination of the value-creation dependent influence factors. To determine the independent parameters more complex methods are necessary.

B. Analytic Hierarchy Process

The analytic hierarchy process, developed by Saaty [31], is a widely used method for multi-criteria decision problems. This method has been applied in comparable decision problems like the selection of enterprise resource planning [32] or the selection of software as a service products [33]. It uses a pairwise comparison of the alternatives to determine ratios and scale priorities. The factors are judged on a 1 to 9 scale. Each factor is compared with every other factor. This kind of comparison improves the decision making within sophisticated problems. On the other hand, with numerous alternatives this leads to an increasing complexity. To reduce this, the alternatives are divided into hierarchies in the AHP. A major advantage with this method is the possibility to check the results for inconsistencies. Through the avoidance of inconsistent answers, it is possible to obtain qualitative better results. However, this requires an increased degree of attention from the participants of a study. The explanation of the particular calculations is omitted at this point.

Despite the relatively simple use of pairwise comparisons, the AHP method can produce reliable results. Due to the high complexity and the high demands placed on the participants, this procedure is only to a limited extent suitable for the utilization in companies. The AHP was chosen to determine the significance of the value-creation independent influence factors. As in already mentioned, a total of 10 experts from different sectors participate in the assignment of these factors. The possibility to detect inconsistent answers helps to ensure the quality of the results. Through the existing segmentation of the framework into hierarchies, the complexity of the decision problem can be reduced.

IV. Application of the Framework

In this section, we present application examples of our IMIS evaluation Framework. For the evaluation of the framework we conducted and analyzed 10 case studies. Thereby, a wide range of companies were involved. This includes, for example, a smaller IT service provider, a medium-sized online travel provider up to a large retailing company. For reasons of space, we only present the results of 3 use cases. The characteristics of the use cases are shown in table I. Aimed by the characteristics the evaluation becomes more comprehensible. In the first part, we determine the weightings of the influence factors, applying the direct ranking method and the AHP. Afterwards, we demonstrate the results of the case studies.

TABLE I. Characteristics of the Analyzed Use Cases

Category	Factor		Local Weight Use Case 1	Local Weight Use Case 2	Local Weight Use Case 3
			Analysis of POS-Data	Real-Time Reporting	Finance Reporting
Analysis	Urgency		Few minutes	Near real-time	Near real-time
	Flexibility of analysis		Ad-hoc	Standard	Standard
	Degree of detail		Medium	Very detailed	High
	Hybrid workload		Yes	Yes	Yes
	Complexity of analysis		High	Very high	Medium
	Source systems		2	1	2
Data	Data volume		Extremely high	Extremely high	Medium
	Data complexity		Only structured data	Mostly structured	Mostly structured
	Data dynamic				
		Frequency of change	Rarely	Frequently	Frequently
		Effects of data changes	Low	High	High
		Range of variation	Moderate	Strong changes	Moderate
Economic	Internal realization conditions		Months or longer	Hours	Days
	Potential added value		High	Very high	Medium
	Target group willingness		Medium	High	Medium
	Technical realization conditions		Low	Low	Medium
	legal realization conditions		Only little regimentation	No regimentation	Highly regimented

A. *Weightings for the Value-Creation Dependent Factors*

To determine the business-related significance of the value-creation dependent factors, it was necessary to include only experts with an appropriate extent of knowledge in the field of data analytics. Therefore, we asked corporate representatives in senior analytic-aware IT positions to rank the importance of each IMIS influence factor. The application of our framework is shown based on 3 selected use cases. The sample use cases have been chosen considering their business and technical characteristics. So, it is possible to illustrate all aspects of a IMIS use case evaluation. The resulting weightings of the use cases are shown in table II.

It becomes clear that the significance of the influence factors vary only a bit in the analysis and data categories.

TABLE II. Weightings of the Value-Creation Dependent Factors

Category	Factor		Local Weight Use Case 1	Local Weight Use Case 2	Local Weight Use Case 3
Analysis	Urgency		0.306	0.316	0.304
	Flexibility of analysis		0.421	0.367	0.353
	Degree of detail		0.272	0.316	0.342
Data	Data dynamic				
		Frequency of change	0.286	0.333	0.300
		Effects of data changes	0.286	0.333	0.400
		Range of variation	0.429	0.333	0.300
Economic	Internal realization conditions		0.177	0.204	0.239
	Potential added value		0.431	0.442	0.324
	Target group willingness		0.104	0.119	0.140
	Technical realization conditions		0.190	0.219	0.257
	legal realization conditions		0.098	0.017	0.039

Significant differences can be seen within the economic factors. As easily predictable, the potential added value is the most important attribute. Nevertheless, the weighting varies quite strongly. The relatively high influence of the other factors illustrates the need for an overall assessment.

B. *Weightings for the Value-Creation Independent Factors*

As already mentioned in section III-B, the mainly technologically driven factors are more complex in their examination. A one-sided investigation from a business perspective does not cover all relevant aspects. It is necessary to involve a broader field of knowledge and experience in this consideration. For this reason, we have included both business experts, scientists and experts from system providers to determine these factors. A strength of the conducted AHP method is the possibility to detect inconsistent answers. The unanimous opinion about the consistency is that only answers with a consistency ratio lower or equal 0.1 has to be considered. For this reason, in each category 2 responses had to be excluded. The aggregated results of the AHP in table III reveal that for the evaluation of the value-creation independent analysis factors the complexity of analysis and the hybrid workload have the main impact. The amount of source systems is in this context only of minor importance. A quite more notable tendency can be seen between the data volume and the data complexity. For the evaluation of the value-creation independent data factors the data volume plays is most relevant.

TABLE III. Weightings of the Value-Creation Independent Factors

Category	Subcategory	Subcategory Weight	Factor	Local Weight
Analysis	Value-Creation independent	0.38	Complexity of analysis	0.42
			Hybrid workload	0.44
			Source systems	0.14
	Value-Creation dependent	0.62		
Data	Value-Creation independent	0.55	Data volume	0.81
			Data complexity	0.19
	Value-Creation dependent	0.45		

C. *Evaluation Examples*

The first chosen example comes from an early adapter of IMIS systems. The analysis of point of sales data in the retail section is one of the first examples in this area. The company participating on our case study is one of the leading retailers in Germany. For reasons of space and legibility we only show some key attributes of the example. The example is characterized by a high demand regarding the urgency, data volume and the complexity of analysis. The calculation includes transactional as well as analytical tasks. Due to the rare and minor data changes, the requirements in this area are quite moderate. The most important obstacle concerning the realization of the potential added value is the long implementation duration.

The second example from the insurance area is characterized by very high requirements in the analysis as well as in the data area. For this use case, it is necessary that the results are based on up-to-date data and are processed in near real-time. The analyzes are based on large amounts of data directly from the transaction system. From an economic point of view, this case is characterized by a very high added value. There are neither internal nor external obstacles that avoid the realization of the results. For this reasons, this example is assessed very high in all categories.

The last example shows very clearly the diverging significance of the influencing factors. The use case comes from a supplier company in the medical field. This company uses IMIS to improve their financial and controlling reports. Despite relatively small changes to the data base, it is important that the data is up-to-date and the results of the analyzes are available very quickly. In comparison to the other use cases, the overall technical requirements are a bit smaller. The same is true for the economical factors. Especially the high legal regimentation stifle/obstruct the economical assessment.

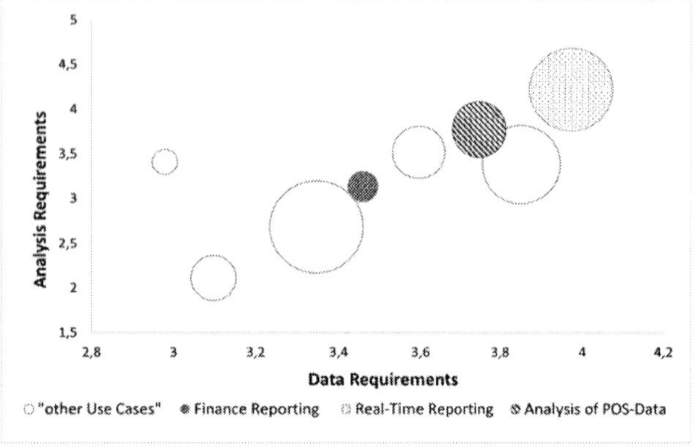

Figure 3. Results of the Use Case Analysis

For a better clarity and easier interpretation we assigned the results of the use case evaluation to a portfolio chart (Figure 3). This chart is comparable to the strategic portfolio matrix of the Boston Consulting Group [34]. The advantage of this chart is the possibility to have a visual indicator for the evaluation of the complex underlying decision problem. The dimensions of the chart are based on the categories of the presented framework. The analysis and data requirements are building the axes of the chart. The radius of a data point reflects the economical assessment as seen in Table I. The chart is an easy to use tool to indicate promising use cases. As seen in Figure 3 the assessment of the use cases is quite diverse. The use case Finance Reporting for instance may be characterized by a rather low economical assessment on side, having medium to low data and analytical requirements on the other side. Although an assessment of a use case scenario is still subjective to the decision maker's assumptions and weights, the chart provides a tool to either choose, rule out or change possible use cases. This may also lead to the decision to only use IMIS in parts of the originally planned scenario or to switch to substitute technologies. So, the process of the application scenario definition, which could be a repetitive process, may also be supported by the framework.

V. Conclusion

Recent research as well as practical applications of In-memory systems has shown a research gap concerning the structured consideration of IMIS use cases. To address all relevant aspects regarding this consideration, a multi-criteria decision framework was introduced. Previous IMIS examples have shown a strongly varying importance of the individual influencing factors. In order to map all factors and their significance, a multi-attribute utility theory model was used. In addition, the factors were subdivided into the two categories value-creation dependent and value-creation independent. The methods for the determination of the weightings were selected according to these categories. The presented framework allows to examine existing, as well as exemplary future use cases with regard to the influence factors of In-memory based IT systems. The approach allows to consider both, the system requirements and the corresponding importance. This makes it possible for decision-makers to investigate IMIS scenarios for their application potential.

In future work, the framework should be extended to other industries. A broad selection framework is also conceivable that shows reasonable conditions for the use of the In-memory technology. With the aid of the framework, catalogs could be created for suitable and tested application scenarios.

References

[1] J. Peppard and J. Ward, "Beyond strategic information systems: towards an is capability," The Journal of Strategic Information Systems, vol. 13, no. 2, 2004, pp. 167–194.

[2] "Top 10 Hot Big Data Technologies," 2016, URL: https://www.forbes.com/sites/gilpress/2016/03/14/top-10-hot-big-data-technologies/ [accessed: 2017-07-11].

[3] "SAP fehlen echte HANA-Business-Cases," 2015, URL: http://www.cio.de/a/sap-fehlen-echte-hana-business-cases,2940526 [accessed: 2017-07-24].

[4] "Lack of SAP HANA use cases stifling demand among ASUG members," 2014, URL: http://diginomica.com/2014/08/08/lack-sap-hana-use-cases-stifling-demand-among-asug-members/ [accessed: 2017-07-24].

[5] "SAP Business Suite powered by SAP HANA," 2014, URL: https://www.pac-online.com/download/9757/125462 [accessed: 2017-07-12].

[6] G. Piller and J. Hagedorn, "Business benefits and application capabilities enabled by in-memory data management." in IMDM, 2011, pp. 45–56.

[7] R. Schütte, "Analyse des einsatzpotenzials von in-memory-technologien in handelsinformationssystemen." in IMDM, 2011, pp. 1–12.

[8] W. H. DeLone and E. R. McLean, "Information systems success: The quest for the dependent variable," Information systems research, vol. 3, no. 1, 1992, pp. 60–95.

[9] H. Garcia-Molina and K. Salem, "Main memory database systems: An overview," IEEE Transactions on knowledge and data engineering, vol. 4, no. 6, 1992, pp. 509–516.

[10] D. J. DeWitt, R. H. Katz, F. Olken, L. D. Shapiro, M. R. Stonebraker, and D. A. Wood, Implementation techniques for main memory database systems. ACM, 1984, vol. 14, no. 2.

[11] F. Färber, S. K. Cha, J. Primsch, C. Bornhövd, S. Sigg, and W. Lehner, "Sap hana database: data management for modern business applications," ACM Sigmod Record, vol. 40, no. 4, 2012, pp. 45–51.

[12] D. J. Abadi, P. A. Boncz, and S. Harizopoulos, "Column-oriented database systems," Proceedings of the VLDB Endowment, vol. 2, no. 2, 2009, pp. 1664–1665.

[13] H. Plattner and A. Zeier, In-memory data management: technology and applications. Springer Science & Business Media, 2012.

[14] D. Abadi, S. Madden, and M. Ferreira, "Integrating compression and execution in column-oriented database systems," in Proceedings of the 2006 ACM SIGMOD international conference on Management of data. ACM, 2006, pp. 671–682.

[15] H. Plattner, "A common database approach for oltp and olap using an in-memory column database," in Proceedings of the 2009 ACM SIGMOD International Conference on Management of data. ACM, 2009, pp. 1–2.

[16] A. Kemper and T. Neumann, "Hyper: A hybrid oltp&olap main memory database system based on virtual memory snapshots," in Data Engineering (ICDE), 2011 IEEE 27th International Conference on. IEEE, 2011, pp. 195–206.

[17] P. Loos, J. Lechtenbörger, G. Vossen, A. Zeier, J. Krüger, J. Müller, W. Lehner, D. Kossmann, B. Fabian, O. Günther et al., "In-memory-datenmanagement in betrieblichen anwendungssystemen," Wirtschaftsinformatik, vol. 53, no. 6, 2011, pp. 383–390.

[18] M. Pezzini, D. Feinberg, N. Rayner, and R. Edjlali, "Hybrid transaction/analytical processing will foster opportunities for dramatic business innovation," Gartner (2014, January 28) Available at https://www. gartner. com/doc/2657815/hybrid-transactionanalytical-processing-foster-opportunities, 2014.

[19] D. J. Abadi, "Query execution in column-oriented database systems," Ph.D. dissertation, Massachusetts Institute of Technology, 2008.

[20] T. Winsemann and V. Köppen, "Kriterien für datenpersistenz bei enterprise data warehouse systemen auf in-memory datenbanken." in Grundlagen von Datenbanken, 2011, pp. 97–102.

[21] G. Piller and J. Hagedorn, "In-memory data management im einzelhandel: Einsatzbereiche und nutzenpotentiale," in Multikonferenz Wirtschaftsinformatik, 2012.

[22] R. Winter, S. Bischoff, and F. Wortmann, "Revolution or evolution? reflections on in-memory appliances from an enterprise information logistics perspective." in IMDM, 2011, pp. 23–34.

[23] J. vom Brocke, S. Debortoli, and O. Müller, "In-memory database business value," 360 - The Business Transformation Journal, vol. 3, no. 7, 2013, pp. 16–26.

[24] J. vom Brocke, "In-memory value creation, or now that we found love, what are we gonna do with it?" BPTrends, vol. 10, 2013, pp. 1–8.

[25] J. vom Brocke, S. Debortoli, O. Müller, and N. Reuter, "How in-memory technology can create business value: insights from the hilti case," Communications of the Association for Information Systems, vol. 34, no. 1, 2014, pp. 151–167.

[26] R. Bärenfänger, B. Otto, and H. Österle, "Business value of in-memory technology–multiple-case study insights," Industrial Management & Data Systems, vol. 114, no. 9, 2014, pp. 1396–1414.

[27] S. Ulbricht, M. Opuszko, J. Ruhland, and M. Thrum, "Towards an analysis and evaluation framework for in-memory-based use cases," in The Twelfth International Multi-Conference on Computing in the Global Information Technology. IARIA, 2017, pp. 22–27.

[28] G. P. Huber, "Multi-attribute utility models: A review of field and field-like studies," Management Science, vol. 20, no. 10, 1974, pp. 1393–1402.

[29] A. R. Hevner, S. T. March, J. Park, and S. Ram, "Design science in information systems research," MIS quarterly, vol. 28, no. 1, 2004, pp. 75–105.

[30] R. Klein and A. Scholl, Planung und Entscheidung. Vahlen, München, 2004.

[31] T. L. Saaty, "What is the analytic hierarchy process?" in Mathematical models for decision support. Springer, 1988, pp. 109–121.

[32] C.-C. Wei, C.-F. Chien, and M.-J. J. Wang, "An ahp-based approach to erp system selection," International journal of production economics, vol. 96, no. 1, 2005, pp. 47–62.

[33] M. Godse and S. Mulik, "An approach for selecting software-as-a-service (saas) product," in Cloud Computing, 2009. CLOUD'09. IEEE International Conference on. IEEE, 2009, pp. 155–158.

[34] D. C. Hambrick, I. C. MacMillan, and D. L. Day, "Strategic attributes and performance in the bcg matrixa pims-based analysis of industrial product businesses1," Academy of Management Journal, vol. 25, no. 3, 1982, pp. 510–531.

A Visual Data Profiling Tool for Data Preparation

Bjørn Marius Von Zernichow and Dumitru Roman
SINTEF Digital
Oslo, Norway
BjornMarius.vonZernichow@sintef.no
Dumitru.Roman@sintef.no

Abstract—**In this paper, we propose a tool that implements visual data profiling capabilities for data preparation – an essential step in the process of linked data generation. Our tool features visual data profiling – a technique that identifies and visualizes potential data quality issues, relevant data cleaning functions, and an interactive spreadsheet table view. The proposed demonstration of the tool will focus on the use of visual data profiling in a scenario of cleaning and transforming tabular weather data – as a pre-processing step for linked data generation.**

Keywords-data preparation; visual data profiling; linked data; usability testing; interactive data cleaning and transformation.

I. INTRODUCTION

Tabular data has been an important type of source for generating linked data, but very often tabular data has quality issues that create challenges in generating linked data [1]. Examples of data quality issues include occurrences of missing values, outliers, inconsistencies, and noisy data [2]. Despite considerable recent research in the area of data quality, there are still opportunities for innovative solutions that can improve data quality and make cleaning and transformation processes more efficient [3][4]. Moreover, there is a need for better solutions and tools to assist users in the data preparation phase that usually comes before the linked data generation process. In this context, visual data profiling is a technique that can support the data preparation process. Visual data profiling systems are used to assess the data quality of datasets, and identify sources of quality issues such as missing and extreme values [2].

We propose a tool that implements visual data profiling capabilities in data preparation by taking as a baseline the Grafterizer framework [1][4][5], a framework for data cleaning and linked data generation – part of the DataGraft platform [4][6][7]. The profiling system checks a selection of a dataset (e.g., a column of values) against a rules matrix to display only possible and relevant charts and data cleaning functions. As an example, number based columns will enable functions (e.g., 'Replace empty cells with median value') and charts (e.g., boxplot) that are not allowed for string columns.

Furthermore, we performed a usability study with 24 users to evaluate usefulness and ease of use of the prototype, while areas of improvement were identified by four expert reviewers. A data preparation scenario was used to compare usefulness and ease of use of the existing version of Grafterizer with the proposed tool that implements visual data profiling capabilities. Drawbacks of the existing Grafterizer framework include usability issues such as a steep learning curve and a complex, less intuitive user interface. To address Grafterizer's usability challenges, we implemented a proof of concept tool that features visual data profiling capabilities to ease the process of data preparation, and improve data quality.

The remainder of this paper is organized as follows. Related work is discussed in Section II, while the implementation of the software prototype is presented in Section III. The demonstration of the tool is outlined in Section IV. Finally, Section V summarizes this paper and outlines avenues for future work.

II. RELATED WORK

Currently, there exists no framework for tabular data cleaning, transformation and linked data generation that targets both data developers and non-developers [1]. Profiler [8], Data Wrangler [11], Trifacta [12] and Talend [13] are examples of systems for data quality analysis that include data mining and anomaly detection techniques in addition to visualizations of relevant data summaries that can be used to evaluate data quality issues. Our data preparation tool is inspired by Profiler, Trifacta, Talend, and the implementation of a spreadsheet table for direct manipulation of data [14][15]. Still, none of these tools for visual data profiling in data preparation target linked data generation. The above-mentioned tools lack specific capabilities that are needed in a linked data transformation process, e.g., the annotation of data with URIs (Uniform Resource Identifiers), and mapping of data into a linked data format that conforms to a specific ontology and data model. Our proposed tool features visual data profiling capabilities that are aimed to be easily integrated in a linked data generation pipeline by replacing the existing version of Grafterizer.

III. SOFTWARE PROTOTYPE

Based on the drawbacks that were identified in the existing version of Grafterizer, the improved tool should provide a) Visual data profiling capabilities, b) Recommendations for relevant data cleaning and transformation functionality, c) A pipeline that reflects the applied data preparation steps, and d) A solution that is useful in data scientists' work activities, and easy to use.

The visual data profiling approach was implemented in a software prototype featuring 14 data cleaning and transformation functions. The implemented data cleaning and transformation process involves the following activities [8]–[10]:

1. The file import (Fig. 1-1): Parsing of the tabular dataset (i.e., in CSV (Comma Separated Values) format).
2. The tabular view (Fig. 1-2): The data can be manipulated directly in the tabular view which features spreadsheet functionality such as 'copy/paste' or 'insert column'.
3. The visual data profiling view (Fig. 1-3): When the user clicks a column in the table, the visual data profiling view returns relevant information about missing values and data distribution of the values in that column.
4. The suggested data cleaning functions (Fig. 1-4): Based on the assessment of data quality, the user selects one of the suggested, relevant data cleaning and transformation functions to improve data quality.
5. The steps pipeline (Fig. 1-5): Finally, the applied data preparation steps are added to a steps pipeline that reflects the data cleaning history.

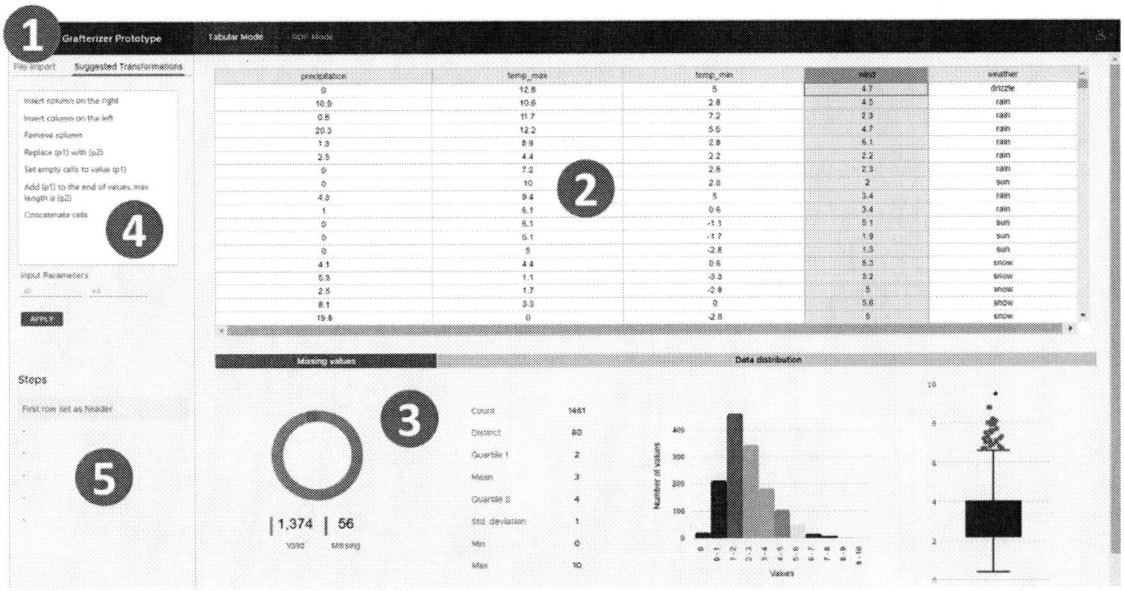

Figure 1. User interface of the visual data profiling tool

1. **Discovery**: Based on the visual data profiling charts and statistical feedback, the user explores the content and structure of the dataset to understand the quality of the data.
2. **Data preparation:** The user applies relevant data preparation functions to the dataset to clean and transform the data.
3. **Validation**: The visual data profiling charts are used to validate that the data is cleaned and transformed according to the intended quality and structure.

The tool consists of five interacting components:

IV. DEMONSTRATION OUTLINE

The visual data profiling prototype will be demonstrated in a scenario that cleans and transforms tabular weather data [16] (precipitation, minimum and maximum temperatures, wind speed, and weather condition). The iterative cleaning and transformation process assisted by the visual data profiling system will include identifying and correcting missing values, and applying transformation functions to the dataset to prepare it for linked data mapping. The demonstration will include all three activities of the visual data profiling process described in Section III, and a typical scenario will include the following steps:

1. The weather dataset is imported [16].
2. The user selects one of the columns, e.g., 'wind', directly in the table view.
3. The data quality, i.e., missing values and data distribution in this case, is assessed by the visual data profiling system. The user reads from the leftmost chart that there are 56 missing values in the 'wind' column.
4. Based on the information about missing values, the user selects a relevant data cleaning function (i.e., 'Replace missing values with a defined value'). In this context, the missing values will be replaced by the median value of all values in the 'wind' column. Alternatively, the function can be selected by right clicking the table view.
5. The rightmost boxplot chart is used to find the median value (i.e., 15.6), and the user applies the data cleaning function to replace all missing values of the column.
6. The user will once more use the profiling charts to assess the current number of missing values. The function has been successfully applied, and the leftmost chart updates to reflect zero missing values.
7. Steps 2 – 6 are repeated to continue improving the quality of the dataset.
8. The resulting dataset is imported to DataGraft and transformed to linked data.

The open source code of the visual data profiling tool is currently available at GitHub [17].

V. CONCLUSION AND FUTURE WORK

This paper proposed a visual data profiling tool that implements visual data profiling capabilities and statistical feedback, recommendations for data cleaning operations, and an interactive spreadsheet table view. The proposed capabilities can improve data quality, and reduce time spent on cleaning and transforming data. Furthermore, the visual data profiling tool has been evaluated in terms of usability, and found to be perceived useful and easy to use [5].

Future work will focus on developing a framework that simplifies the technical user specification in a domain specific language. This will be achieved by implementing a visual recommender system for data profiling, and a semi-automated data preparation approach to guide the user through an incremental process of cleaning and transforming data.

ACKNOWLEDGEMENTS

The work in this paper is partly supported by the EC funded projects proDataMarket (Grant number: 644497), euBusinessGraph (Grant number: 732003), and EW-Shopp (Grant number: 732590).

REFERENCES

[1] D. Sukhobok et al., "Tabular Data Cleaning and Linked Data Generation with Grafterizer," ESWC (Satellite Events), pp. 134–139, 2016.

[2] J. Han, J. Pei, and M. Kamber, Data mining: concepts and techniques. Elsevier, 2011.

[3] J. M. Hellerstein, "Quantitative Data Cleaning for Large Databases," United Nations Economic Commission for Europe (UNECE), Feb. 2008.

[4] D. Roman et al., "DataGraft: One-Stop-Shop for Open Data Management," To appear in the Semantic Web Journal (SWJ) – Interoperability, Usability, Applicability (published and printed by IOS Press, ISSN: 1570-0844, DOI: 10.3233/SW-170263), 2017.

[5] B. M. V. Zernichow and D. Roman, "Usability of Visual Data Profiling in Data Cleaning and Transformation," To appear in the proceedings of ODBASE 2017 - The 16th International Conference on Ontologies, DataBases, and Applications of Semantics, Springer, 24-25 October 2017, Rhodes, Greece, in press.

[6] D. Roman et al., "Datagraft: Simplifying open data publishing," in ESWC (Satellite Events), pp. 101–106, 2016.

[7] D. Roman et al., "DataGraft: A Platform for Open Data Publishing," In the Joint Proceedings of the 4th International Workshop on Linked Media and the 3rd Developers Hackshop. (LIME/SemDev@ESWC), 2016.

[8] S. Kandel, R. Parikh, A. Paepcke, J. M. Hellerstein, and J. Heer, "Profiler: Integrated Statistical Analysis and Visualization for Data Quality Assessment," in Proceedings of the International Working Conference on Advanced Visual Interfaces, New York, NY, USA, pp. 547–554, 2012.

[9] J. Heer, J. M. Hellerstein, and S. Kandel, "Predictive Interaction for Data Transformation.," in CIDR, 2015.

[10] S. Chen, "Six Core Data Wrangling Activities eBook," Trifacta, 2015.

[11] S. Kandel, A. Paepcke, J. Hellerstein, and J. Heer, "Wrangler: Interactive visual specification of data transformation scripts," in Proceedings of the SIGCHI Conference on Human Factors in Computing Systems, pp. 3363–3372, 2011.

[12] M. Heinsman, "Data Wrangling | Prepare Raw & Diverse Data Faster," Trifacta. [Online]. Available: https://www.trifacta.com/. [Accessed: 2017.09.28].

[13] "Talend Data Preparation: Self-Service Data Prep for Analytics," Talend Real-Time Open Source Data Integration Software.

[14] E. Bakke and D. R. Karger, "Expressive query construction through direct manipulation of nested relational results," in Proceedings of the 2016 International Conference on Management of Data, pp. 1377–1392, 2016.

[15] "Microsoft Excel 2016 Spreadsheet Software." [Online]. Available: https://products.office.com/en/excel. [Accessed: 2017.09.28].

[16] GitHub - vega-datasets: Common repository for datasets used by Vega-related projects. Vega, 2017.

[17] GitHub - data-fixer: Tool for tabular data cleaning, preparation and transformation. DataGraft, 2017.

Contents Popularity Prediction by Vector Representation Learned from User Action History

Naoki Nonaka, Kotaro Nakayama, Yutaka Matsuo
Graduate School of Engineering
University of Tokyo
Tokyo, Bunkyo 7-3-1
Email: {nonaka,k-nakayama,matsuo}@weblab.t.u-tokyo.ac.jp

***Abstract*—The anime and manga industry is important in Japan, and its popularity has been increasing overseas in recent years. Under such circumstances, predicting the popularity of media contents is important for content holding companies. Popularity prediction research has, so far, rarely considered the multifaceted information of media contents based on consumer preferences. In this study, we extracted users' preferences from Wikipedia and obtained a vector representation with multifaceted content information. We qualitatively analyzed learned vector representations and showed that accuracy is improved by 2 to 3 % in a popularity prediction task.**

Keywords–Popularity prediction, Wikipedia, Vector representation, MLP

I. Introduction

The anime and manga industry is important in Japan, and its popularity has been increasing overseas in recent years. In 2016, the market size of the animation industry grew at a large rate of 12.0% over the previous year [1]. In addition, it is expected that the scale of overseas content markets will continue to expand [2].

Under such circumstances, popularity prediction of media content is an important task for companies considering secondary use of content and content holders. If overseas copyright buyers can obtain accurate popularity information regarding media contents and information useful for predicting trends, promotion of content work to overseas will be enhanced. Predicting the number of product units sold and the future popularity of a product is important for company decisions such as marketing [3], and many studies have been conducted in this regard [4]-[5]. Representative research includes research predicting movie sales [4][6] and predicting future stock prices [5]. In research on popularity prediction of media contents, Hozumi [7][8] made a prediction using search query volume in search engine, Twitter and Wikipedia data. These studies use information regarding social media that has developed rapidly in recent years, for the purpose of prediction. In addition, accuracy is improved by using consumers' word-of-mouth information for predicting subjects in future prediction [9].

When predicting product sales, multifaceted information considering multiple degrees of similarity, such as product categories, based on consumer preferences, is equivalent in importance to consumers' word-of-mouth information. Collaborative filtering, a typical method in product recommendation, is a model that reflects user preferences, such as recommending based on a product and user vector representation [10], [11]. Thus, in the recommendation problem, a model that considers consumer preference has achieved admirable results. In the popularity prediction task, popularity prediction of movies using features obtained from word-of-mouth information [4] and popularity prediction using feature quantities extracted from prediction targets [12] existed, but there is little research in which the degree of similarity was considered for multiple scales based on a user's preference toward objects.

In this study, we aim to extract users' preferences from Wikipedia and obtain multifaceted information, such as genre and fashion age, regarding media contents. Wikipedia, which covers a wide range of contents, is one of the social media that are used and edited by many users. In Wikipedia, since the user edits pages relating to items of high interest to them, the items edited by each user are considered to reflect user preferences. Therefore, by considering the preferences of various users obtained from their editing histories, multifaceted information can be obtained for content works, taking similarity into account for multiple scales such as genre of contents or fashion age.

In summary, in this study, we learn multifaceted information of media content based on consumer preference from the history of a user's actions with regard to media contents and predict the popularity of contents using multifaceted information. More specifically, we apply Word2vec [13], a popular tool in the field of natural language processing, to the editing history of Wikipedia regarding content and obtain a vector representation of the content. Subsequently, popularity prediction is performed using Wikipedia's number of inbound links as an popularity index of each contents. The overview of this research is shown in Figure 1. The number of inbound links is used to estimate the popularity and importance of blogs [14] and webpages [15]. We also perform qualitative analysis on the vector representation aquired from the editing history.

The contribution of this study is as follows.

- We show that vector representation of media content can be learned from a user's action history on the web.
- We show that prediction accuracy improves as a result of using vector prediction learned from the editing history in media content popularity prediction.
- We analyze the difference between the case in

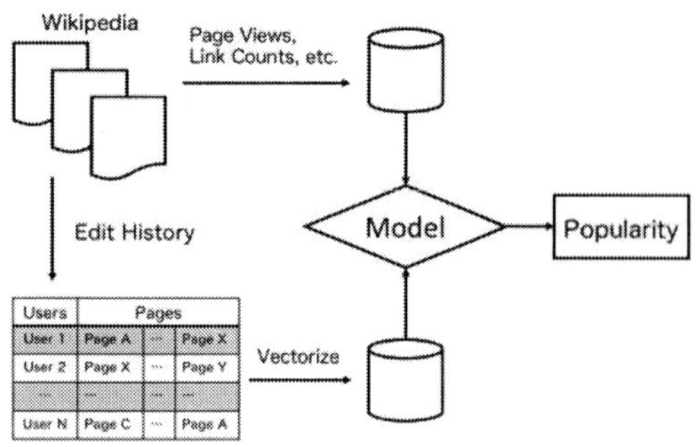

Figure 1. Overview of proposed method.

which prediction accuracy improves and that in which it deteriorates, by performing clustering on contents.

The remainder of the paper is organized as follows. Section 2 discusses related research, and Section 3 explains the proposed method. Section 4 describes preliminary experiments to verify the prerequisites of the proposed method, Section 5 describes experiments to verify the effectiveness of the proposed method, and Section 6 discusses experimental considerations and the development of the method. Section 7 presents the conclusions.

II. Related work

In this section, we describe research related to the proposed method. After discussing research on popularity prediction, we describe research related to Wikipedia editing and the learning of vector representations. Finally, we describe research measuring the popularity of pages from the number of inbound links.

A. Product sales and popularity prediction

Popularity prediction of products and media contents is important in deciding on a marketing strategy [3]. With the spread of the Internet and smartphones, a vast amount of data is available. Thus, many studies on popularity or sales prediction using these data have been conducted. For instance, Choi [16] used volume of queries searched in search engine to predict sales and some economic indicators, and Hozumi [7] used data obtained from various social media to predict popularity.

It has been shown that prediction accuracy can be improved using word-of-mouth information on the problem of sales and popularity prediction of products [9]. For example, Liu [17] attempted to explain the transmission of word-of-mouth information and the revenue of a movie, and Garber [18] predicted the degree of success of new products using word-of-mouth information. In addition, Yu [6] performed sentiment analysis on user information posted on the review site, and then predicted movie revenue.

Considering multifaceted information of products based on consumer preferences is similarly important to consumer word-of-mouth information. Collaborative filtering, a typical method in product recommendation, is a model that reflects user preferences[10][11]. There is a self-reinforcing aspect in the popularity of products, and popularity is known to affect consumer decision-making [19][20]. From this, it seems that consumer preference is relevant to product popularity. However, in the research that predicts the sales and popularity of products, only a few cases took consumer preferences into consideration.

In this study, we aim to conduct popularity prediction considering multifaceted information, such as genre, based on user preference.

B. Studies of Wikipedia

The online encyclopedia Wikipedia is a social medium that is used and edited by many users. Wikipedia covers a wide range of contents, and many studies has been conducted. Specifically, Milne [21] and Strube [22] used Wikipedia as a large corpus of knowledge and its relationships with a link structure as a knowledge base, and Welser [23] and Butler [24] focused on social aspects related to Wikipedia.

Among studies on Wikipedia, there are also studies that focus particularly on editing and editing behaviors. Both registered users and unregistered general users can be Wikipedia editors. Nov [25] examined their motivation by conducting questionnaires for registered users of Wikipedia. In addition, Welser [23] analyzed the social role of registrants' editing behaviors. In the context of popularity prediction, Hozumi [7] used the number of page edits as a prediction feature.

C. Learning multifaceted vector representation

Attention has been paid to a method of acquiring multifaceted information, such as semantic representation in a word with respect to each element, when the series data is given as an input. Word2vec [13], which acquires a distributed representation of words, and [26], which derived from that research and acquires the representation of sentences, has become a major tool. It has been shown that the vector representation learned by Word2vec contains the semantic representation of the word, and the learned vector representation is used for various tasks.

Methods for learning vector representation have also been proposed in fields other than natural language processing, for example, Node2vec [27] takes a graph structure as input and returns a vector representation of each node in the graph. In addition, Barkan [28] learned vector representations related to products from a user's product browsing history and used it for recommendation problems.

D. Link structure as a popularity indicator

The idea of a method for estimating the importance, quality, and popularity of each page from the link structure of a web page has been proposed. PageRank [15], which considers a page with a several links or a page to which a link is affixed from an important page as an important page, and then positions it on a higher level is one typical method. PageRank was introduced to Google's search engine as an index of the popularity or attention degree of a webpage, with positive results.

Examples of using the link structure as an index of popularity or importance are also available outside webpages. Leskovec [29] showed that link structure in blogs follows a power law, and Wu [14] uses link structure to rank blogs. In addition, Kliegr [30] treated the number of links on each page in Wikipedia as a popularity index.

III. Proposed method

In this section, we explain the proposed method. We obtain vector representations of media contents from Wikipedia editing history. Then, we use the obtained vector representation to predict the popularity of the contents.

A. Learning content vectors

This section describes a method for learning vector representations of contents (content vectors) from the editing history of Wikipedia. Each user is assumed to edit pages based on his or her interests. In addition, contents adjacent to each other in a user's editing sequence are considered to be similar contents based on that user's interests.

In the proposed framework, every content is mapped to a unique vector, represented by a column in a matrix C. The column is indexed by the position of the content in the content space. The editing history for each user is arranged in chronological order, and the concatenation or sum of the vectors is then used as feature for prediction of the next content in an edit sequence. More formally, given a sequence of content edits $c_1, c_2, c_3, ..., c_T$, a vector expression of each content c is learned so that c_t can be predicted by the content $c_{t-k}, ..., c_{t+k}$ existing before and after that. Let C be the matrix that maps each content c to a single vector. Learning of mapping matrix C is performed using continuous bag-of-words (CBOW) or skip-gram [31].

B. Popularity prediction

Popularity prediction is performed by providing model features obtained from Wikipedia and a vector representation of contents, as described in the previous section. The features obtained from Wikipedia, including the numbers of page views, edits, and inbound links, are used.

Multilayer perceptrons (MLPs) are used for monthly features and features from content vectors. Let e_c^t be the monthly number of edits during a month t for a content c, v_c^t be the number of page views, and l_c^t be the number of inbound links. The monthly feature $\boldsymbol{X}_{c,M}^t$ is structured as

$$\boldsymbol{X}_{c,M}^t = [e_c^t, v_c^t, l_c^t] \quad (1)$$

and provided as an input to an MLP for monthly feature, MLP_m.

In addition, let T_c be the vector representation of c obtained from C learned from the content edit history. The MLP for content vector, MLP_c is provided with T_c as an input separately from MLP_m. The outputs obtained from respective MLPs are concatenated and transmitted to a new MLP, MLP_p, as an input to obtain the popularity as the final output.

We provide $\boldsymbol{X}_{c,M}^t$, T_c, and the correct label y (number of inbound links) to the model and jointly train MLP_c, MLP_m and MLP_p.

IV. Preliminary experiment

In this section, we analyze the preconditions of points to be verified when using the proposed method. Experiments are conducted using the Japanese version of Wikipedia, and the popularity prediction targets are media contents such as anime, manga, and games. The premise of popularity prediction using the proposed model is the assumption that user's preferences are reflected in the sequence of Wikipedia's editing history. In addition, preprocessing of obtained data used in experiments is explained. The data used for popularity prediction are obtained during September 2015 to the end of July 2016.

A. Data

The Wikipedia data are acquired from MediaWiki [32]. We collect hourly page views of Japanese Wikipedia pages from dump data. Based on the acquired hourly data, the total value of the page views for 24h is calculated and taken as the data of daily page views.

As for the monthly data, the average value of page views in the previous month and the total number of edits are calculated. In addition, the number of inbound links on the first day of each month is calculated as monthly data. That is, as the value of each feature in October 2015, average page views and total edit counts are calculated based on data from September 1 to 30, 2015, and the number of inbound links for October 2015 is the value for October 1, 2015.

The editing history of the page by the editors is acquired as follows. First, Wikipedia-registered editors who edited Wikipedia pages concerning the anime, manga, and game categories is selected. Then, to secure a sequence length long enough to enable the learning of content vectors, editors with long edit histories are selected. As a result, 2,500 editors corresponding to the the top 5% of the total number of editors are selected and analyzed. The lowest number of editing times by a selected user is 86.

After learning the content vector using the edited sequence of the selected user, future popularity prediction is made using the created monthly data and content vector.

B. Preprocessing

1) Title integration: On the Wikipedia pages of media contents that are serialized for a long time, there are character pages, and related work pages in addition to the main page. Since the contents originally described on one page are distributed and described on multiple pages, the main page of such titles is distributed to related pages, with the result that the number of pages viewed and the number of inbound links are reduced. This also reduces the apparent page views and the number of inbound links. To solve this problem, we use "Path Navi" to describe how the structure of a Wikipedia page relates the page to the main page. If there is a page with "Path Navi" among all pages to be analyzed, then "Path Navi" is analyzed and correspondence with the main page is acquired. When there is "Path Navi," we address the problem that the apparent value decreases by adding the number of edits, page views, and the number of inbound links used for prediction to be added to the value of the main page (in the absence of "Path Navi," this is not done).

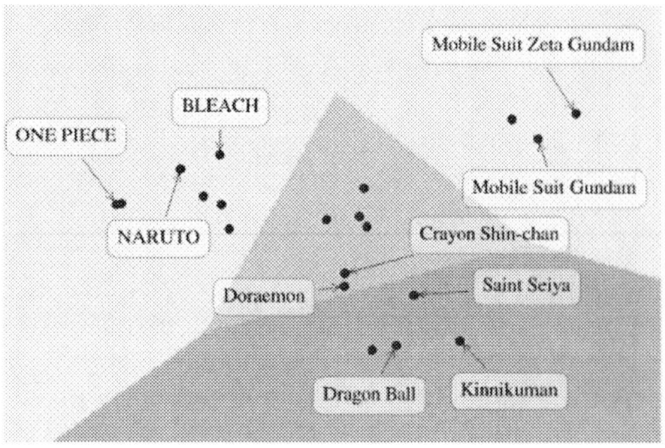

Figure 2. Clustering result of content vector.

2) Selecting target titles: In this study, animation, manga, and games are subjected to popularity prediction. The acquisition of the title to be predicted is carried out in two stages. First, a page listed under the Wikipedia categories "Anime," "Manga," or "Game" other than pages listed under category "List of xx" is obtained. Subsequently, contents are integrated based on "Path Navi," and those with the top 2,000 inbound links are selected. Then, contents that, are not included in a trained vector and whose inbound links shift more than 10% within a month are excluded, because the case in which the number of inbound links fluctuates suddenly is excluded from the prediction by the current model. As a result of narrowing down, 1,547 works are analyzed.

C. Qualitative analysis of Wikipedia editor

In this study, we focus on the top 2,500 editors who registered as editors before October 2015. As a prerequisite for vectorization, the user preferences must be reflected in the editing series, and titles similar in some way must be adjacent in the editing series. Three editors are randomly selected from the 2,500 editors, and a qualitative analysis is performed on a portion of their editing series.

In vectorization, we use the surrounding 10 titles to obtain a vector representation of a content. Accodingly, fragments of the editing history of 10 sequence lengths are selected and analyzed. We randomly specify a position from the edit series of a randomly selected editor, and then select 10 titles to be edited later. Table I shows titles that are included in the selected sequences.

As a result of selecting three series, works related to "Lupin the Third" and those such as "The Kindaichi Case Files" were arranged in series 1. In series 2, gag comics of 2010 such as "One-Punch Man" and "The Disastrous Life of Saiki K." are lined up. In series 3, works related to "JoJo ' s Bizarre Adventure" and many games related to American comics are seen.

In summary, adjacent titles in the editing series tend to have similar genres, authors, fashion ages, and categories as products, and similar common features, reflecting the user's preferences. This result suggests that a vector of target titles can be represented using a vector representation of adjacent titles in an editing sequence.

D. Obtaining a content vector

We describe a method for learning a vector representation of each content from the editing history of a Wikipedia editor. An edit series from editors with several edits of pages belonging to categories targeted for popularity prediction is used. Because it is difficult to learn from an editor's data with few edits, top 5% editors in terms of number of edits is targeted for vectorization. The number of edits by the selected editor is between 86 and 20,793.

The number of epochs is 50,000, the window size is 10, and number of appearances of contents in the editing series is 10 or more in vectorization. CBOW and skip-gram [31] are used as models for vectorization and the size of vector is set to 50.

After learning, qualitative analysis is performed on the obtained vector. To verify the effectiveness of the learned vector, four contents are selected and the top five contents, which are most similar to each content, are acquired. As for the contents related to the query content, contents that are broadcasted or serialized at the same time or contents with similar tendencies are selected. Table II lists the queried contents and top 5 closest contents for each query.

In addition, the results of the kernel principal component analysis on the top 20 inbound link contents' vector are shown in Figure 2. The background color is obtained using k-means clustering. In the area on the left, popular content ranks from content of interest to users in their late teens to age 20, such as "Pokemon", "ONE PIECE", and "NARUTO". In the central area, many contents for children, such as "Crayon Shin-chan" and "Doraemon," are seen. In the upper right area, contents related to "Mobile Suit Gundam", "Mobile Suit Z Gundam", and "Gundam series" are located, and in the lower right area, contents popular in the 1980s and 90s such as "Dragon Ball", "Saint Seiya", and "Dr. Slump" are located. Contents having similar characteristics, such as target age and age of broadcasting, are placed in each area. This result indicates that the vector learned contains information such as the genre of each work and the fashion age.

V. Experiment

In this section, based on the result of the preliminary experiments, popularity prediction of content is performed using a content vector. Moreover, we show that prediction accuracy improves siginificantly as a result of adding a content vector as a feature, compared to the baseline.

A. Popularity prediction

Popularity prediction is performed by a model that takes as input the features and content vectors obtained from Wikipedia, using the number of links of each content work page in Wikipedia as a popularity index. The number of inbound links is used as an index of the degree of importance of pages on the web [15] or an index of the popularity of blogs [14]. Therefore, in this research, based on Kliegr [30], the number of inbound links on each page in Wikipedia is used as an indicator of content popularity.

The prediction model consists of three multilayered perceptrons (MLP_m, MLP_c, MLP_p), given monthly data $\boldsymbol{X}^t_{c,M}$, a content vector T_c, or output of MLP_m and MLP_c

TABLE I. Edit history of content pages (examples).

	editor1	editor2	editor3
1	Lupin the Third	One-Punch Man	Marvel vs Capcom (Game)
2	The Kindaichi Case Files	Chagecha	JoJo's Bizarre Adventure (Game)
3	Lupin the Third and Detective Conan	The Disastrous Life of Saiki K.	JoJo's Bizarre Adventure (Manga)
4	Lupin the Third (Movie)	Chagecha	Deleted page
5	Lupin the Third and Detective Conan	The Disastrous Life of Saiki K.	Street Fighter: Sakura Ganbaru!
6	Lupin the Third (Movie)	Blue Exorcist	Oh! Edo Rocket
7	Lupin the Third and Detective Conan	The Disastrous Life of Saiki K.	Spider-Man
8	Lupin the Third (Movie)	Assassination Classroom	X-Men vs. Street Fighter
9	The Kindaichi Case Files	The Disastrous Life of Saiki K.	Marvel Super Heroes (video game)
10	Lupin the Third (Movie)	NARUTO (Movie)	X-Men: Children of the Atom (video game)

TABLE II. Example of contents vector.

original title	SLAM DUNK	Dragon Ball (Anime)	NARUTO (Manga)	Doraemon
1	Yu Yu Hakusho	Dragon Ball (Manga)	NARUTO (Computer game)	Doraemon (Movie)
2	Touch (manga)	Dragon Ball (Anime; Special)	NARUTO (Movie)	Crayon Shin-chan
3	Dr. Slump	Dragon Ball (Movie)	FAIRY TAIL	Doraemon (Movie)
4	Kimagure Orange Road	Dr. Slump	NARUTO (Computer game)	Doraemon (Movie)
5	I"s	Dragon Ball (Anime; Special)	D.Gray-man	21emon

as an input respectively. As the content vector, we use either T_{sg} which is trained using skip-gram, or T_{cbow} which is trained using CBOW. In addition, a prediction based on a model that does not use a content vector is set as a baseline and compared with the proposed method.

MLP_m has a structure consisting of two layers, with each layer having eight units. MLP_c has two layers, with each layer having 32 units, and a dropout layer inserted between the adjacent layers. The outputs of the two MLPs are combined and provided as input to the MLP layer with 24 units to obtain the final output. ReLU [33] is used for the activation function of the layer except for the final layer, and a linear function is used in the final layer. Only MLP_m and MLP_p are included in the baseline model.

Learning is performed by using back propagation, and optimization is performed using RMSprop. The learning rate is set to 0.0001, the number of epochs is set to 800, and the experiments are conducted using early stopping. Here epoch is number of times that data are passed into the model.

For the content that is analyzed, data from October 2015 to March 2016 are used as training data, and those from April 2016 to July 2016 are used as test data. Next, test data are provided to the model, prediction for three months for each content is performed, and the deviation from the actual value is evaluated using the mean absolute percentage error (MAPE). Since an animation, which is a typical content work, has one occurrence that lasts for three months, we set the prediction period to three months in this study.

$$MAPE = \frac{100}{n} \sum_{i=1}^{n} \left| \frac{y_{true} - y_{pred}}{y_{true}} \right| \quad (2)$$

The average of MAPE values for all contents is shown in Table III for the cases with and without a content vector. Random seeds are fixed and five experiments are performed. In the case in which the content vector is used, the average MAPE value is reduced by 2.0% in both T_{cbow} and T_{sg}, compared to the baseline. In addition, the p-value

TABLE III. Result of popularity prediction.

# Seed	MAPE ($\times 10^2$)		
	Proposed T_{sg}	Proposed T_{cbow}	Baseline
1	0.153	0.148	0.150
2	0.147	0.148	0.154
3	0.146	0.149	0.150
4	0.147	0.148	0.151
5	0.147	0.147	0.151
Average	0.148	0.148	0.151
p-value (vs Baseline)	0.004	0.051	-

by the t test is 0.004 for T_{cbow} and 0.051 for T_{sg}. When T_{cbow} is used, the value of MAPE significantly decreases at a significance level of 1%. The following are the results obtained by T_{cbow}.

B. *Prediction term and prediction accuracy*

Next, the relationship between the length of the prediction period and the accuracy of the prediction using the proposed method is investigated. The number of inbound links after zero, one, two, three months is predicted for the model with T_{cbow} and the baseline, and prediction accuracy was calculated. Data from October 2015 to September 2016 was used, of which those from July to September 2016 are used as test data for each prediction. Experiments are conducted five times with different random seeds, and the average value is taken as the final result.

Table IV shows the relationship between the prediction period length and the accuracy of the proposed method. In both the proposed and the baseline methods, a longer prediction period is associated with lower prediction accuracy. In the prediction after zero months, the difference in prediction accuracy between the two methods is small, and the t test reveals no significant difference between the proposed method and the baseline. In prediction after one, two, three months, the p-value decreases as the prediction period increases, but only prediction after three months shows a significant difference at the significance level 1%.

TABLE IV. Prediction period and prediction accuracy.

# seed	MAPE ($\times 10^2$)							
	month 0		month 1		month 2		month 3	
	T_{cbow}	baseline	T_{cbow}	baseline	T_{cbow}	baseline	T_{cbow}	baseline
1	1.31E-02	8.12E-03	7.61E-02	7.78E-02	1.19E-01	1.21E-01	1.48E-01	1.50E-01
2	2.11E-02	2.77E-02	7.71E-02	7.86E-02	1.19E-01	1.22E-01	1.48E-01	1.54E-01
3	1.45E-02	9.96E-03	7.63E-02	8.47E-02	1.19E-01	1.21E-01	1.49E-01	1.50E-01
4	3.93E-02	1.93E-02	8.05E-02	8.00E-02	1.23E-01	1.21E-01	1.48E-01	1.51E-01
5	8.45E-03	1.41E-02	8.03E-02	7.97E-02	1.19E-01	1.30E-01	1.47E-01	1.51E-01
Average MAPE	1.93E-02	1.58E-02	7.81E-02	8.02E-02	1.20E-01	1.23E-01	1.48E-01	1.51E-01
p-value (vs baseline)	0.607	-	0.211	-	0.137	-	0.004	-

TABLE V. MAPE value of each cluster.

cluster id	ratio	# contents	cluster id	ratio	# contents
1	19.73	61	9	4.36	31
2	5.27	318	10	-36.09	22
3	1.00	119	11	3.29	183
4	17.72	22	12	-2.07	31
5	-5.64	120	13	11.96	31
6	18.92	1	14	1.36	246
7	2.66	132	15	4.81	23
8	3.20	192			

C. *Prediction accuracy of cluster*

As a result of calculating MAPE, there are contents with improved accuracy and contents without, compared with the baseline. To analyze the difference between them, clustering by content vector is performed, and the average MAPE value for each cluster is calculated. After that, the accuracy of prediction for each cluster with or without a content vector is compared. Table V shows the number of contents included in each cluster and the average MAPE improvement over the baseline. Clustering is conducted using k-means, and the number of centroids is set to 15 with respect to the total number of contents of 1,547.

As a result of clustering, the number of contents included in each cluster is between 22 and 318 except for cluster six. Of the clusters consisting of 50 or more contents, we focus on five, cluster 1, 2, 5, 8, and 11, in which the average MAPE value is greatly improved over the baseline, and we examined the top 20 inbound link contents in each cluster.

VI. Discussion

In this section, we discuss experimental and observational results obtained from the editing history analysis, vectorization of contents, popularity prediction, and clustering analysis of popularity prediction.

A. *Edit history sequence*

As a prerequisite for vectorizing the media contents, it is required that the contents adjacent to each other in the input sequence be similar. Because Wikipedia editors edit pages with which they are familiar, it is expected that adjacent contents in an editing history sequence are similar in some sense. Editors who edit Wikipedia pages related to media content are selected randomly, and a qualitative analysis is performed on a portion of their editing history.

As a result, it becomes clear that adjacent contents are pages relevant to the same contents, contents having the same genre, contents having the same author, or contents related in some other sense. Vector representation of content trained by using an editing series is found to contain information, such as genre, author information, and fashion age.

B. *Vectorization*

After evaluation of editing history, two qualitative analysises of the content vector are conducted. First, the nearest content of the selected title is retrieved, and their similarity is discussed. Second, contents with the most inbound links are selected and their position in the vector space is projected and visualized. As shown in the Table II, the contents located around a query content in the learned vector space have some relevance to query content. The most frequent relationship is that between the targeted content and its related work. In addition, if the authors are the same person ("Dragon Ball" and "Dr. Slump", "Doraemon" and "21 Emon") or contents are broadcasted in the same era ("Slam Dunk" and "Yu Yu Hakusho"), they are close in the vector space. There is also a tendency that similar genres or target age contents are located closer in the vector space.

Figure 2 shows a two dimensional projection of vector representations of the top 20 contents in terms of the number of inbound links among the contents targeted. We perform k-means clustering using the values of the first and second components obtained by the kernel principal component analysis. As a result, the first cluster (left) contains popular contents in a wide range of layers, primarily in late teens and 20s men, such as "Pokemon", "NARUTO", "ONE PIECE". The second cluster (center) contains a contents, such as "Crayon Shin-chan" and "Doraemon", that are familiar to a wide age group, that have persisted for a relatively long time. The third cluster (top right), contains the series related to "Mobile Suit Gundam." This suggests that the Gundam series has a large distance from other clusters and different user layers. In fact, the "Gundam series" is known to have substantial support from middle-aged and older men. The last cluster (bottom right), contains content, such as "Dragon Ball" and "Saint Seiya", that prevailed from the 1980s to the early 1990s. It seems that the differences among clusters are the main strata or age of fashion. From the above results, it is considered that the content vector learned using the editing history represents multifaceted information of contents considering the degree of similarity for multiple scales, such as content genre and age, based on the user's preference.

C. Popularity prediction

For the contents analyzed, the number of inbound links of Wikipedia in three months is predicted. In addition to the monthly input features, content vectors learned using CBOW or skip-gram methods from the editor's history are provided to the model. As a result, prediction accuracy improves by 2.0% in both the CBOW and skip-gram cases as compared to the baseline. This is because the user's preference for the target content is incorporated into the model by inputting the targeted content information as the content vector. Monthly features, such as the number of page views, provided to the model are considered to capture short-term fluctuations. However, those monthly features cannot consider the user's preference for the content formed over the long term. The content vector is trained from the editing history of Wikipedia, and it is considered that the content vector provides information regarding the user's preferences to the contents formed over the long term and information on the user layer that supports the target content, to the prediction model. As a result, it is considered that prediction accuracy is improved by giving the content vector to the model in the popularity prediction.

D. Prediction term and prediction accuracy

We also investigate the relationship between the prediction accuracy improvement and the prediction period using the proposed method. In the prediction after zero months, the model can use the number of inbound links of the current month, which is the prediction target, and hence, no significant difference in MAPE value between the proposed method and the baseline is seen. The accuracy of the proposed method is lower than that of the baseline because the proposed model has more features, which is unnecessary for this case. From the prediction results after one, two and three months, it is clarified that the prediction accuracy declines as the prediction period increases in both the baseline and proposed method. From the results of the statistical significance test between the proposed and baseline methods, the p-value in the statistical test between the two methods clearly decreases with a longer prediction period. When the prediction period is short, prediction based on features of the current month is relatively easy, while when the prediction period becomes longer, fluctuations due to characteristics of the target content tend to become larger, and this makes prediction by the proposed method effective. In this experiment, the proposed method significantly exceeds the baseline method at 1% significance level in the prediction three months after. In addition, with regard to prediction over a period of four or more months, since the animation work that occupies the majority of content subject to this research is broadcast every three months, we do not make predictions because new releases might not be made more than three months before the beginning of the broadcast.

E. Cluster analysis

Content is clustered based on the content vector obtained, and clusters whose prediction accuracy is substantially improved or degraded compared to the baseline are examined. We focus on clusters containing more than 50 contents among clusters with large changes in accuracy and analyze them by checking the top 20 inbound link contents in each cluster. In the case of using a content vector, prediction accuracy improves as the genre of the work and the supporting user layer are strongly included in the content vector. In contrast, it is considered that prediction accuracy decreases when the user layer deployed in a plurality of media and the supporting user layer becomes wider.

VII. Conclusion and future work

In this study, we learned multifaceted information considering multiple degrees of similarity, such as product categories, based on consumer preferences, and made popularity prediction of contents using them. Specifically, we applied a low-dimensional vector representation acquisition method using Word2vec to a user's editing history in Wikipedia. After that, we showed that the accuracy of the popularity prediction improves by providing a learned vector representation to popularity prediction model. The prediction accuracy using the proposed method significantly improved when the prediction period was long. This was probably because if the prediction period is long, not only the current popularity provided as input but also information regarding the content become important. In addition, it is suggested that prediction accuracy becomes higher as the acquired vector representation strongly includes factors such as the genre of the content and the user layer that supports it, based on the comparison result of prediction accuracy for each cluster.

In this experiment, we used the editing history in Wikipedia as the user's action history on the web. However, the proposed method can be applied as long as it can acquire sequence data on objects considered to be of interest to users. Therefore, it can be applied not only to the editing history but also to the action history of a wide range of users, such as the posting history of the review text at a review site and the browsing history of a page at an online shopping site. Thus, a possible extension of this work is to learn vector representation of other user action histories and apply learned vector to other tasks.

Acknowledgment

This work was supported by JSPS KAKENHI Grant Number JP25700032, JP15H05327, JP16H06562.

References

[1] "Anime Industry Data, The Association of Japanese Animations (AJA)," http://aja.gr.jp/english/japan-anime-data, accessed: 2017.07.15.

[2] "Current status of content industry and direction of future development, Ministry of Economy, Trade and Industry," http://www.meti.go.jp/policy/mono_info_service/contents/downloadfiles/shokanjikou.pdf, accessed: 2017.07.15.

[3] R. J. Kuo and K. Xue, "A decision support system for sales forecasting through fuzzy neural networks with asymmetric fuzzy weights," Decision Support Systems, vol. 24, no. 2, 1998, pp. 105–126.

[4] G. Mishne and N. S. Glance, "Predicting movie sales from blogger sentiment." in AAAI Spring Symposium: Computational Approaches to Analyzing Weblogs, 2006, pp. 155–158.

[5] J. Bollen, H. Mao, and X. Zeng, "Twitter mood predicts the stock market," Journal of computational science, vol. 2, no. 1, 2011, pp. 1–8.

[6] X. Yu, Y. Liu, X. Huang, and A. An, "Mining online reviews for predicting sales performance: A case study in the movie domain," IEEE Transactions on Knowledge and Data engineering, vol. 24, no. 4, 2012, pp. 720–734.

[7] J. Hozumi et al., "Consumer trend prediction system using web mining," The Japanese Society for Artificial Intelligence, vol. 29, no. 5, 2014, pp. 449–459.

[8] "Asia Trend Map," http://asiatrendmap.jp/en, accessed: 2017.07.15.

[9] C. Dellarocas, X. M. Zhang, and N. F. Awad, "Exploring the value of online product reviews in forecasting sales: The case of motion pictures," Journal of Interactive marketing, vol. 21, no. 4, 2007, pp. 23–45.

[10] P. Resnick, N. Iacovou, M. Suchak, P. Bergstrom, and J. Riedl, "Grouplens: an open architecture for collaborative filtering of netnews," in Proceedings of the 1994 ACM conference on Computer supported cooperative work. ACM, 1994, pp. 175–186.

[11] U. Shardanand and P. Maes, "Social information filtering: algorithms for automating " word of mouth "," in Proceedings of the SIGCHI conference on Human factors in computing systems. ACM Press/Addison-Wesley Publishing Co., 1995, pp. 210–217.

[12] A. Khosla, A. Das Sarma, and R. Hamid, "What makes an image popular?" in Proceedings of the 23rd international conference on World wide web. ACM, 2014, pp. 867–876.

[13] T. Mikolov, I. Sutskever, K. Chen, G. S. Corrado, and J. Dean, "Distributed representations of words and phrases and their compositionality," in Advances in neural information processing systems, 2013, pp. 3111–3119.

[14] Y. Wu and B. L. Tseng, "Important weblog identification and hot story summarization." in AAAI Spring Symposium: Computational Approaches to Analyzing Weblogs, 2006, pp. 221–227.

[15] L. Page, S. Brin, R. Motwani, and T. Winograd, "The pagerank citation ranking: bringing order to the web." 1999.

[16] H. Choi and H. Varian, "Predicting the present with google trends," Economic Record, vol. 88, no. s1, 2012, pp. 2–9.

[17] Y. Liu, "Word of mouth for movies: Its dynamics and impact on box office revenue," Journal of marketing, vol. 70, no. 3, 2006, pp. 74–89.

[18] T. Garber, J. Goldenberg, B. Libai, and E. Muller, "From density to destiny: Using spatial dimension of sales data for early prediction of new product success," Marketing Science, vol. 23, no. 3, 2004, pp. 419–428.

[19] M. J. Salganik, P. S. Dodds, and D. J. Watts, "Experimental study of inequality and unpredictability in an artificial cultural market," science, vol. 311, no. 5762, 2006, pp. 854–856.

[20] Y. Chen, Q. Wang, and J. Xie, "Online social interactions: A natural experiment on word of mouth versus observational learning," Journal of marketing research, vol. 48, no. 2, 2011, pp. 238–254.

[21] D. Milne and I. H. Witten, "Learning to link with wikipedia," in Proceedings of the 17th ACM conference on Information and knowledge management. ACM, 2008, pp. 509–518.

[22] M. Strube and S. P. Ponzetto, "Wikirelate! computing semantic relatedness using wikipedia," in AAAI, vol. 6, 2006, pp. 1419–1424.

[23] H. T. Welser et al., "Finding social roles in wikipedia," in Proceedings of the 2011 iConference. ACM, 2011, pp. 122–129.

[24] B. Butler, E. Joyce, and J. Pike, "Don't look now, but we've created a bureaucracy: the nature and roles of policies and rules in wikipedia," in Proceedings of the SIGCHI conference on human factors in computing systems. ACM, 2008, pp. 1101–1110.

[25] O. Nov, "What motivates wikipedians?" Communications of the ACM, vol. 50, no. 11, 2007, pp. 60–64.

[26] Q. V. Le and T. Mikolov, "Distributed representations of sentences and documents." in ICML, vol. 14, 2014, pp. 1188–1196.

[27] A. Grover and J. Leskovec, "node2vec: Scalable feature learning for networks," in Proceedings of the 22nd ACM SIGKDD International Conference on Knowledge Discovery and Data Mining. ACM, 2016, pp. 855–864.

[28] O. Barkan and N. Koenigstein, "Item2vec: Neural item embedding for collaborative filtering," arXiv preprint arXiv:1603.04259, 2016.

[29] J. Leskovec, M. McGlohon, C. Faloutsos, N. Glance, and M. Hurst, "Patterns of cascading behavior in large blog graphs," in Proceedings of the 2007 SIAM international conference on data mining. SIAM, 2007, pp. 551–556.

[30] T. Kliegr, V. Svátek, K. Chandramouli, J. Nemrava, and E. Izquierdo, "Wikipedia as the premiere source for targeted hypernym discovery," Wikis, Blogs, Bookmarking Tools Mining the Web 2.0, 2008, p. 38.

[31] T. Mikolov, K. Chen, G. Corrado, and J. Dean, "Efficient estimation of word representations in vector space," arXiv preprint arXiv:1301.3781, 2013.

[32] "MediaWiki," https://dumps.wikimedia.org/, accessed: 2017.07.15.

[33] X. Glorot, A. Bordes, and Y. Bengio, "Deep sparse rectifier neural networks," in Proceedings of the Fourteenth International Conference on Artificial Intelligence and Statistics, 2011, pp. 315–323.

A Novel Approach to Information Spreading Models for Social Networks

Burcu Sayın, Serap Şahın
Department of Computer Engineering, Izmir Institute of Technology, Izmir, Turkey
Email: burcusayin@iyte.edu.tr, serapsahin@iyte.edu.tr

***Abstract*— Analyzing and modelling the spreading of any information through a social network (SN) is an important issue in social network analysis. The proposed solutions for this issue do not only help with observing the information diffusion, but also serve as a valuable resource for predicting the characteristics of the network, developing network-specific advertising, etc. Up-to-date approaches include probabilistic analysis of information spreading and the information cascade models. In this paper, we propose a hybrid model, which considers an information spreading model, and combines it with cascades and social behavior analysis. We propose a new hybrid usage approach to represent a real-world modelling for the information spreading process.**

Keywords-social network analysis; information spreading; information cascades.

I. INTRODUCTION

Information spreading on social networks (SNs) is getting more popular in social network analysis. Thanks to the developing technology, information has become quickly accessible, especially via SNs. This situation creates new domains on SNs, such as advertising, marketing, etc. Hence, it is important to have an information spreading model for predicting the effect of the information on SNs.

In the literature, there are many models that either support or modify the Susceptible – Infected – Removed (*SIR*) model [1], [2], [3] or adopt it to new approaches. We selected some of the most current ones and presented them in Section 3. However, it is hard to find a model that matches real-life scenarios because SNs are dynamic platforms and SN users act with their emotions. Therefore, models should also represent SN users' real behaviors. Developing such a model serves as a solution to problems in many areas, like security. For example, in the case of any malicious information existing in the network, we can predict its spreading area and pattern. In this way, we can take precautions against a possible crisis. These are the reasons for which we would like to propose a real-world information spreading model.

In this paper, we present out work in progress as well as our opinion. The existing models do not provide a complete solution to reflect real SN user's decisions for spreading the information. We point out the deficient points on proposed studies and propose an alternative hybrid model.

The paper is organized as follows. Section 2 proposes some of the current requirements for a realistic information spreading model. Section 3 gives an overall explanation of the basis information spreading model "*SIR*" in the literature and its current applications, with some modifications and new approaches. Section 4 includes our proposed hybrid solution for a real-world modelling of information spreading. We conclude the paper and outline our future research directions in Section 5.

II. IDENTIFIED REQUIREMENTS OF A REALISTIC INFORMATION SPREADING MODEL

As SNs have a dynamic characteristic, it is hard to model the spreading of information only with a probabilistic approach. Current information spreading models should focus on a user-specific approach and consider SN users' behavioral effects, because SN users shape the diffusion of any information on the network.

Based on our research, we noted some requirements, as listed below, for a realistic information spreading model with behavioral analysis:

- **Popularity of the source:** Popularity level of the information source affects SN users' decisions on whether to spread that information or not. This factor can also be related with the trustworthiness and credibility of the source.
- **Strength of relations among users:** Strong relations/features (such as similar political views, education, gender, etc.) among SN users cause information to spread faster.
- **Content of the information:** If a SN user gives importance to the content of any information, he/she is more likely to spread it.
- **Personal interests:** If a SN user's interests are related to the information, he/she becomes more likely to spread it.
- **Privacy preferences:** Privacy preferences of a SN user in his/her profile have an impact on information spreading. For example, if the user is conservative about his/her privacy, then he/she is more likely to abstain from spreading information.

Each mentioned requirement affects the information spreading on SNs with a probability. However, the value of this probability may vary according to each user. Hence, developing models for information spreading should take into account these real-world conditions.

III. Information Spreading Models

In SNs, information spreads via posts from one user to another. This spreading continues until it loses actuality and attractiveness to users. In literature, researchers proved that the information spreading process and epidemics resemble each other [4]. Hence, the *SIR* model reflects epidemics. We present this model in the following section and then provide an overview of up-to-date information spreading models.

A. *SIR Model*

The *SIR* Model is based on epidemics. Epidemics spread for a time and then lose their effect. The size of the area affected by the epidemics depends on population size. It is obvious that the probability of the disease spreading in a crowded area is higher than in a deserted area. Hence, population size is an important determinant in the spreading process of epidemics [5]. Similarly, in SNs, a post spreads quickly if the owner of the post has lots of connections.

In epidemics, time evolution of a disease is managed by a threshold; information spreading also has a threshold theorem. The Threshold Theorem of Kermack–McKendrick [1], [2] defines the evolution process of epidemics. This theorem models the population with three types: Susceptible (*S*), Infected (*I*), and Removed (*R*), which constitutes the *SIR* model. Each variable/state refers to the number of people in the related group. Susceptible ones are ignorant, which means that they are not yet infected but have a potential to be an Infected. Infected ones have the disease and they can infect the Susceptible ones. Removed ones have recovered from the disease and stopped the spreading process.

The theorem consists of two differential equations which define transitions between *S*, *I* and *R* states [1], [2]:

- Transition from Susceptible state to Infected state,
- Transition from Infected state to Removed state.

A critical point here is to model the transition from the Infected state to Removed. Researchers first proposed a counter value (*ctr*) to control this process [4], [6]. The main idea behind this value is that it counts the number of users who became infected, and it stops spreading when this number reaches to the *ctr* value. The value is determined before the spreading process and is valid for each user in the network. Unsurprisingly, if we choose a big value for *ctr*, information reaches a bigger portion of the network, but more rounds are required to complete the spreading process. Eventually, *ctr* controls the termination of the spreading process and the size of spreading area in a network.

In addition, information can be observed in two different ways within a spreading process; (i) static information and (ii) dynamic information. During the whole spreading process, if the information does not have any revision, it is accepted as static information. In the contrary case, it becomes dynamic information [7]. When we consider this concept in SNs, users may revise someone's post and publish it as a new post, so information in SNs is dynamic. Hence, we need some modifications to the *SIR* model, or we need new approaches to model the current information spreading processes.

B. *Current Information Spreading Models*

Although most current studies consider the *SIR* model as a baseline and modify it according to today's requirements, some of them also propose new approaches, such as cascades. Information cascades allow us to predict how well the information will spread. This section first summarizes the studies that focus on the adaptation of the *SIR* model and then describes an information spreading model with cascades. We do not provide an algorithmic comparison between the current studies, because our aim is not to find an algorithm which provides the best performance. Instead, we focus on how well the proposed algorithms represent real-world circumstances. In this study, we consider the effectiveness of the algorithms as the achievement level of realistic modelling.

Bao et al. [8] criticizes the *SIR* model in terms of the idea behind the Infected state. They propose that an infected user does not have to believe/accept the information; may also oppose that information. Hence, they divided the infected state into two distinct ones: (i) positive infected (supports the information) and (ii) negative infected (opposes the information). They named this model Susceptible – Positive Infected – Negative Infected – Removed (*SPNR*). According to the *SPNR* model, when an ignorant user receives information from a positive/negative spreader, becomes a new positive/negative spreader with a probability value [8]. In the same way, there is a probability that a positive spreader may affect a negative spreader or vice versa. If a positive/negative spreader gets the information from a stifler (removed user), becomes a stifler, also with a probability. They define the transition from a spreader state to a removed one with a spreading threshold. This model is an enhanced version of *SIR* that takes into account users' decisions to believing the information. However, they only use this decision as a probabilistic value; they do not consider the mentioned requirements.

Serrano et al. [9] consider that a SN user may have a first impression about an information before being infected by other users. In this model, they modified *SIR* and proposed the following four states: (i) neutral (initial state), (ii) infected (believe the information), (iii) vaccinated (believe the anti-information before being infected) and (iv) cured (believe the anti-information after being infected). According to this model, all users are initially neutral. Then, they assign some of them as infected. Infected ones start to infect their neutral neighbors with a given probability. To simulate cured or vaccinated ones, they define a time as delay. At that time, a randomly selected infected user starts to spread anti-information, which says the opposite of the original information in the network. Hence, they try to cure or vaccinate their neighbors with a probability of accepting or denying (probAcceptDeny). Finally, cured and vaccinated ones try to cure or vaccinate their neighbors with the value of probAcceptDeny. This model uses an agent-based modelling so that it can reflect the real world better than *SIR*. However, it is still insufficient to be applied to SNs today.

Cordasco et al. [10] consider the infected state of the *SIR* model from a different aspect. They propose that a user may not immediately start spreading just after it is infected; they define a new state for this situation: "aware". They claim that there should be a threshold that controls the transition from being aware to start spreading. This model resembles the Susceptible – Exposed – Infected – Removed (*SEIR*) epidemic model [11], which differs from *SIR* model with the additional "Exposed" state. This state contains people who had contact with an infected user but have not yet started to infect other people. Similarly, Cordasco et al. [10] propose three states: (i) ignorant, (ii) aware and (iii) spreading. As usual, all users are ignorant at the beginning. When an ignorant user takes information from a spreader, it becomes aware. To be a spreading one, any aware user should take the information from more than a pre-defined number (threshold value) of spreading users. This model has no state for removed, but they define a termination rule in the original paper [10]. Although this model considers the transition process from being aware to start spreading, the model is not sufficient to represent today's information spreading process.

Tong. et al. [12] describes an information cascade model in SNs. First, they provide an extensive study on cascade scales, the scope of the cascade subgraphs, and topological attribute of spread tree. Then, based on the evaluation results, they analyze the spread of the user's decisions for city-wide activities. Decisions include "want to take part in the activity" and "be interested in the activity". This study introduces three mechanisms to use for making a decision:

- **Equal probability:** A user has an equal probability to make any of two decisions.
- **Similarity of users:** Similarity of users is the criteria to make a decision for any user.
- **Popularity of users:** Popularity of users affects users' decision.

Experimental results show that the popularity of users is an important criterion for information spreading. Although this study evaluates some user-specific parameters, such as popularity of the information source and similarity of users to model information spreading on SNs, it does not satisfy all the requirements proposed in Section 2 and it does not consider an epidemic approach.

When we examine the existing studies, we notice that most of them consider a behavioral effect/model on the information spreading process and so modify the *SIR* model to represent this effect in some way. However, they do not propose the factors that affect this behavioral model; they just take it as a probabilistic value for the behavior decision. Indeed, there are many factors (some of which were proposed in Section 2 as the requirements) that affect SN users' behavior on the information spreading process, and they are completely interrelated. Hence, we need to consider them all as a complete impact on users' decisions for the spreading process.

IV. A Hybrid Information Spreading Model

We propose to develop a hybrid model, which considers the models of Bao et al. [8] and Cordasco et al. [10] but modifies their threshold idea by using information cascade characteristics to meet requirements mentioned in Section 2. Novelty comes from using such a hybrid model, which combines epidemic models with up-to-date approaches like cascades to represent behavioral effect on SNs. Considering this effect together with the proposed requirements is so important to observe information spreading on SNs because it affects users' decision on spreading the specific information or not. By using this approach, we can make more realistic transitions between different states of our model. In addition, we will use the idea of Bao et al. [8] regarding the infected state. We will also divide our infected state into two: positive infected and negative infected, because there is a probability that a user will reject an information.

Figure 1 shows the state transitions of our model. The proposed model includes the following properties:

- There will be five states: (i) ignorant (user is not aware of the information), (ii) aware (user is aware of the information but he/she has not started to spread it), (iii) positive infected (user believes the information and spreads it) (iv) negative infected (user opposes the information and tries to convince other people in this way) and (v) removed (user stops spreading).

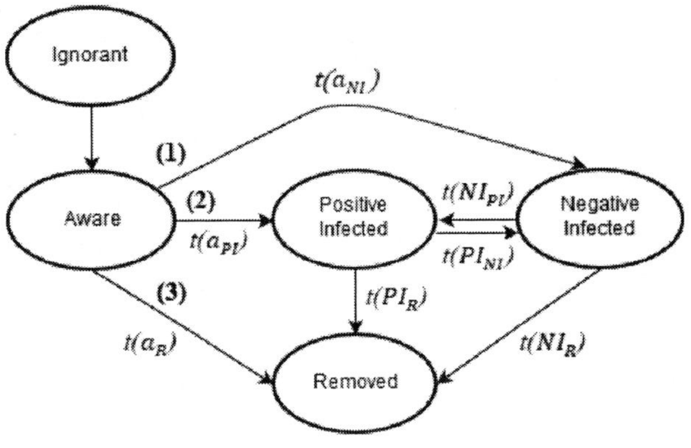

Figure 1. A Hybrid Information Spreading Model

- Initially, we assume that all users are ignorant. Then, some of them are selected as positive infected and some as negative infected. This selection may be important for some domains. For example, if we are working in the advertising or marketing sectors, it is important to reach more users in a short time. Hence, the selection process of initial positive/negative infected users should be performed according to the topology of the network. After this selection, information starts to be spread in the network.

- If an ignorant user takes the information from a positive/negative infected user, he/she becomes aware. After being an aware, the user passes to one of three possible states: (1) he/she may believe that the information is true and pass to a positive infected state via function "$t(a_{PI})$: transition from aware state to positive infected state", (2) he/she may refuse the information and decide to infect others negatively by passing to a negative infected state via function "$t(a_{NI})$: transition from aware state to negative infected state", and (3) an aware user may prefer not to infect any other user either positively or negatively. In this case, that user may pass directly to the removed state via transition function $t(a_R)$.
- After being a positive/negative infected, there may be a transition between those two infected states, which can be controlled with "$t(NI_{PI})$: transition function from negative infected state to positive infected state" or "$t(PI_{NI})$: transition function from positive infected state to negative infected state." Alternatively, they may pass to removed state via "$t(NI_R)$: transition function from negative infected state to removed state" and "$t(PI_R)$: transition function from positive infected state to removed state".
- All transition functions will have a threshold value, including the effect of cascading mechanisms and behavioral effects to meet all five requirements. Hence, these functions will depend on a user-specific approach. We will first analyze each user based on the requirements and define user-specific behavioral effect values for them (training phase). This means that each SN user will have a behavioral impact value and this value will be used in the information spreading process. Hence, users will make a decision based on this impact value for any transition in our model.

Consequently, we will base our hybrid model on the modified version of the *SIR* model and generate a new formulation by also using information cascades and users' social behavior analysis. To verify our model, we will implement both referred models [8], [10] and our proposed model in a real SN dataset to observe effectiveness, and then we will compare them in terms of success and failure rates on real-world modelling.

V. CONCLUSION

In this paper, we discussed the main information spreading model *SIR* and the current modifications of it. We also emphasized that information cascades are important to adjust information spreading models to SNs to create more realistic structures. Hence, we are working on developing a hybrid information spreading model which can meet the presented requirements and dynamism of SNs. Because users' decisions on spreading any information also depend on social behavioral factors, we will include behavioral analysis of SN users in our model. What we expect from this research is that anyone will be able to use our model to predict the spreading area and pattern of an information so that they can measure the effect of it on SNs. Additionally, this model can be used for interaction analysis among SN users.

As this paper proposes our preliminary work, we roughly provided our model. We will continue with the formulation, validation, and simulation phases of the model.

REFERENCES

[1] W. O. Kermack, and A. G. McKendrick, "A Contribution to the Mathematical Theory of Epidemics", Proceedings of the Royal Society of London A: Mathematical, Physical and Engineering Sciences, Volume 115, pp. 700-721, 1927. DOI: 10.1098/rspa.1927.0118.

[2] F. Brauer, "The Kermack–McKendrick epidemic model revisited", Mathematical Biosciences, Volume 198, Issue 2, pp. 119-131, ISSN 0025-5564, 2005. DOI: http://dx.doi.org/10.1016/j.mbs.2005.07.006.

[3] C. Nowzari, V. M. Preciado, and G. J. Pappas, "Analysis and Control of Epidemics: A Survey of Spreading Processes on Complex Networks," IEEE Control Systems, Volume 36, Issue 1, pp. 26-46, 2016. DOI:10.1109/MCS.2015.2495000.

[4] A. Demers et al., "Epidemic algorithms for replicated database maintenance", In Proceedings of the sixth annual ACM Symposium on Principles of distributed computing (PODC '87), Fred B. Schneider (Ed.). ACM, New York, NY, USA, pp. 1-12, 1987. DOI=10.1145/41840.41841 http://doi.acm.org/10.1145/41840.41841.

[5] D. J. Daley and D. G. Kendall, "Stochastic Rumours", IMA Journal of Applied Mathematics (Institute of Mathematics and Its Applications) 1, pp. 42-55, 1965. DOI: 10.1093/imamat/1.1.42.

[6] N. T. J. Bailey, "The Mathematical Theory of Infectious Diseases and its Applications", Hafner Press, Second Edition, 1975.

[7] Y. Zhang, S. Zhou, Z. Zhang, J. Guan, and S. Zhou, "Rumor Evolution in Social Networks". Physical Review E, vol. 87, no. 3, Article ID 032133, 2013.

[8] Y. Bao, C. Yi, Y. Xue, and Y. Dong, "A new rumor propagation model and control strategy on social networks", In Proceedings of the 2013 IEEE/ACM International Conference on Advances in Social Networks Analysis and Mining (ASONAM '13). ACM, New York, NY, USA, pp. 1472-1473, 2013. DOI:http://dx.doi.org/10.1145/2492517.2492599.

[9] E. Serrano, C. Á. Iglesias, and M. Garijo, "A Novel Agent-Based Rumor Spreading Model in Twitter", In Proceedings of the 24th International Conference on World Wide Web (WWW '15 Companion). ACM, New York, NY, USA, pp. 811-814, 2015. DOI: http://dx.doi.org/10.1145/2740908.2742466.

[10] G. Cordasco, L. Gargano, A. A. Rescigno, and U. Vaccaro, "Brief Announcement: Active Information Spread in Networks", In Proceedings of the 2016 ACM Symposium on Principles of Distributed Computing (PODC '16). ACM, New York, NY, USA, pp. 435-437, 2016. DOI: http://dx.doi.org/10.1145/2933057.2933069.

[11] J. Zhang, J. Li, and Z. Ma, "Global Dynamics of an SEIR Epidemic Model with Immigration of Different Compartments", Acta Mathematica Scientia, Volume 26, Issue 3, pp. 551-567, ISSN 0252-9602, 2006. DOI: http://dx.doi.org/10.1016/S0252-9602(06)60081-7.

[12] C. Tong, W. He, J. Niu, and Z. Xie, "A novel information cascade model in online social networks", Physica A: Statistical Mechanics and its Applications, Volume 444, pp. 297-310, 2015. DOI:10.1016/j.physa.2015.10.026.

A Graph Theoretical Approach for Identifying Fraudulent Transactions in Circular Trading

Priya, Jithin Mathews, K. Sandeep Kumar, Ch. Sobhan Babu
Department of Computer Science
Indian Institute of Technology Hyderabad
India
Email: {cs15resch11007, cs15resch11004, cs15mtech11017, sobhan} @iith.ac.in

S.V. Kasi Visweswara Rao
Department of Commercial Taxes
Government of Telangana
India
Email: svkasivrao@gmail.com

***Abstract*—Circular trading is an infamous technique used by tax evaders to confuse tax enforcement officers from detecting suspicious transactions. Dealers using this technique superimpose suspicious transactions by several illegitimate sales transactions in a circular manner. In this paper, we address this problem by developing an algorithm that detects circular trading and removes the illegitimate cycles to uncover the suspicious transactions. We formulate the problem as finding and then deleting specific type of cycles in a directed edge-labeled multigraph. We run this algorithm on the commercial tax dataset provided by the government of Telangana, India, and discovered several suspicious transactions.**

***Keywords*—social network analysis; fraud detection; circular trading; value added tax.**

I. Introduction

A tax is a mandatory financial charge or some other type of levy imposed upon an individual or a legal entity by a state in order to fund various public expenditures. There are mainly two types of tax structures, direct tax and indirect tax. In this paper, we focus on the indirect tax structure. The indirect tax (Value added Tax (VAT) [3] and Goods and Services Tax (GST) [13]) is a tax collected by an intermediary (such as a retail store) from the person who bears the ultimate economic burden of the tax (such as the consumer).

A. Value Added Tax

VAT is a consumption tax that is collected incrementally based on the value added to the goods at each stage of production. Figure 1 explains the transfer of tax from the consumer to the government.

- The manufacturer purchases raw material of value ₹ 1000 from the seller (Here, we represent currency in the form of Indian currency denoted by the symbol ₹ or *Rs.*). He pays ₹ 1100 (₹ 1000 towards raw material and ₹ 100 towards tax, at the tax rate of 10%) to the seller. The seller remits the tax he collected from the manufacturer (₹ 100 rupees) to the government.
- The retailer purchases goods of value ₹ 1200 from the manufacturer. He pays ₹ 1320 (₹ 1200 towards the goods and ₹ 120 towards tax, at the tax rate of 10%) to the manufacturer. The manufacturer remits the difference between the tax he collected from the retailer and the one paid to the raw material seller, which is ₹ 120 - ₹ 100 = ₹ 20, to the government.
- The end user purchases goods of value ₹ 1500 from the retailer. He pays ₹ 1650 (₹ 1500 towards goods and ₹ 150 towards tax, at the tax rate of 10%) to the retailer. The retailer remits the difference between the tax he collected from the end user and the one paid to the manufacturer, which is ₹ 150 - ₹ 120 = ₹ 30, to the government.

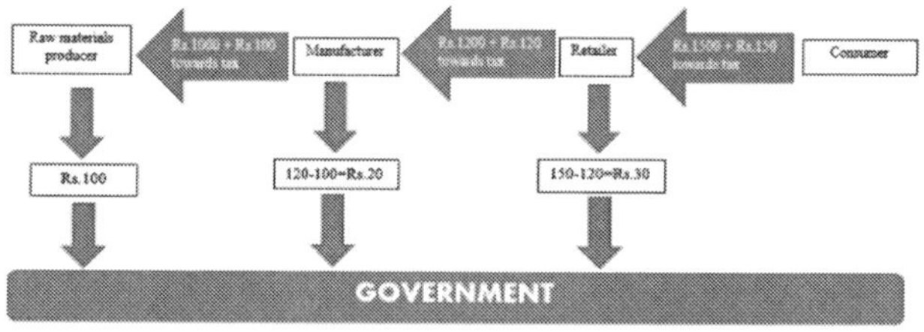

Figure 1. Cash flow diagram of VAT

Note that the total tax received by the government is ₹ 150, which is paid by the consumer.

B. VAT Evasion Methods

Illegal evasion of VAT often entails taxpayers deliberately misrepresenting the true state of their business affairs to the tax authorities to reduce their tax liability and includes dishonest tax reporting. The dealers will try to reduce their liability to pay tax by indulging in some of the following practices.

- Do not collect the tax.
- Evade tax by collecting the tax but not reporting it to the government and thus pocketing the tax.
- Show fake exempt transactions, i.e., branch transfer.
- Show fake sales to other states/countries to claim lower tax rate.

- Bill trading is an organized crime [10]. In this approach, one dealer sells goods to a buyer without issuing an invoice but collecting tax. He then issues a fake invoice to another dealer, who uses it to minimize his tax liability.

To hide these manipulations, which are easily detectable by tax authorities, dealers exchange goods (can be fictitious goods) among themselves without any value-add. This tax evasion technique is called *circular trading* [2] [4] [8].

C. Circular Trading

One of the major malpractices to VAT evasion is *circular trading*. The motivation for circular trading is to hide suspicious sales/purchase transactions, which can be detectable by sales authorities. They hide these suspicious transactions by doing several illegitimate sale transactions among themselves in a short duration in a circular manner without any *value-add*, as shown in Figure 2. Since there is no value-add for the illegitimate transactions, they do not pay VAT on these illegitimate transactions and confuse the tax authorities about suspicious transactions. In this manner, they complicate the process of identifying suspicious transactions.

Some of these fraudulent traders who are part of circular trading can be fictitious (dummy) traders created by malicious real traders.

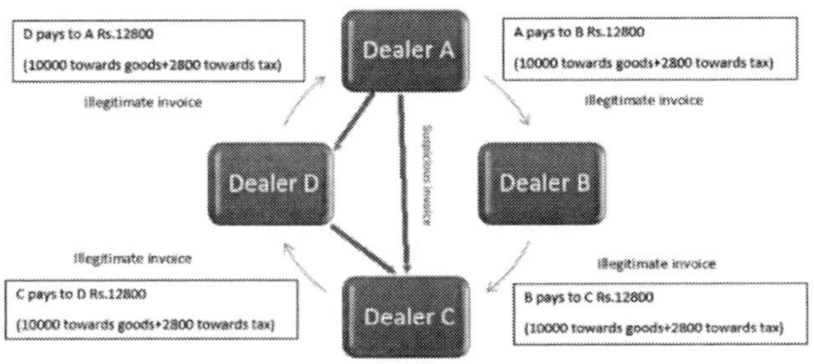

Figure 2. circular flow of sales/purchases

In Figure 2, transactions shown in thick line from A to D, A to C and D to C are suspicious transactions. In order to complicate the process of detection of these suspicious transactions by tax authorities, dealers superimpose illegitimate transactions on the suspicious transaction, as shown using thin lines. Note that the superimposition of thin lines transactions did not change the tax liability of any dealer.

The problem that we address in this paper is to identify suspicious sales transactions, which are superimposed by several illegitimate sales transactions.

The difficulties in identifying suspicious sales transactions are the large size of sales database, complex sequence of illegitimate sales transactions, large number of traders, unknown number and identity of traders in the circular trading. In this paper, we propose algorithms to remove illegitimate sales transactions, which are superimposed on suspicious sales transactions. This allows tax authorities to identify suspicious transactions in an easy manner.

The structure of the paper is as follows. In Section II, several approaches which are available in literature to detect circular trading have been described. In Section III, the problem is formulated as finding specific type of cycles in directed edge-weighted multigraph and an overview of the solution is given. In Section IV, a detailed algorithm along with its proof of correctness is given. In Section V, we have taken up a case in which eight dealers are doing heavy circular trading among themselves and analyzed the case in detail using our proposed algorithm.

II. Related Work

Most approaches for detecting circular trading are concentrated on stock market trading. In [4], a graph clustering algorithm specially tailored for detecting collusion sets in stock market is given. A novel feature of this approach is the use of Dempster–Schafer theory of evidence to combine the candidate collusion sets. In [7], a method is proposed to detect the potential collusive cliques involved in an instrument of future markets by first calculating the correlation coefficient between any two eligible unified aggregated time series of signed order volume, and then combining the connected components from multiple sparsified weighted graphs constructed by using the correlation matrices where each correlation coefficient is over a user-specified threshold. In [5], the authors proposed an approach to detect collusion sets using Markov Clustering Algorithm (MCL). Their method can detect purely circular collusions as well as cross trading collusions. They have used MCL at various strength of "residual value" to detect different cluster sets from the same stock flow graph. Classic centrality functions for graphs are able to identify the key players of a network or their intermediaries. However, these functions provide little information in large and heterogeneous graphs. Often the most central elements of the network (usually too many) are not related to a collections of actors of interest, such as a group of drug traffickers or fraudsters. Instead, its high centrality is due to the good relations of these central elements with other honorable actors. In [14], the authors introduced complicity functions, which are capable of identifying the intermediaries in a group of actors, avoiding core elements that have nothing to do with this group. These functions can classify a group of criminals according to the strength of their relationships with other actors to facilitate the detection of organized crime rings. In [11], the authors presented a statistics-based method for detecting value-added tax evasion by Kazakhstani legal entities. Starting from features selection they performed an initial exploratory data analysis using Kohonen self-organizing maps; this allowed them to make basic assumptions on the nature of tax compliant companies. Then they selected a statistical model and proposed an algorithm to estimate its parameters in an unsupervised manner. In [9], the authors presented a case study of a pilot project that was developed to evaluate the use of data mining in audit selection for the Minnesota Department of Revenue (DOR). They described the manual audit selection process used at the time of the pilot project for Sales and Use taxes, discussed the data from various sources, addressed issues regarding feature selection, and explained the data mining techniques used.

Several approaches are available in the literature to detect cycles in directed graphs. Traditional methods rely on depth-first searches (DFS)[1], exploiting the fact that a graph has a cycle if and only if the DFS finds a so-called back edge. Recent works on the topic include distributed algorithms that aim at maintaining an acyclic graph when new links are added to an initially acyclic graph [6]. In [15], the authors introduced a new problem, cycle detection and removal with vertex priority. It proposes a multithreading iterative algorithm to solve this problem for large-scale graphs on personal computers. In [12], the authors considered the problem of detecting a cycle in a directed graph that grows by arc insertions, and the related problems of maintaining a topological order and the strong components of such a graph.

III. Problem Formulation

A. Sales Database Format

Table 1 contains a few fields of the sales transaction database.

Table I. SALES TRANSACTIONS DATABASE

S.NO	Seller	Buyer	Time of Sales	Sales in Rupees
1	Dealer A	Dealer B	2017/01/03/10:30	10000
2	Dealer C	Dealer D	2017/01/03/12:00	15000
3	Dealer A	Dealer D	2017/01/04/09:00	12000
4	Dealer B	Dealer C	2017/01/04/10:00	14000
5	Dealer C	Dealer A	2017/01/04/10:30	10000

The actual sales transactions database contains many other details like, quantity of sales, vehicle used for transporting, etc. Each record in this sales transactions database refers to a single sales transaction.

B. Time-stamped directed graphs

Using the sales database, we construct a directed edge-labeled multigraph called *sales flow graph*, denoted by $G_s = (V, E, \Phi)$, where V is the set of vertices(each vertex is labeled by a dealer name), E is the set of directed edges and Φ is the function that associates a 2-tuple for each edge, where first element of the tuple is the time of sales of this transaction and second element is the value of sales of this transaction. Figure 3 shows the sales flow graph of Table I.

Let us define a few notations. Note that each edge in the graph has two parameters, one is the time of sale and the other is the value of sales. The *end time* of a cycle is defined as the time of most recent transaction among all the transactions corresponding to edges in the given cycle. The end time of the cycle *ABC* in Figure 3 is *2017/01/04/10:30* of the edge

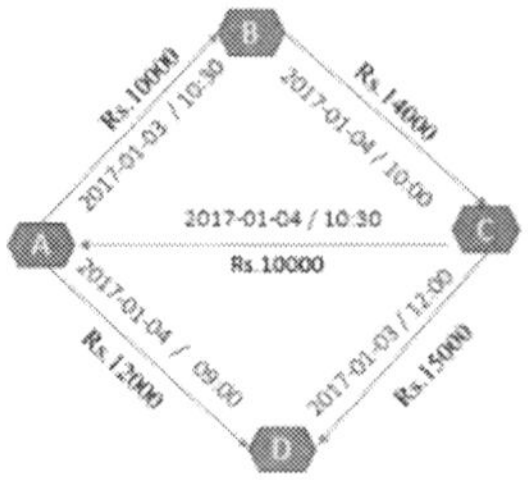

Figure 3. Sales Flow Graph

CA. The *start time* of a cycle is defined as the time of least recent transaction among all the transactions corresponding to edges in the given cycle. The start time of the cycle *ABC* in figure 3 is *2017/01/03/10:30* corresponding to the edge AB. The *span* of a cycle is defined as the difference between *end time* and *start time*. The span of the cycle *ABC* in figure 3 is *2017/01/04/10:30 - 2017/01/03/10:30 = 24:00*. The *bottle neck value* of a path is defined as the time of least recent transactions among all transactions corresponding to edges in the given path. The *bottleneck* value of the path *BCAD* in Figure 3 is *2017/01/04/9:00*.

C. Overview of the solution

From the in-depth research by taxation authorities, it is observed that dealers do illegitimate sales transactions among themselves in a very short period of time. Any illegitimate cycle should satisfy the following conditions since for any dealer the net tax liability due to illegitimate transactions should be zero.

- For a dealer in any illegitimate cycle the tax he pays on illegitimate purchase transaction should be same as the tax he collects on illegitimate sales transaction. This makes net tax liability due to illegitimate transactions zero.
- The quantity of goods involved in an illegitimate purchase should be the same as the quantity of goods of illegitimate sale. Otherwise, it is easy for tax authorities to detect these illegitimate transactions.

To meet the above two conditions the price of one unit of goods should be the same in every illegitimate transaction. Since the market price of goods can vary from day to day dealers perform all illegitimate transactions in a very short period of time. This means that the *span* of any illegitimate sales cycle is very small.

Our objective is to remove all illegitimate cycles from the sales flow graph. Then the remaining graph is a directed acyclic graph(DAG). Note that the resultant DAG contains all suspicious transactions. This make the fraud detection process easier and we can perform an in-depth analysis on suspicious transactions to identify tax evaders.

In the proposed algorithm, we remove illegitimate cycles from the *sales flow graph* one after the other in increasing order of their *end time*. If two cycles have the same *end time*, then we remove them in the increasing order of their *span*. Following is a brief sketch of the algorithm.

1) Select a cycle C in sales flow graph G_s with the following conditions:
   - *Condition 1: end time* of C is minimum among all the cycles in G_s
   - *Condition 2:* With respect to the condition one, *span* of C is minimum
2) Let m be the minimum of the values of sales of all the edges in C. Subtract m from values of sales of all edges in C.
3) Remove any edge from C whose value of sales becomes zero.
4) Repeat steps one to three, as long as G_s contains a cycle.

IV. ALGORITHM

A. Bottleneck Edge Computation Algorithm

The objective of Algorithm 1 is to find a path between the given source and destination vertices in a sales flow graph such that the *bottleneck* value is maximized.

Time Complexity: Assuming that there are V vertices in the graph, the queue Q may contain $O(V)$ vertices. Every time the *while* loop executes, one vertex is extracted from the queue Q and added to S. This operation takes $O(logV)$ time assuming the heap implementation of priority queues. So the total time required to execute the *while* loop itself is $O(VlogV)$.

Assuming that there are E edges in the graph,the inner *for* loop will be executed E times. Each iteration takes $O(logV)$ time assuming the heap implementation of priority queues. So, time complexity of this algorithm is $O(E * logV)$.

Proof Of Correctness:

Theorem 4.1: Let S be the set of visited vertices.

- For every vertex $v \in S$, bt[v] is the maximum among bottleneck values of all the paths from vertex a to vertex v.
- For every vertex $v \in V(G_s) - S$, if we consider only those paths from vertex a to vertex v where predecessor of v is in S, bt[v] is the maximum among bottleneck values of all such paths.

Proof Proof by induction on $|S|$.

Base case ($|S|$= 1): the only time $|S|$= 1 is when $S = \{a\}$. In this case

- bt[a] $= \infty$.
- For every $v \in V(G_s) - S$, which is adjacent to a, bt[v] is the time of sales of the edge av.

Inductive hypothesis: Let u be the last vertex moved from Q to S. Assume that theorem is true for the set $S' = S - \{u\}$.

Data: sales flow graph G_s and two vertices a, b in G_s
Result: A path from a to b such that *bottle neck value* is maximum, and the corresponding bottle neck value.

```
# Set the bottleneck value of source vertex a to ∞;
bt[a] = ∞;

# Set the predecessor of source vertex to NULL;
pred[a] = NULL;

# Set the bottleneck values of all other vertices to −∞;
For (all v ∈ V(Gs) − a){
bt[v] = −∞;
pred[v] = NULL}

# S be the set of visited vertices, initially it is empty;
S = ∅;

# Q be the queue of unvisited vertices, initially it contains all vertices;
Q = V(Gs);

while Q ≠ ∅ do
    Let u be a vertex in Q with maximum bottleneck value ;

    # Move the vertex u from queue Q to processed set S;
    S = S ∪ {u} ;
    Q = Q − u;

    For (all v ∈ neighbours(u))
    {
      # Note that there can be more than one edge from vertex u to vertex v. We take the edge whose time of sales is most recent;
      # If the bottleneck value of vertex v is less than the minimum among the bottleneck value of vertex u and the time of sales of the edge uv, then replace the bottleneck value of vertex v;

    if ((min(bt[u],time of sales of the edge uv) > bt[v]) then
        bt[v]= min(bt[u],time of sales of the edge uv);
        pred[v]=u;
    end
    }
end
```

Algorithm 1: Bottleneck Edge Computation Algorithm

Lemma 4.2: bt[u] is the maximum among bottleneck values of all paths from a to u

Proof Let $a, s_1, s_2, \ldots, s_k, q_1, \ldots, u$ be a path from a to u in G_s such that bottleneck value is maximum. Assume that $\{a, s_1, s_2, \ldots, , s_k\} \subseteq S'$ and $q_1 \in V(G_s) - S'$. Note that the bottleneck value of path $a, s_1, s_2, \ldots, s_k, q_1, \ldots, u$ is less than or equal to the bottleneck value of the path $a, s_1, s_2, \ldots, s_k, q_1$, which is less than or equal to $bt[q_1]$. Since we selected u such that $bt[u] \geq bt[v]$, for all $v \in V(G_s) - S'$, $bt[q_1] \leq bt[u]$. So, the bottleneck value of the path $a, s_1, s_2, \ldots, s_k, q_1, \ldots, u$ is less than equal to $bt[u]$. Since $a, s_1, \ldots, s_k, q_1, \ldots, u$ is a path from a to u in G_s such that bottleneck value is maximum, bottleneck value of the path $a, s_1, s_2, \ldots, s_k, q_1, \ldots, u$ is equal to $bt[u]$

Lemma 4.3: For every vertex $v \in V(G_s) - S$, if we consider only those paths from vertex a to vertex v where predecessor of v is in S, $bt[v]$ is the maximum among bottleneck values of all such paths.

Proof The proof is based on the fact that every vertex $v \in S$, bt[v] is the maximum among bottleneck values all path from a to v.

This proves the theorem.

B. Minimum Span Cycles Removal Algorithm

The objective of this algorithm is to remove illegitimate cycle in sales flow graph. This algorithm uses the Algorithm 1 to find a cycle with minimum span.

Data: sales flow graph G_s
Result: Forest G_t, which is obtained by removing all cycles in G_s

G_t = Edgeless graph whose vertex set is $V(G_s)$;
Let $l_1, l_2, \ldots, l_m$ be a sequence of all edges in G_s ordered by non decreasing order of time of sales;
for $i = 1 \ldots m$ **do**
  insert the edge l_i in the graph G_t;
  while *(G_t contains cycle)* **do**
    Assume that the edge l_i is from vertex b to vertex a in G_t;
    Let $a, v_1, \ldots, v_k, b$ be a path from a to b in G_t such that the bottleneck value is maximum;
    Let cycle $C = a, v_1, \ldots, v_k, b$;
    Let p be the minimum among price of sales of all edges in C;
    Subtract p from price of sales of all edges in C;
    Remove all edge from G_t whose price of sales is zero;
  end
end

Algorithm 2: Cycle Removal Algorithm

V. CASE STUDY

We had taken up a synthetic data set in which few dealers are doing heavy circular trading among themselves. Figure 4 shows the details of this circular trade. The value of each edge represents the value of sales in lakhs (one *lakh* is equal to 0.1 million), and note that it is the sum value of several transactions between two particular dealers directed from one to the other.

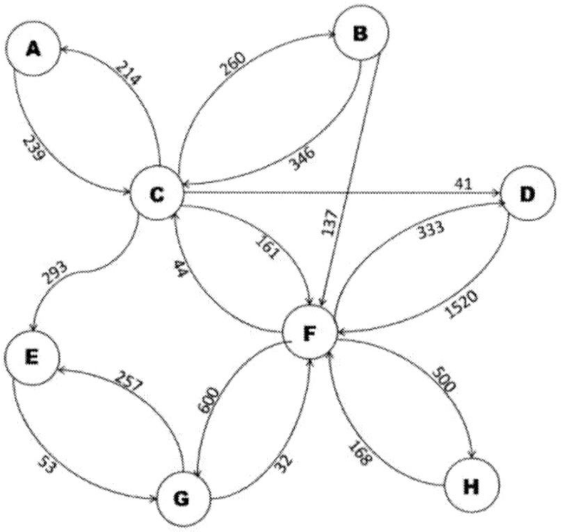

Figure 4. Sales flow graph

As given in Figure 4, there are numerous cycles among this group of dealers and these cycles are considered as undesirable patterns by domain experts. Cycles are undesired in these transactions since a cycle indicates the buying of the same goods by a dealer which (s)he has previously sold. According to domain experts, this kind of flow of goods is not valid for the particular commodity which these people are trading among themselves. These cycles indicate that there is a great chance for tax evasion. As mentioned in Sub-section C of Section III, the dealers involved in a circular trade need to fabricate these cycles in a short duration of time. We used the proposed algorithm to delete the illegitimate cycles. Figure 5 shows the directed acyclic graph obtained after deleting all cycles from the graph given in Figure 4. The novelty of our technique over the others in deleting cycles is that since we delete cycles that forms in a short duration of time, with high accuracy we delete the illegitimate edges used to form these cycles. This would not be the case if we had deleted the cycles using other techniques. Recall that the objective of the illegitimate transactions were to hide these suspicious transactions, and the directed acyclic graph (DAG) given in Figure 5 contains the suspicious transactions. Analysis of this DAG gives significant information which can be used by the taxation authorities for conducting further investigations.

By studying the purchases/sales they did it is observed that they should have paid huge tax, buy they paid only negligible amount of tax by showing fictitious exports and inter state

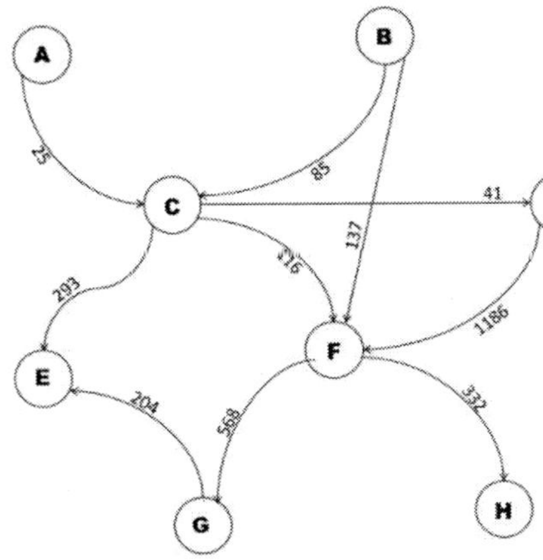

Figure 5. Suspicious transactions

sales. To hide this fictitious sales they created a web of sales and purchase transactions among themselves.

VI. Conclusion

In this paper, we stated and formalized an important practical problem in the commercial taxation system called *circular trading*. *Circular trading* is the method in which a set of traders do heavy illegitimate sales/purchase transactions in a circular manner among themselves in a short duration without any *value-add*. The problem of removing these type of cycles is important because, tax authorities can easily detect suspicious transactions once the cycles are removed. Here, we proposed an algorithm to remove such type of illegitimate cycles. As further work, we are investigating to find more effective ways of removing cycles.

VII. Acknowledgement

We would like to express our deep thanks towards the government of Telangana, India, for allowing us to use the Commercial Taxes Data set and giving us constant encouragement and financial support.

References

[1] E. W. Dijkstra and S. S. Scholten. "Termination detection for diffusing computations". In: *Information Processing Letter* 11 (1980), pp. 1–4.

[2] M. Franke, B. Hoser, and J. Schröder. "On the analysis of irregular stock market trading behavior". In: *Data Analysis, Machine Learning and Applications*. ISBN: 978-3-540-78239-1, URL: https://link.springer.com/chapter/10.1007/978-3-540-78246-9_42. Springer, Jan. 2007, pp. 355–362.

[3] Alan Schenk and Oliver Oldman, eds. *Value Added Tax: A Comparative Approach*. ISBN: 978-1107617629. Cambridge University Press, Jan. 2007.

[4] G. K. Palshikar and M.M. Apte. "Collusion set detection using graph clustering". In: *Data Mining and Knowledge Discovery*. ISSN: 1384-5810, URL: https://link.springer.com/article/10.1007/s10618-007-0076-8. Springer, Apr. 2008, pp. 135–164.

[5] N. Md. Islam et al. "An approach to improve collusion set detection using MCL algorithm". In: *Computers and Information Technology*. ISBN: 978-1-4244-6284-1, URL: http://ieeexplore.ieee.org/abstract/document/5407133/. IEEE, Dec. 2009, pp. 237–242.

[6] B. Haeupler et al. " Incremental cycle detection, topological ordering, and strong component maintenance". In: *ACM Transactions on Algorithms* vol. 8, no. 1 (2012), pp. 1–33.

[7] J. Wang, S. Zhou, and J. Guan. "Detecting potential collusive cliques in futures markets based on trading behaviors from real data". In: *Neurocomputing* 92 (2012), pp. 44–53.

[8] K. Golmohammadi, O.R. Zaiane, and D. Díaz. " Detecting stock market manipulation using supervised learning algorithms". In: *Data Science and Advanced Analytics*. ISBN: 978-1-4799-6991-3 , URL: http://ieeexplore.ieee.org/document/7058109/. IEEE, Nov. 2014, pp. 435–441.

[9] Hsu KW.and Pathak N. et al. "Data Mining Based Tax Audit Selection: A Case Study of a Pilot Project at the Minnesota Department of Revenue". In: *Real World Data Mining Applications*. ISBN: 978-3-319-07811-3, URL: https://doi.org/10.1007/978-3-319-07812-0_12/. Springer, Nov. 2014, pp. 221–245.

[10] B. Baesens, V.V. Vlasselaer, and W. Verbeke, eds. *Fraud Analytics Using Descriptive, Predictive, and Social Network Techniques: A Guide to Data Science for Fraud Detection*. ISBN: 978-1-119-13312-4. Wiley, Aug. 2015.

[11] Zhenisbek Assylbekov et al. "Detecting Value-Added Tax Evasion by Business Entities of Kazakhstan". In: *Intelligent Decision Technologies 2016*. ISBN: 978-3-319-39629-3, URL: https://doi.org/10.1007/978-3-319-39630-9_4/. Springer, 2016, pp. 37–49.

[12] Michael A. Bender, Jeremy T. Fineman, and Robert E. Tarjan Seth Gilbert. "A New Approach to Incremental Cycle Detection and Related Problems". In: *ACM Transactions on Algorithms* Volume 12 Issue 2 (2016), p. 22.

[13] S. Dani. "A Research Paper on an Impact of Goods and Service Tax(GST) on Indian Economy". In: *Business and Economics Journal* 7 (2016). ISSN: 2151-6219, p. 264.

[14] E. Vicente, A. Mateos, and A. Jiménez-Martín. "Detecting stock market manipulation using supervised learning algorithms". In: *Modeling Decisions for Artificial Intelligence*. ISBN: 978-3-319-45655-3, URL: https://link.springer.com/chapter/10.1007/978-3-319-45656-0_17. Springer, Sept. 2016, pp. 205–216.

[15] Huanqing Cui et al. "A Multi-Threading Algorithm to Detect and RemoveCycles in Vertex- and Arc-Weighted Digraph". In: *Algorithms 2017* 10 (2017), p. 115.

When Teachers and Machines Achieve the Best Combination: A National Comparative Study of Face-to-face and Blended Teaching and Learning

Cecilia Marconi
Data Analytics Section
Plan Ceibal
Av. Italia 6201 - CP 11500
Montevideo, Uruguay
Email: cmarconi@ceibal.edu.uy

Juan José Goyeneche
Instituto de Estadística
Fac. de C. Econ. y de Adm.
Universidad de la República
Eduardo Acevedo 1139 - CP 11200
Montevideo, Uruguay
Email: jjgoye@iesta.edu.uy

Cristóbal Cobo
Center for Research
Ceibal Foundation
Av. Italia 6201 - CP 11500
Montevideo, Uruguay
Email: ccobo@fundacionceibal.edu.uy

***Abstract*—This paper analyzes a national technology and education program in Uruguay known as Plan Ceibal. This work studies a sample of over 105,000 students from 4th, 5th, and 6th grade of public primary education in that country. This work aims to assess the impact of technology on teaching and learning of English. The method adopted is based on log-file data to compare two different modalities of English teaching (a face-to-face and a blended model). Additionally, we explored the correlation between a common measure of online engagement when using the Learning Management System (LMS) and an adaptive English assessment. We examined the impact of the teaching modalities on the students engagement and to what extent the engagement can contribute to enhance the student learning of English. This work documents the steps followed to elaborate the common measure of engagement to ensure transparency and its replicability (or improvement). A strength of this work, in comparison with previous studies, is the number of cases analyzed as well as the age of the target population (primary school students). The results indicate that engagement is affected by at least three key factors: socio-cultural context, teaching modality, and the role that teachers play. In fact, the higher the engagement level, the larger the proportion of students who achieve a better learning outcome in the assessment. This study shows that the use of LMS enhanced the learning experience when this tool is integrated within the ecosystem of the teaching and learning process. The findings of this study are consistent with previous works in the field, for instance: the relevance of the context as well as the role of teaching. Although the measurement of engagement can help to understand students performance noteworthy that as a stand-alone dimension it is a poor predictor of performance. To consider additional factors associated with learning is still necessary.**

***Keywords*—Plan Ceibal; Online learning; LMS Engagement; Learning Analytics; Adaptive test**

I. Introduction

This study analyzes a national technology and education program in Uruguay known as Plan Ceibal. In particular, this work aims to assess the impact of technology on teaching and learning of English in public primary schools. Previous research works have shown that the deployment of educational technology as such, can not necessarily be translated into better learning outcomes [1]. So, it is critical to consider associated factors such as the context, the teachers training, the pedagogical strategies among other factors which can play a relevant role during learning [2].

Since the Plan Ceibal works at a national level, it must manage and analyze large-scale platforms and datasets gathered from the whole public educational system. This wealth of data becomes a unique opportunity for conducting data analytics exploration. For instance, it opens the opportunity for combining and analyzing dimensions such as: access to technology, type of use of the devices in different modalities of teaching, frequency of use, among others [3] [4]. All these dimensions are relevant, but, as previous research shows, in order to play a meaningful role during the educational process, it is critical that students are engaged in the use of the technology during their learning experience. That is why our work aims to analyze students engagement during their learning experience [5]. It is relevant for our work to build a common measure of online engagement. This measure can be particularly useful to analyze from a comparative perspective how the different teaching modalities of English (a face-to-face and a blended one) have an impact on students engagement and to what extent this measure of engagement when using the LMS can contribute to enhance the student learning of English. This analysis focuses on the online interactions with the LMS platform, which includes over 13.7 million records, of 4th, 5th, and 6th grade students in two teaching modalities of English from the public educational system of Uruguay during 2015.

The study is structured as follows. Sections II describes the two different modalities of teaching English and the national evaluation. Sections III presents the methodological aspects of this work. Section IV includes the results and a discussion of the results obtained. Finally, Section V summarizes the conclusions and and suggests further work.

II. Educational context

In Uruguay, the teaching of English in primary schools is conducted under two different modalities. We are comparing two EFL (English as a Foreign Language) programs. One is delivered entirely face-to-face and the other uses a blended modality.

A. Face-to-Face modality

The Second Language Program runs a face to face teaching program. This modality consists of 3 hours per week for 4th, 5th and 6th graders. The pedagogical activities of the class are defined by each teacher. In this modality, there is no prescriptive definition regarding the use of technology (face-to-face classes can be enhanced by the use of LMS or other platforms).

B. Blended modality

"Ceibal en Inglés" is a program conducted since 2012 in partnership between Plan Ceibal and British Council to overcome the shortage of qualified EFL teachers in Uruguay. It offers a blended approach integrating remote teaching via video conference, LMS and traditional face-to-face instruction. It was designed for primary school learners in 4th, 5th and 6th grades, who have English lessons three times a week [6]. This blended model enabled to conduct multidimensional data analysis, offering useful information for both the academic community and the policy makers.

C. National evaluation of both modalities

Since 2014, the National Educational System (ANEP, by its Spanish acronym), Plan Ceibal and the British Council implemented an annual EFL adaptive test applied to children in both teaching modalities (face-to-face and blended). Performance levels were designed in accordance with the standards defined by the The Common European Framework of Reference for Languages: Learning, Teaching, Assessment (CEFR) for the teaching and learning of Foreign Languages [7]. The students' EFL learning is assessed through an adaptive online test, including the following domains: Vocabulary, Reading, Grammar (VRG), Listening and Writing. The assessment adapts to the level of knowledge of the test taker. Depending on the accuracy of the student answers to previous questions, the assessment displays either a more difficult or an easier question as subsequent test items.

The scores patterns indicate that the best results are obtained by students from higher socio-cultural contexts, as defined by ANEP. In addition, the higher the student grade level, the better the results [8]. A subset of the sample of 21.989 students who completed both 2014 and 2015 tests was analyzed. The results showed significant improvements from 2014 to 2015, across all three grades, regardless of students socio-cultural contexts. However, the learning outcomes gap between students from high and low socio-cultural context remain throughout these years.

III. Methodological Aspects

In this section, we present the objectives of this study, a summary of the state of the art and the different methodological steps implemented to reach our goals. Particularly, we present our proposal of an engagement index and the characteristics of our dataset.

A. Key questions

The main question of this study is: what is the effect of the teaching modality (blended vs face-to-face) on the level of LMS engagement. We also considered a subsidiary question: to what extent the use of this technology contributes to enhance the learning outcomes of learners?

B. Previous research

Using LMS data is often at the heart of learning analytics studies. It is also one of the most popular research orientations due to its ubiquity in many educational institutions [9]. Although the expectation is that students' use of the LMS features have a positive effect on student performance, previous research works show mixed results: basic LMS data does not predict student academic performance [10]. LMS usage is at best a poor proxy for actual user-behaviour of students. The challenge is to build a more comprehensive understanding of online practices. Previous works indicate that a combination of LMS data with data from assessments can be a better predictor for students learning outcome or engagement [11] [12]. More and more studies of online education have begun to focus on student engagement, noting that engagement is also influenced by the learning context and by the instructor who plays a significant influence in online (or blended) education [13] [14] [15] [16]. Student engagement can be represented by the time and effort students devote to their learning experience, but also based on the activities conducted online [17] [18]. When analyzing student engagement in the online learning environment, it is necessary to select the indicators to measure online engagement [19] [20]. As previous studies have explored [21], the integration of LMS into an English language course can offer a flexible and convenient space for learning, also called a "third space" for education. Likewise, recent works have examined different styles on the engagement patterns [22]. As Wintrup et al. report, previous studies have analyzed how learners engagement online varies according to their learning experience [23]. Previous works present an alternative methodology based on latent class models instead of computing a single index score [5] [24]. Having revised and analyzed the existing literature in the field [5] [6] [7] [8], this article develops a methodological approach grounded on data mining strategies using log-file data. One of the key contributions found in the literature is the measurement of students engagement using log data which is both minimally disruptive and highly scalable [8].

C. Data sources, sample and index computation

In order to answer our key questions, we used data from different sources. Our main dataset was the data from the logs of the LMS platform, 13.7 million records of events of the students activity during 2015. Administrative information was collected and merged from Ceibal (grade, school, classroom and the socio-cultural context of the school). In addition, for each student, we added the achieved score from the annual EFL adaptive online test. The test was applied to 4th, 5th and 6th grade students from primary education who attended either one of the two modalities of English teaching (blended and face-to-face). The assessment was not universal, although it reached 62% (65,699 students) of the total number of students [8]. This subset included members of all the socio-cultural contexts and grade levels. The proportion of students in each grade and in each socio-cultural level in this subsample were similar to the values of the total population.

The universe considered in this study are students from 4th, 5th and 6th grade of public primary education (105,715 students: 76,752 blended students, and 28,963 face-to-face students) from all (942) urban schools. Despite the large number of students and events registered, we managed the volume of the data with the standard libraries in R (base, stats) [25]. The original data was read using the library RODBC [26] to connect to Structured Query Language (SQL) Server.

The second step was to generate an index in order to systematize the students performance in the LMS, the Engagement Index (IEG, in Spanish). This index provided a combined indicator of key activities: students access, type of usage in the LMS and intensity of use. This index is used to establish a common measure to compare both English teaching modalities.

The properties considered during the elaboration of the index were (a) it should be increasing with higher level of engagement, (b) it must be bounded, preferably between 0 and 1, and (c) it should be on a logarithmic or relative scale.

In order to summarize the students activity on the platform, a subset of 13 variables were selected from the dataset. These variables computed the number of times that a certain task was done (logging in, uploading files, etc.) and the number of different days when those tasks were done. Since some of these variables were highly correlate, we selected those that showed less correlation (less than 0.8) in order to represent the various aspects of the multivariate analysis. The variables used in the index were: x_1 = number of assignments submitted, x_2 = number of files uploaded, x_3 = number of comments, x_4 = number of comments on submissions, x_5 = number of days in which comments on submissions are made, and x_6 = number of days in which some activity took place.

The computation of the IEG includes two steps: aggregation of the six variables involved, and re- scaling and smoothing of the result. First, we computed $\pi = \prod_{i=1}^{6}(1+x_i)$, which takes a minimum value of 1 when all variables are zero. Then, we transform the product of the six functions of the variables:

$$IEG = (\delta + 1)/\delta \times [(\pi/(\delta + \pi) - 1/(\delta + 1)],$$

where δ is a smoothing parameter (after some calibration we set $\delta = 90$ for the IEG). It can be seen that $IEG = 0$ if $\pi = 1$ and $IEG \to 1$ as $\pi \to \infty$. After having obtained the index, the following step was to analyze the behavior of the IEG at different levels of analysis (student-level vs classroom-level) according to the English teaching modalities.

Finally, in order to answer the second research question, we explored the correlation between IEG and the adaptive English test scores. From the total number of students (65,699) who completed the computerized adaptive test, 46,776 were blended students enrolled in the LMS, so our correlational analysis focused particularly on this subset.

IV. Results and Discussion

The findings of this study are structured in two sections, in order to answer the questions, followed by a discussion. First, we conduct a comparative analysis to explore to what extent the teaching modality (blended vs face-to-face) defines the level of engagement in the use of the LMS. Second, we present to what extent the use of the LMS enhances the learning outcomes of learners. Finally, we discuss the results.

A. Relation between engagement and teaching modalities

Based on a comparative analysis of the coverage rate for access to the platforms done by learners according to the modality of English teaching, it was observed that blended students registered the highest student coverage rates (82% blended versus 52% face-to-face). We interpret that these results, in addition to the proportion of blended students (76,752) in the total number (105,715), indicate that the access to the LMS can be explained mostly by the role the platform plays in the remote teaching of English. It was also observed that the coverage rate increases with the student grade level: 65.7%, 67.5% and 73.3% for 4th, 5th and 6th, respectively.

The differences identified in the coverage rate according to the modality of English teaching can be also observed in terms of the intensity of use of the platform. Figure 1 shows the engagement index obtained per student for the two teaching modalities. The engagement index reflects a higher participation and interaction of blended students, with an average of 0.5 and a median of 0.5, whereas for the face-to-face students the average is 0,3 and the median is 0. Furthermore, as seen in other studies [27], we found a positive correlation between students engagement and the socio-cultural context. The medians for the IEG for each one of the socio-cultural quintiles are: $Q_1 = 0.11, Q_2 = 0.22, Q_3 = 0.41, Q_4 = 0.57$, and $Q_5 = 0.85$, where Q_1 is the most critical and Q_5 is the least critical context.

Figure 1 shows that for approximately 30% of the blended students the interaction with the LMS is zero or very low. These low values at the beginning of the curve are notably extended in the graphic corresponding to face-to-face students; more than half of them have zero or very low levels of IEG. It can be seen that the proportion of students with higher engagement is more relevant in the case of the blended students. Finally, the index illustrates that, in the case of the blended students, the distribution between the students with high and low engagement is very similar, while in the case of the face-to-face students the largest proportion of the students register a very low engagement index. For illustrative purposes, a student with a IEG greater than 0.985 is a student who does at least 12 comments in 3 differents days, has 24 assignments submitted, 12 files uploaded, 4.2 comments on submissions and the standard activity frequency is 32 days per year when some activity took place.

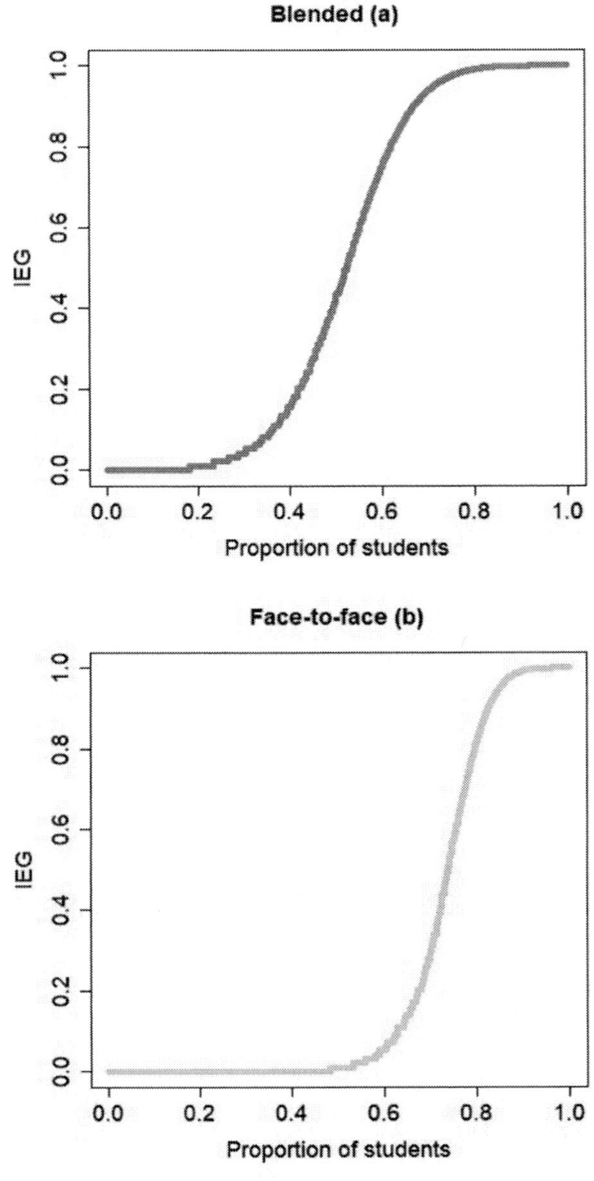

Figure 1. Blended (a) and Face-to-face (b): IEG distribution by modality of English teaching.

In the field of education, the data from schools have typically been considered as well-defined units with students "nested" or grouped within schools. The same happens at the classroom-level. The analysis at the classroom level contributes to examine what role do the teachers play in the engagement of their students.

For each student, an indicator was computed showing if they submitted any assignments. The new indicator, $y_1 = 1$ if $x_1 > 0$ and $y_1 = 0$ otherwise, was aggregated at the classroom level by computing its average for all the students in each classroom. A classroom with an average of 0.50 would mean that half of the students submitted at least one assignment and the rest of the students did not submit any. Figure 2 shows for each classroom the percentage of students with at least one assignment submitted. It can be seen that in both histograms, for the students in blended classrooms and for the ones in face-to-face classrooms, a U-shaped graph appears. The U-shaped graph shows that the average of y_1 for the classrooms do concentrate either near 0% or 100% suggesting the teachers effect on the level of students engagement. There are some teachers who do use the LMS, and therefore almost all of their students use it, and there are some teachers who do not use the LMS and neither do their students.

The engagement on the LMS is influenced by the modality of English teaching: more groups from blended than face-to-face registered a higher engagement (IEG). This indicates that the students' activity is not only determined by the teaching modality but also by the role played by the classroom teacher.

B. *Relationship between engagement and performance levels*

The correlation was computed between IEG and the adaptive online EFL test score. Performance levels of the test are designed in accordance to those of CEFR. The analysis was done with 46,776 blended students.We found a moderate correlations, namely, the Pearson correlation was 0.24 for all students. We compared the distribution of the levels reached by the students in the English assessment according to their level of IEG (see Table I). The analysis shows that the higher the IEG level, the larger the proportion of students that reach the highest levels of the test results. Only 32% of the blended students who have no activity in the LMS (IEG = 0) achieve the A2 level in the EFL test, whereas this percentage increases to 62% when we consider the students with a high level of engagement (IEG greater than 0.985).

The results obtained are observed in the comparison of the different estimated density functions of the obtained score for each IEG level. Figure 3 represents the blended students grouped based on their engagement performance. As mentioned before, the higher the IEG the higher their VRG score. The range of the score of the adaptive test is from 0 to 1500. The score was standardized with an average of 500 and a standard deviation of 100. After that, cut-off points were established to determine the levels in accordance to the CEFR. Figure 3 shows a shift to the right of the curves that represent a higher level of IEG.

TABLE I. ADAPTIVE EFL TEST (VRG) LEVELS OBTAINED BY LEVELS OF IEG.

	A0	*A1-*	*A1+*	*A2-*	*A2+*	*Total*
$IEG = 0$	1%	32%	35%	31%	1%	100%
$0 < IEG \leq 0.3$	1%	26%	32%	41%	1%	100%
$0.3 < IEG \leq 0.8$	0%	19%	28%	50%	2%	100%
$0.8 < IEG \leq 0.985$	0%	16%	27%	54%	3%	100%
$IEG \geq 0.985$	0%	10%	23%	62%	5%	100%

In order to compare the distribution of the VRG scores according to their level of IEG, we run Kolmogorov-Smirnov

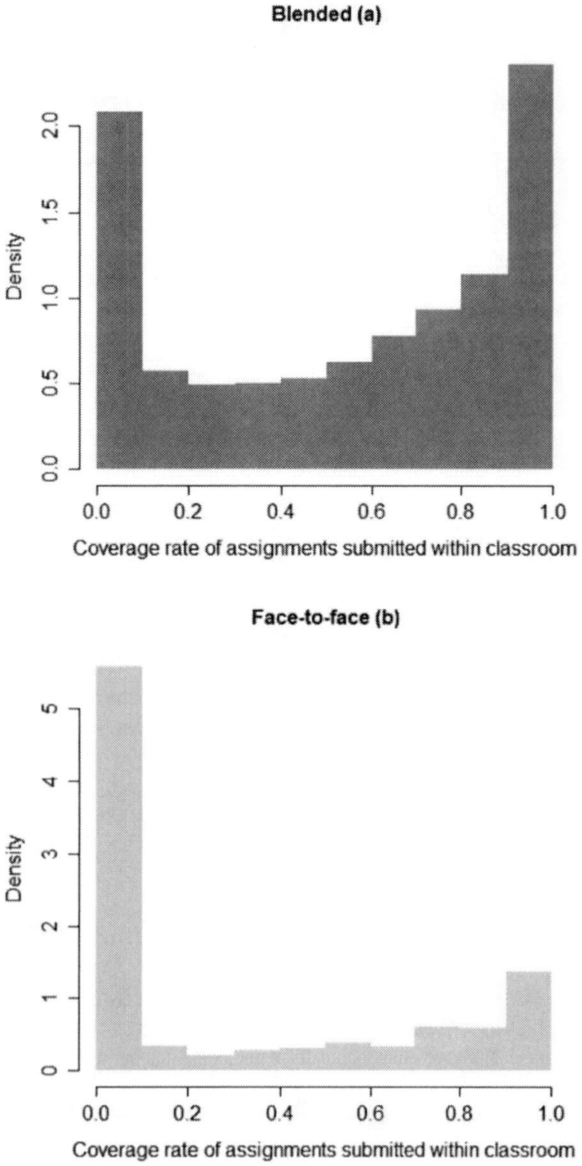

Figure 2. Blended (a) and Face-to-face (b): Percentage of students within a classroom with at least one submission by modality of English teaching.

tests in R for each pair of densities. The five distributions are significantly different (all of the *p-values* are less than 10^{-13}).

V. Discussion

The modality of teaching plays a relevant role during the learning of English. The results are consistent with previous works which suggest that online engagement is enabled or influenced by the role played by teachers or tutors [28] [29]. In other words, it is not only the deployment or access to the educational technology but the human factor which enables students participation or engagement. This study illustrates the advantages of an appropriate integration between the use of

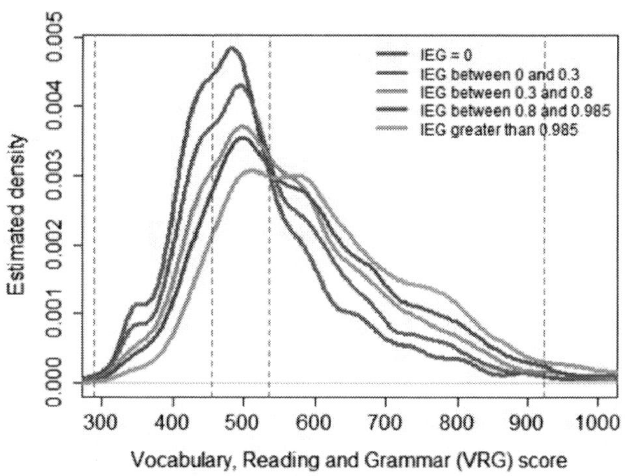

Figure 3. Blended students: estimated VRG score density by levels of IEG.

educational technology and face-to-face practices in primary level education. The majority of research works we reviewed address higher levels of education. However, in this case the analysis focused on K-12 students and the results showed to be consistent with the results of more advanced levels of education. Additionally, previous works have indicated that only small, positive relationship was identified between engagement and performance at the student's level [30]. In our work, we tested these results but aimed for a larger sample (national scale outside of the context of Massive Open Online Course) in order to explore the replicability of this trend. We identified low to moderate correlation between the use of the LMS (based on the engagement index) and the students performance on the adaptive test. This is aligned with what Gašević et al. (2016) [10] suggest that under specific circumstances engagement can be correlated with student performance, when measuring the use of LMS. However, engagement can not be understood as a unequivocal predictor of performance. In that sense, it is important to state that our results do not indicate causality on student performance but they suggest the usefulness of the LMS during the learning experience.

This study follows guidelines of previous works which have focused on engagement as a critical dimension to study students learning and/or participation [5] [23] [24] . One contribution of this study has been to document the elaboration of the engagement index. The input that our work provides is to document the steps followed during the selection of different variables as well as the weight that these values have in the elaboration of the IEG. This was done with two major purposes in mind: to ensure the transparency of the indexs elaboration, and to simplify the replicability (or improvement) of the IEG in future works.

VI. Conclusion and Further Work

This study aimed to analyze a large sample of 4th, 5th, and 6th grade primary students in Uruguay.We elaborated an Engagement Index to compare two different teaching modalities for learning English. One of them, more traditional based on face-to-face interaction where the teachers deliver the lessons in dialogue with learners. The other is conducted under a blended model, combining remote video conference, the use of a LMS and face-to-face interaction.

One of the findings that arises from the comparative analysis is that socio-cultural context and teaching modality are correlated with engagement. Students from higher socio-cultural contexts present higher levels of engagement. We identified that engagement increases with student grade level. In other words, the higher the students grade, the higher their LMS participation. Blended students registered a higher index of engagement in comparison to the face-to-face students. This could indicate that, when technological resources are well embedded in the design of the program, students engagement increases. The contribution of technology was registered even when the English proficiency of teachers was not high.

Regarding the learning outcome (test results) and the Engagement Index, we identified a consistent correlation in all groups analyzed, between frequency of use of the LMS and the English learning outcome. Although this result does not indicate causality, it suggests the usefulness of the platform. Engagement can help to understand students performance; however, as a stand-alone dimension, it is a poor predictor of performance. It is still necessary to consider additional factors associated with learning.

As shown in the analysis, IEG tries to capture the effect of the teaching modality (face-to face vs blended) in the integration of the LMS during the teaching practices. The results indicate that the use of LMS by 4th, 5th, and 6th grade students enhanced the learning experience when this tool is integrated within the ecosystem of the teaching and learning process.

Based on the findings, we present some reflections regarding the introduction of technology in educational practices with students in primary education. Although this study is exploratory based on data analysis, it is important to emphasize the role of teachers in relation to the use of the platforms at the primary level. Academic work exploring the impact of technology in education has usually studied large scale interventions in secondary and tertiary education, e.g., Massive Open Online Courses. It is expected that this study can contribute to future research in the field when exploring the role of technology with students in primary level.

One limitation of this research is that we can not claim that the sample is representative of the population. Although this study included a high number of students, the participants were self-selected (the ones assessed in the national adaptive test).

Future research can also revise the analysis of log data (optimizing the engagement index) in order to improve student outcomes. Additional studies could explore if it is possible to optimize the IEG measurement by capturing non-structured data, e.g., contents of the comments, quality of assignments from the LMS as well as using social network analysis. Further research can investigate the possibility to replicate the analysis using the 2016 log-data in order to verify the consistency of the patterns found. Finally, it would be interesting to identify the critical variables which explain and/or predict learning performance.

ACKNOWLEDGMENT

We would like to thank Hernán Silva and Sofía Doccetti who are part of the technical team. They would also like to thank Plan Ceibal, Ceibal en Ingleés and the Departamento de Segundas Lenguas for their support, and Claudia Brovetto, Gabriela Kaplan and Cecilia Aguerrebere for their valuable contributions.

REFERENCES

[1] F. Avvisati, "Students, Computers and Learning: Making the Connection," *OECD Publishing*, 2015.

[2] J. S. Brown and P. Duguid, "The Social Life of Information: Updated, with a New Preface," *Harvard Business Review Press*, 2017.

[3] M. Bailón, M. Carballo, C. Cobo, S. Magnone, C. Marconi, M. Mateu, and H. Susunday, "How can Plan Ceibal Land into the Age of Big Data?" *DATA ANALYTICS 2015, The Fourth International Conference on Data Analytics*, pp. 126–129, 2015.

[4] C. Cobo, M. Mateu, M. Gomez, and C. Aguerreberre, "Strategies for Data and Learning Analytics Informed National Education Policies: the Case of Uruguay," *7th Learning Analytics and Knowledge (LAK) conference organized by the Society for Learning Analytics Research (SOLAR) and the Simon Fraser University*, 2017.

[5] C. R. Henrie, "Measuring Student Engagement in Technology-Mediated Learning Environments," *All Theses and Dissertations*, vol. Paper 5949, 2016.

[6] C. Brovetto, "Ceibal en Inglés: Enseñanza de Inglés por videoconferencia en Educación Primaria. Aprendizaje Abierto y Aprendizaje Flexible. Más allá de formatos y espacios tradicionales," *Plan Ceibal*, pp. 210–229, 2013.

[7] "Common European Framework of Reference for Languages: learning, teaching,assessment, Language Policy," 2001, URL: https://www.coe.int/t/dg4/linguistic/Source/Framework_EN.pdf.

[8] C. Marconi and M. Luzardo, "Adaptive English evaluation in the Uruguayan educational system, 2015," *Plan Ceibal, CODICEN, British Council and CEIP, (S. Rovegno, Trans.)*, 2016.

[9] Y. Park and I. H. Jo, " Development of the Learning Analytics Dashboard to Support Students' Learning Performance," *J. UCS*, pp. 110–133, 2015.

[10] D. Gašević, S. Dawson, T. Rogers, and D. Gašević, "Learning analytics should not promote one size fits all: The effects of instructional conditions in predicting academic success," *The Internet and Higher Education*, vol. 28, pp. 68–84, 2016.

[11] A. Wolff, Z. Zdrahal, A. Nikolov, and M. Pantucek, "Improving retention: Predicting at-risk students by analysing clicking behaviour in a virtual learning environment," *In Paper presented at the proceedings of the third international conference on learning analytics and knowledge*, 2013.

[12] D. T. Tempelaar, B. Rienties, and B. Giesbers, " In search for the most informative data for feedback generation: Learning Analytics in a data-rich context," *Computers in Human Behavior*, vol. 47, pp. 157–167, 2015.

[13] J. Ma, X. Han, J. Yang, and J. Cheng, "Examining the necessary condition for engagement in an online learning environment based on learning analytics approach: The role of the instructor," *The Internet and Higher Education*, vol. 24, pp. 26–34, 2015.

[14] M. L. Hung and C. Chou, "Students' perceptions of instructors' roles in blended and online learning environments: A comparative study," *Computers and Education*, vol. 81, pp. 315–325, 2015.

[15] B. J. Calder, E. C. Malthouse, and U. Schaedel, "An experimental study of the relationship between online engagement and advertising effectiveness," *Journal of Interactive Marketing*, vol. 23(4), pp. 321–331, 2009.

[16] I. P. Cvijikj and F. Michahelles, "Online engagement factors on Facebook brand pages," *Social Network Analysis and Mining*, vol. 3(4), pp. 843–861, 2013.

[17] J. M. Jennings and T. E. Angelo, "Student engagement: Measuring and enhancing engagement with learning," *[Proceedings of a symposium], New Zealand Universities Academic Audit Unit*, 2006.
[18] G. D. Kuh, "What we're learning about student engagement from NSSE: Benchmarks for effective educational practices," *Change: The Magazine of Higher Learning*, vol. 35(2), pp. 24–32, 2003.
[19] S. Kinash, M. Judd, V. Naidu, E. Santhanam, J. Fleming, M. Tulloch, B. Tucker, and S. Nair, "Measuring and improving student course engagement and learning success through online student evaluation systems," *Learning and Teaching papers*, vol. Paper 113, 2015.
[20] J. D. Gobert, R. S. Baker, and M. B. Wixon, "Operationalizing and detecting disengagement within online science microworlds," *Educational Psychologist*, vol. 50, pp. 43–57, 2015, doi:10.1080/00461520.2014.999919.
[21] N. Sanprasert, "The application of a course management system to enhance autonomy in learning English as a foreign language," *System*, vol. 38, pp. 109–123, 2010, iSSN 0346-251X.
[22] S. Bhat, P. Chinprutthiwong, and M. Perry, "Seeing the Instructor in Two Video Styles: Preferences and Patterns," *International Educational Data Mining Society*, 2015.
[23] J. Wintrup, K. Wakefield, and H. C. Davis, "Engaged learning in MOOCs: a study using the UK Engagement Survey," 2015.
[24] A. Voight and J. Torney-Purta, "A typology of youth civic engagement in urban middle schools," *Applied Developmental Science*, vol. 17(4), pp. 198–212, 2013.
[25] R Core Team, *R: A Language and Environment for Statistical Computing*, R Foundation for Statistical Computing, Vienna, Austria, 2017. [Online]. Available: https://www.R-project.org/
[26] B. Ripley and M. Lapsley, *RODBC: ODBC Database Access*, 2017, r package version 1.3-15. [Online]. Available: https://CRAN.R-project.org/package=RODBC
[27] J. Kormos and T. Kiddle, "The role of socio-economic factors in motivation to learn English as a foreign language: The case of Chile," *System*, vol. 41(2), pp. 399–412, 2013.
[28] D. Gedera, J. Williams, and N. Wright, "Identifying factors influencing students motivation and engagement in online courses," *Springer, Singapore*, pp. 13–23, 2015.
[29] K. Larkin, "Course redesign to improve pre-service teacher engagement and confidence to teach mathematics: A case study in three parts," *International Journal for Mathematics Teaching and Learning*, vol. 17(1), 2016.
[30] M. Wells, A. Wollenschlaeger, D. Lefevre, G. D. Magoulas, and A. Poulovassilis, "Analysing engagement in an online management programme and implications for course design," *In Proceedings of the Sixth International Conference on Learning Analytics and Knowledge*, pp. 236–240, 2016.

Integrating the Balanced Scorecard and Web Analytics for Strategic Digital Marketing: A Multi-criteria Approach using DEMATEL

Dimitris K. Kardaras
School of Business, dept. of Business Administration
Athens University of Economics and Business
Athens, Greece
e-mail: kardaras@aueb.gr

Bill Karakostas
VLTN GCV
Antwerp, Belgium
e-mail: Bill.karakostas@vltn.be

Stavroula Barbounaki
Merchant Marine Academy of Aspropyrgos,
Aspropyrgos, Greece
e-mail: sbarbounaki@yahoo.gr

Anastasios Papadopoulos
School of Business, dept. of Business Administration
Athens University of Economics and Business
Athens, Greece
e-mail: anastasiopapadopoulos@gmail.com

Stavros Kaperonis
Dept. of Communication Media and Culture
Panteion University
Athens, Greece
e-mail: skap@panteion.gr

***Abstract*—Web analytics tools provide a wide range of information regarding the performance of a company. This information is valuable for assessing the strategic performance of a company. However, Web analytics tools at their current state of development fall short in providing all the necessary information and data analysis functionality that is required to assess the strategic performance and the digital marketing priorities of businesses. This paper utilizes DEMATEL (i.e. Decision Making Trial and Evaluation Laboratory) method in order to investigate how the Balanced Scorecard Model can be associated with data collected from the Google analytics. The data in this study are collected from the management and the Website of a company that provides tourism services in Greece. This research also examines the potential of using Web analytics in strategic decision analysis.**

Keywords-Google analytics, DEMATEL, Digital Marketing Analytics, Multi-Criteria Analysis.

I. INTRODUCTION

Information that can be found on Web analytics tools relates to the number of visitors, their demographics, their location, the paths of Web pages they visited, etc. Such information is valuable in assessing the current performance of a firm but also in planning its future development. Firms have already recognized that business activities on the Web are of particular importance for their growth. Subsequently they increasingly invest in digital marketing [1], [2]. Indeed, spending in digital marketing, including paid search, display advertising, social media advertising, online video advertising and email marketing will account to 46% of all advertising in five years from 2017, and it is expected to reach $120 billion by 2021 according to [3]. In another survey, by [4], 65% of marketing leaders surveyed in the US plan to increase their spending on digital advertising, due to factors that impose a continuing and consistent shift of offline media spending to digital advertising, a decline of organic social in favor of paid social and the rising importance of video, which is more expensive than other digital techniques.

On the other hand, a large number of strategic planning frameworks, such as the Balanced Scorecard (BSC), have been developed with the aim to assist top management designing the future development of their businesses across business sectors. For example, in logistics services, within the context of the SELIS ('Towards a Shared European Logistics Intelligent Information Space') research project, it is important to establish the conceptual links between Web analytics and business performance, i.e. to identify the appropriate KPIs (Key Performance Indicators) and model their interrelationships. Despite the large number of studies pertaining to strategic decision making, little research has attempted to integrate business strategic frameworks with Web analytics. Few are also the studies who attempt to explore the potential of Web analytics in strategic planning. [1], [2], and [5] argue there is very little academic or empirical work examining how Web analytics might impact an organization and what benefits they might bring. They have examined the strategic use of Web analytics but they did not investigate how Web analytics affect or affected by business metrics and KPIs defined in strategic frameworks such as the BSC. The need to develop a BSC model that takes into consideration the recent developments in e-business and Web analytics has already been recognized. An application for a "balanced web analytics scorecard" patent has been submitted in the US in 2014 by SAP (Systems, Applications and Products) AG (Aktiengesellschaft (i.e. in German: Stock Corporation) [6]. A balanced Web analytics scorecard considers perspectives, objectives and (KPIs) based on Web analytics. According to the patent application, the balanced Web analytics scorecard suggests at least one perspective related to Web-based activities, such as a traffic generation perspective, a visitor engagement perspective, a growth and innovation perspective or an e-commerce perspective. Scores for Web analytic-based measures are calculated based on the Web analytics, while the patent suggests that updated balanced Web analytics scorecards can be stored and be made available on a computing device. The consideration of multiple KPIs implies multi-criteria methods' suitability for assessing the business strategic performance. This paper suggests the use of DEMATEL, which is well established and used in similar studies [7]. The DEMATEL is proposed for it allows decision makers, e.g. business managers, to express their beliefs regarding the inter-relationships among KPIs, as well as to indicate their business priorities. In addition, the DEMATEL produces the cause-effect model that can be used to simulate several strategic scenarios and investigate their impact on the KPIs in consideration.

Thus, this research aims to:

- Propose a multi-criteria approach for identifying and assessing the interactions among the perspectives defined in the Balanced Scorecard model and Web analytics.
- Evaluate analytics tools, such as the Google analytics, as strategic analysis tools, and suggest ways for their improvement.

II. THE BALANCED SCORE CARD

The BSC is considered, by many managers, as an important tool in strategic management [8]. The use of the BSC is based on the visualization, through a specific drew up shape, of a company's strategic management plan [8]. The BSC is a model for the measurement and the performance analysis of all types of businesses. It was developed by Kaplan and Norton [9], [10]. They argued that the mere consideration of the established financial criteria was not enough to measure the business performance, since financial criteria could not represent all aspects of businesses. Therefore, they suggested that the (KPIs) of a company should also include measures related to the products, the company's interaction with its customers, the holistic view of company's internal processes and the outcome of the organization's activity to improve, innovate and develop its business procedures [9], [10]. The combined consideration of both financial and non-financial criteria offers the company's management a comprehensive list of measures that reflect various aspects of the business and its current outcomes as well as indicate the potential for the business to react or even preempt against the fast changing requirements of the market's environment [11]. The BSC can be used as an additional supportive asset for the company management during decision making and it can directly contribute to the formulation of long term value based relationships with the stakeholders [8]. A BSC considers four perspectives namely, the Financial, the Customer, the Internal Business Processes and the Learning and Growth, with the associated (KPIs) for each perspective. An example of a BSC is shown in Figure 1.

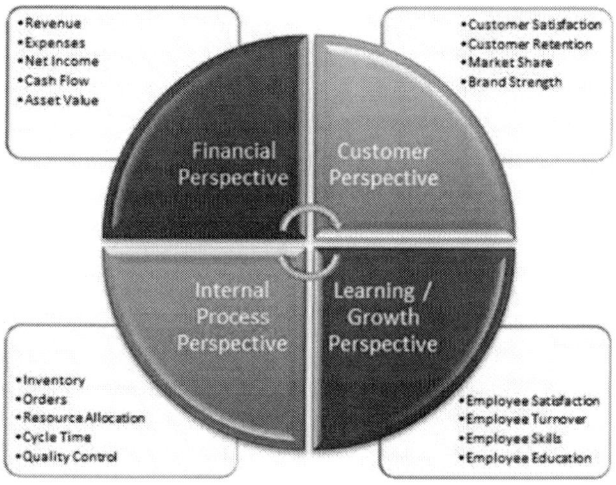

Figure 1. [12]

In order to examine its research objectives, this study focuses on the financial and customer perspectives, for simplicity reasons.

III. METHODOLOGY AND METHODS

3.1 *Methodology for evaluating business strategy based on Web analytics*

This study proposes a multi-criteria approach in order to assess the business strategic performance by utilizing the BSC and the information that is available on Web analytics platforms. Data is collected from two sources. Firstly, from the management of the company that participated in our case study, and, secondly, from the company's Google analytics tool. The data is analyzed by utilizing the DEMATEL multicriteria analysis method. In recent years, many researchers adopted Multi-Criteria Decision Making (MCDM) approaches for solving problems such as assessing alternative solutions, selection problems, strategic analysis [13] etc. The steps of the proposed methodology adopted follow.

Step 1: Collect data from the business management regarding strategic priorities (management data). The data in our study are selected from a company that operates in the tourism industry in Greece. Through its website, the company allows tourists of higher income to book luxurious villas for their holidays. A group of five (5) managers, dealing with digital marketing and business development, had agreed to participate in our study. At first, the managers were asked to review the BSC and specify a list of KPIs that would represent the BSC perspectives most appropriately to their business. Next, the managers were asked to review the Google analytics data set of the company and to select a list of parameters they would consider most important. The group of managers was also presented with a comprehensive list of Web analytics KPIs as found in [2]. The Fuzzy Delphi method [13] was utilized in order to prioritize and finally select managers' suggestions. The final list of parameters is shown in Table I:

TABLE I. THE SELECTED KPIS RELATED TO THE BSC PERSPECTIVES AND THE GOOGLE ANALYTICS TYPE STYLES

The selected BSC and Google Analytics Criteria and their abbreviations used in Figure 2
Reduce cost (RC)
Revenue growth (RG)
Customer satisfaction (CS)
New customers (NC)
Sales (SALES)
Views (VIEWS)
Nationality of visitors (NATIO)
Device used by visitors (DEV)
Returning users (RU)
Products that visited on Website and attracted the interest of users (PR)
Network through which visitors reached the Website (NET)
Navigation program used (NavPr)

A questionnaire was developed and sent to five (5) managers of the company that participated in this case study. The questionnaire consisted of questions that referred to the extent the selected criteria affect each other. A 5-point Likert scale ranging from 0 to 4 representing the 'no influence' to 'very strong influence' scale was used for the respondents to report their beliefs regarding the interactions among the criteria considered in the study. The sample size of five is adequate for applying DEMATEL, since a group ranging between 5 and 15 experts is more appropriate [14].

Step 2: Apply DEMATEL and construct a strategy causal model. The selected criteria were evaluated by utilizing the DEMATEL method, so that importance priorities for each criterion are calculated and their interactions are specified in the DEMATEL causal model.

Step 3: Collect Google analytics data. Data from the company's Google analytics are selected and analyzed.

Step 4: Assess the strategic performance of the company. Examine the proposed model's ability to produce results upon which conclusions can be drawn regarding the strategic performance of the company.

3.2. The DEMATEL Method

The DEMATEL method was developed by the Battelle Geneva Institute [16]. DEMATEL is a multi-criteria method which is used to model and analyze complex relationships among factors pertaining to a particular domain. The method is applied to real life problems where the consideration of the interactions among important criteria is needed. DEMATEL produces causal models that show how interrelated factors affect each. The method can equally handle qualitative and quantitative factors. The DEMATEL method has been extensively used in MCDM problems such as marketing strategies, e-learning evaluations, control systems, safety problems, and environment watershed plans [17]-[26]. The steps of DEMATEL are shown below:

Step 1: Generate the Direct Relation Matrix. The direct relation matrix is calculated based on experts' responses. The experts comment on the influence a factor exerts on another by using the following scale: 0 for no influence, 1 for somewhat influence, 2 for medium influence, 3 for high influence and 4 for very high influence. The direct relation matrix $A=[a_{i,j}]$ is a nxn matrix, where $a_{i,j}$ indicates the degree to which factor (i) affects factor (j). In the case of a group of experts, all responses are averaged to produce the average matrix Z, where $Z = [z_{i,j}]$, with i,j indicating performance criteria.

Step 2: Calculate the normalized initial Direct- relation matrix D. The Matrix D is calculated using the following formulas.

$$D = \lambda * Z$$

where,

$$\lambda = \min\left[\frac{1}{max\sum_{j=1}^{n}(z_{i,j})}, \frac{1}{max\sum_{i=1}^{n}(z_{i,j})}\right],$$

and

$$1 \leq i \leq n \; and \; 1 \leq j \leq n.$$

Step 3: Derive the Total relation matrix T.

Where,

$$T = D(I-D)^{-1}.$$

Step 4: Calculate the sums of rows and columns of matrix T. The sum of rows is calculated by $r = r_i[i,j]_{nx1} = \sum_{j=1}^{n} t(i,j)$ and the sum of columns is calculated by $c = c_j[i,j]_{1xn} = \sum_{i=1}^{n} t(i,j)$. The value of r(i) indicates the total effect given by criterion (i) both directly and indirectly. The value of c(j) shows the total effect received by criterion (j) both directly and indirectly. If (j = i), the value of (ri+ci) represents the total effects both given and received by factor (i), while the value of (ri-ci) shows the net contribution by factor (i) on the system. If (ri-ci) is positive, then factor (i) is a net cause, which means factor (i) affects other factors of the model. If (ri-ci) is negative, then factor (i) is a net receiver that implies factor (i) is affected by other factors of model.

Step 5: Set a threshold value (α). The threshold is calculated with the formula,

$$a = \frac{\sum_{i=1}^{n}(t_{i,j})\sum_{j=1}^{n}(t_{i,j})}{n^2},$$

where n is the number of criteria. The threshold is used to cut-off the most important criteria, which will be included in the DEMATEL causal model.

Step 6: Build the DEMATEL causal model. A cause and effect relationship diagram, by mapping all coordinate of $(r_i + c_i, r_i - c_i)$. The causal model indicates the importance of the most important criteria, i.e. those above the threshold and the degree of influence among criteria.

IV. Empirical Study and Data Analysis

After all responses from the group of the five managers were collected, the average matrix Z was calculated. The matrix Z is shown in Table II.

TABLE II. THE AVERAGE MATRIX Z

	REDUCE COST	REVENUE GROWTH	CUSTOMER SATISFACTION	NEW CUSTOMERS	SALES	VIEWS	NATIONALITY	DEVICE	RETURNING USERS	PRODUCTS	NETWORK	NAVIGATION PROGRAM
REDUCE COST	0	3,2	2,4	3,2	2,6	2,6	1,6	3,2	3,4	2,4	1,8	2,8
REVENUE GROWTH	3,8	0	4	4,2	4,2	3,4	1,6	2,6	3,8	3,6	2,6	2,8
CUSTOMER SATISFACTION	2,4	3,8	0	3,6	4,6	3,8	2,2	3	5	3,6	3	3,2
NEW CUSTOMERS	2,6	4,4	3,8	0	4,2	4	2,2	3,4	4	3,4	2,4	2,4
SALES	2,6	4,6	4,6	4,4	0	4	2,8	3,4	4,2	4,4	2,6	2,8
VIEWS	2,6	3,6	3,6	3,8	4,2	0	2,6	4	4,4	4	3,2	3,6
NATIONALITY	1,8	1,8	2,2	2,4	2,8	2,4	0	2,8	2,6	2,6	1,6	2,4
DEVICE	3	2,8	2,6	3,2	3,6	4,4	2,2	0	2,2	3,2	3,6	2,2
RETURNING USERS	3	4	5	4	4,6	4,4	2,8	2,2	0	4,2	3	3,2
PRODUCTS	2,6	4	4	3,8	4,8	4,2	2,2	3,4	4,2	0	2	2,6
NETWORK	2	2,6	3	2,4	3	3,2	2,2	3,6	2,6	2,2	0	1,8
NAVIGATION PROGRAM	2,6	3	3,4	2,4	2,8	3,4	2,2	4	3,2	3,8	1,8	0

By applying the formulas in steps 2, 3 and 4 the T matrix, shown in Table III, is calculated.

TABLE III. THE T MATRIX

$T = D(I-D)^{-1}$	REDUCE COST	REVENUE GROWTH	CUSTOMER SATISFACTION	NEW CUSTOMERS	SALES	VIEWS	NATIONALITY	DEVICE	RETURNING USERS	PRODUCTS	NETWORK	NAVIGATION PROGRAM
REDUCE COST	0,308218001	0,470585822	0,461211103	0,465791869	0,4911302	0,474115612	0,299228817	0,437481	0,489522449	0,44809138	0,337539571	0,378653706
REVENUE GROWTH	0,466686964	0,497317094	0,594040815	0,583023242	0,6300065	0,597157979	0,36322684	0,51418853	0,600439849	0,56883708	0,42601984	0,455634668
CUSTOMER SATISFACTION	0,453856301	0,602290567	0,52854184	0,581757323	0,6618552	0,622546236	0,390734308	0,5416982	0,646352489	0,59073621	0,450782508	0,480858462
NEW CUSTOMERS	0,444832259	0,5967115	0,593823454	0,494705648	0,6345533	0,60800876	0,378570753	0,53362557	0,6079082	0,56887394	0,425478468	0,49028677
SALES	0,47802957	0,644053585	0,65417287	0,63954735	0,58962	0,63313874	0,419544723	0,57340771	0,657288031	0,63180911	0,461348046	0,492535878
VIEWS	0,467774704	0,613073854	0,620814995	0,60769135	0,6668291	0,551783551	0,407369915	0,57466733	0,646429787	0,61089322	0,464407435	0,498794632
NATIONALITY	0,309924567	0,389796473	0,404752625	0,398303473	0,4400911	0,416813171	0,229001781	0,38290786	0,419923451	0,40217051	0,29523227	0,329862719
DEVICE	0,409419787	0,567093907	0,510616757	0,530157553	0,5605604	0,557865385	0,342217335	0,40883165	0,511376862	0,50863649	0,40940187	0,401465457
RETURNING USERS	0,485513525	0,631907946	0,662326711	0,625068085	0,689812	0,660424093	0,419716851	0,54934075	0,505829931	0,6277185	0,468949811	0,501424492
PRODUCTS	0,456017354	0,603806125	0,613344594	0,599642703	0,6629532	0,627696778	0,388549796	0,54721554	0,627668866	0,50806716	0,427971857	0,466356439
NETWORK	0,346176758	0,447543762	0,46307883	0,439242527	0,4890355	0,476432212	0,306306639	0,43751163	0,462621509	0,43391927	0,289784715	0,349518747
NAVIGATION PROGRAM	0,400246217	0,509197737	0,52562471	0,4958617	0,5428635	0,536065483	0,340776164	0,48431194	0,53064973	0,52006352	0,369916815	0,349763895

The shadowed numbers are those who exceed the threshold (a=0,49). The (ri+ci) and the (ri-ci) for each criterion are calculated and shown in Table IV.

In Table IV, the criteria that give effects (positive ones) and those who receive effects (negative ones) are represented in different colors. The results in the Total matrix (T) show how business criteria conceptualized in the BSC are associated, affect or affected, with data from the Google analytics. For example, "cost reduction"" and "revenue growth" are interacting with the "number of views", the "number of the returning users", which are data collected from the company's Website. Equally important, the T matrix shows how Web analytics data, e.g. the "number of the returning users", affect business criteria such as "sales", "cost", "revenue growth", etc.

Therefore, the utilization of DEMATEL constitutes a way to unveil and study the interactions among business and Web analytics data, regarding the performance of a firm.

TABLE IV. THE TOTAL EFFECTS GIVEN AND RECEIVED AND THE IMPORTANCE OF EACH CRITERION

Sum of r(rows)	Sum of c(columns)		r+c	r-c	Business and Google Analytics Data
5,061629505	5,026695907	REDUCE COST	10,08832541	0,0349336	-2%
6,290996263	6,510298112	REVENUE GROWTH	12,80129437	-0,219302	5%
6,561748218	6,631848803	CUSTOMER SATISFACTION	13,19359702	-0,070101	7%
6,337270655	6,434792725	NEW CUSTOMERS	12,77206338	-0,097522	5%
6,889022248	7,059012203	SALES	13,94803445	-0,16999	3%
6,72698575	6,776622343	VIEWS	13,50360809	-0,049637	35%
4,418880139	4,285243924	NATIONALITY	8,704124064	0,1336362	data on certain nationalities
5,638143416	5,995208339	DEVICE	11,63335176	-0,357065	data on certain devices
6,887633076	6,766495643	RETURNING USERS	13,65412872	0,1211374	2%
6,523279002	6,419672744	PRODUCTS	12,94295175	0,1036063	5%
4,940732114	4,826335149	NETWORK	9,767067263	0,114397	data on certain network providers
5,611351369	5,155445864	NAVIGATION PROGRAM	10,76679723	0,4559055	data on certain browsers

In addition, by focusing on the (r+c) the results show that the top 5 of the most important performance criteria in the e-tourism industry are the "sales" which is the foremost important factor, followed by the "number of the returning users", the "number of views" of the Website and the "customer satisfaction", thus indicating the importance of the Web channel for companies to improve their performance. By examining the (r-c) column, the results indicate that the most affected criteria, those with negative (r-c), i.e. criteria affected by other are the "type of device", the "revenue growth", the "sales", the "returning users" and the "number of views". The results also show the important role of the "navigation program" that users use, in affecting other criteria such as the "sales". Although outside the scope of this study, this could possibly be an indication that the browser and the type of device that users use could be features of the users' profile.

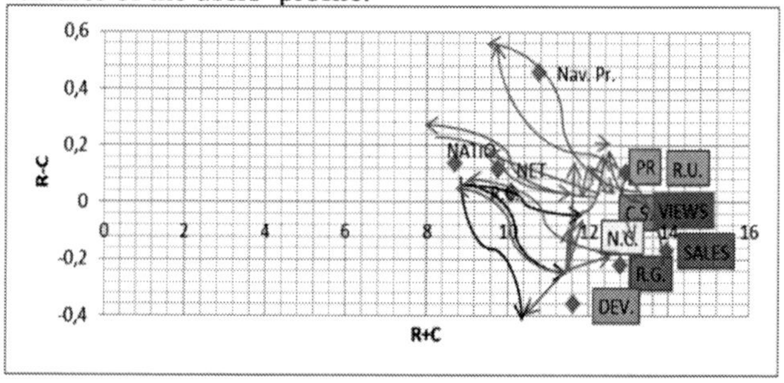

Figure 2. The DEMATEL Causal Model.

The causal model shown in Figure 5 is produced by applying the threshold in order to distinguish the criteria with higher than the threshold interactions. The causal model shows how each KPI affects or is affected by other KPIs. This model does not only show the interactions among KPIs but it can be used in scenarios simulations that investigate the impact of alternative business strategies on selected KPIs.

As T matrix in Table III shows, the criteria "nationality" and "device" do not affect or are not affected by any criteria with impacts higher than the threshold. It implies that the management of the company does not have any particular interest in distinguishing customers based on their nationality or the network provider they use. In other circumstances these interactions would have been different if specialized promotion programs had been in place to address customers from certain countries or network providers. The application of the threshold also shows in Table III that the "reduce cost" criterion is not affected significantly by other criteria, but it affects sales.

Finally, by reviewing the actual performance of the company as shown in the "Business and Google Analytics Data" column in Table IV, the management can contrast their priorities with the real outcomes. Management can compare and contrast the (r+c) column with their top priorities and judge to what extent their expectations have been realized. For example, Table IV shows that the "number of views" which is the third most significant priority exhibited the top actual performance. Similarly, "customer satisfaction" which is the fourth most important priority, is actually the second most successful area. However "sales", which is the top priority, did not return the results that the company anticipated, thus indicating that sales related policies should be reviewed.

V. CONCLUSIONS

Web analytics play an important role in assessing the effectiveness of business development and strategy. Currently Web analytics tools do not provide the comprehensive KPIs set that is needed to address the complexity of business decisions making. This study used the BSC as business strategic framework and examined how it can be integrated with the Web analytics data sets. By utilizing the DEMATEL method, this research proposes how to identify and comprehensively analyze the interactions among business criteria as defined within the BSC framework and Web analytics data. It also identifies the most important Web analytics KPIs in e-tourism. This research also indicates that DEMATEL can be used to highlight and contrast the strategic priorities and expectations of the management with the actual performance of the company, as this is reflected in the Web (Google) analytics data. Furthermore, this research suggests that, Web analytics tools should improve their functionality by combining MCDM methods such as the DEMATEL method, with strategic frameworks such as the BSC in order to enhance their value in assessing digital marketing strategies.

The proposed approach will also be tested within the context of the SELIS research project, in order to examine its applicability in linking Web analytics and strategic performance evaluation in the logistics service sector.

Future research should focus on developing Web analytics methods and tools that provide the necessary data sets and the required functionality in analyzing and managing the interactions among data generated online within the context of business strategy and development.

ACKNOWLEDGMENT

The research described in this project has been partially funded by the Horizon 2020 Project SELIS ('Towards a Shared European Logistics Intelligent Information Space') Grant agreement no: 690588.

REFERENCES

[1] J. Järvinen, and H. Karjaluoto, "The use of Web analytics for digital marketing performance measurement." Industrial Marketing Management Vol 50, pp. 117-127, 2015.

[2] D. Jayarama, A. Manrai, and L. Manrai, L. "Effective use of marketing technology in Eastern Europe: Web analytics, social media, customer analytics, digital campaigns and mobile applications." Journal of Economics, Finance and Administrative Science, Vol 20, pp. 118-132, 2015.

[3] Forbes, "US Digital Marketing Spend Will Near $120 Billion By 2021." Available from URL: https://www.forbes.com/sites/forrester/2017/01/26/us-digital-marketing-spend-will-near-120-billion-by-2021/#4aa2e6b278bb, 2017, last viewed 31/7/2017.

[4] Gartner, "Gartner CMO Spend Survey 2016-2017 Shows Marketing Budgets Continue to Climb." Available from URL: http://www.gartner.com/smarterwithgartner/gartner-cmo-spend-survey-2016-2017-shows-marketing-budgets-continue-to-climb/, 2016, last viewed 31/7/2017.

[5] A. Phippen L. Sheppard and S. Furnell, "A practical evaluation of Web analytics", Internet Research, Vol. 14, pp. 284 -293, 2004.

[6] Balanced Web Analytics Scorecard. Available from URL: http://www.freepatentsonline.com/20140052502.pdf, 2014, last viewed 1/8/2017.

[7] A. Keramati, and F. Shapouri, "Multidimensional appraisal of customer relationship management: integrating balanced scorecard and multi criteria decision making approaches." Information Systems and e-Business Management, Vol 14, pp. 217-251, 2016.

[8] J. Jassbi, F. Mohamadnejad, and H. Nasrollahzadeh, "A Fuzzy DEMATEL framework for modeling cause and effect relationships of strategy map." Expert Systems with Applications Vol 38, pp.5967–5973, 2011.

[9] R. Kaplan, and D. Norton, "The balanced scorecard-measures that drive performance." Harvard Business Review Vol 70, pp.71–79, 1992.

[10] R. Kaplan, and D. Norton, "Using the Balanced Scorecard as a Strategic Management System," Harvard Business Review, January-February, pp.35-48, 1996.

[11] M. Tseng, "Implementation and performance evaluation using the fuzzy network balanced scorecard." Computers & Education, Vol 55, pp. 188-201, 2010.

[12] Figure 1. Balanced Score Card (URL: http://bi-insider.com/wp-content/uploads/2012/05/Balanced-Scorecard-Four-Perspectives.png).

[13] N. Moghaddam, M. Sahafzadeh, A. Alavijeh, H. Yousefdehi, H. Hosseini, "Strategic Environment Analysis Using DEMATEL Method Through Systematic Approach: Case Study of an Energy Research Institute in Iran." Management science and engineering, Vol 4, pp. 95-105, 2010.

[14] Y. Kuo, and P. Chen, "Constructing performance appraisal indicators for mobility of the service industries using Fuzzy

Delphi Method." Expert Systems with Applications, Vol 35, pp. 1930-1939, 2008.

[15] J. Teng, "Project evaluation: Methods and applications. Taiwan, National Taiwan Ocean University," 2002.

[16] E. Fontela, and A. Gabus, (1976) The DEMATEL observer, DEMATEL 1976 Report. Battelle Geneva Research Center, Geneva, 1976.

[17] Chang, H. H. and Chen, S. W. (2008). The impact of online store environment cues on purchase intention: Trust and perceived risk as a mediator. Online information review, 32(6), 818-841.

[18] Chang, H. H. and Chen, S. W. (2009). Consumer perception of interface quality, security, and loyalty in electronic commerce. Information and management, 46(7), 411-417.

[19] Y. C. Chen, H. Lien, G. Tzeng, and L. Yang, "Fuzzy MCDM approach for selecting the best environment-watershed plan." Applied soft computing, Vol 11, pp. 265-275, 2010.

[20] S. Hori, and Y. Shimizu, "Designing methods of human interface for supervisory control systems." Control engineering practice, Vol 7, pp. 1413-1419, 1999.

[21] C. Lin, C. Chen, and G. Tzeng, "Planning the development strategy for the mobile communication package based on consumers' choice preferences." Expert systems with applications, Vol 37, pp. 4749-4760, 2010a.

[22] C. Lin, M. Hsieh, and G. Tzeng, "Evaluating vehicle telematics system by using a novel MCDM techniques with dependence and feedback." Expert systems with applications, Vol 37, pp. 6723-6736, 2010b.

[23] C. Lin, and G. Tzeng, "A value-created system of science (technology) park by using DEMATEL." Expert systems with applications, Vol 36, pp. 9683-9697, 2009.

[24] J. Liou, G. Tzeng, and H. Chang, "Airline safety measurement using a hybrid model." Journal of air transport management, Vol 13, pp. 243-249, 2007.

[25] O Yang, H. Shieh, J. Leu, and G. Tzeng, "A novel hybrid MCDM model combined with DEMATEL and ANP with applications." International journal of operations research, Vol 5, pp. 160-168, 2008.

[26] G. Tzeng, C. Chiang, and C. Li, "Evaluating intertwined effects in e-learning programs: A novel hybrid MCDM model based on factor analysis and DEMATEL." Expert systems with applications, Vol 32, pp. 1028-1044, 2007.

Optimization of the Revenue of the New York City Taxi Service using Markov Decision Processes

Jacky P.K. Li, Sandjai Bhulai

Vrije Universiteit Amsterdam,
Faculty of Science,
Amsterdam, The Netherlands
Email: jacky.li@vu.nl, s.bhulai@vu.nl

Theresia van Essen

Delft Institute of Applied Mathematics,
Delft, The Netherlands
Email: J.T.vanEssen@tudelft.nl

***Abstract*—Taxis are an essential component of the transportation system in most urban centers. The ability to optimize the efficiency of routing represents an opportunity to increase revenues for taxi drivers. The vacant taxis cruising on the roads are not only wasting fuel consumption, the time of a taxi driver, and create unnecessary carbon emissions but also generate additional traffic in the city. In this paper, we use Markov Decision Processes to optimize the revenues of taxi drivers by better routing. We present a case study with New York City Taxi data with several experimental evaluations of our model. We achieve approximately 10% improvement in efficiency using data from the month of January. The results also provide a better understanding of the several different time shifts. These data may have important implications in the field of self-driving vehicles.**

Keywords–New York taxi service; revenue optimization; optimal routing; Markov decision processes

I. Introduction

In New York City, there are over 485,000 passengers taking taxis per day, equating to over 175 million trips per year [1]. Creating an efficient way to transport passengers through the city is of utmost importance. Taxi drivers cannot control a passenger's destination but can make better decisions using optimal routing. This consequently leads to reductions of costs and of the carbon emissions.

Previous studies have focused on developing recommendation systems for taxi drivers [2]–[7]. Several studies use the GPS system to create recommendations for both the drivers and the passengers to increase the profit margin and cutting the time for seeking [4], [6]–[8]. Ge et al. [9] and Ziebart et al. [10] gather a variety of information to generate a behavior model to improve driving predictions. Ge et al. [2] and Tseng et al. [11] measure the energy consumption before finding the next passenger. Castro et al. [8], Altshuler et al. [12], Chawla et al. [13], Huang et al. [14] and Qian et al. [15] learn knowledge from taxi data for other types of recommendation scenarios such as fast routing, ride-sharing, or fair recommendations.

Most of the papers above focus on optimizing the measures for the immediate next trip. Rong et al. [3] investigate how to learn business strategies from the historical data to increase revenues of the taxi drivers using Markov decision processes (MDPs). Their research model uses historical data to estimate the probability of finding a passenger and its location for drop-off as the necessary parameters for the MDP model. For each one-hour time slot, the model learns a different set of parameters for the MDP from the data and finds the optimal move for the vacant taxi to maximize the total revenues in that time slot. At each state, the MDP model uses a combination of location, time, the current and the previous actions. The vacant taxi can travel to its neighboring locations and cruise through the grid to seek for the next passenger. Using dynamic programming to solve the MDP, the output of the model recommends the best actions for the taxi driver to take at each state.

Tseng et al. [11] examine the viability of electric taxis in New York City by using MDPs. Due to the usage limitation of electric taxis before each charge, they examine the profitability of replacing taxi with internal combustion engines by electric taxis. The research model uses OpenStreetMap (OSM) to assign each pick-up and drop-off into the nearest junctions. The advantage of using OSM is to be able to identify the number of available taxis at the junction without extra calculations. The research is concentrated on energy consumption; the actions become infeasible if the electric vehicle runs out of battery.

Analysis of real taxi data shows that there are significant differences in demand between certain periods of the day. The aforementioned research has not taken the effect of this demand variation into account. The contribution of our model is that we extend the research by Rong et al. [3] in this direction. We analyze the New York City Taxi data and study the differences in optimal policies and revenues for the demand between weekdays, weekends, day shifts, and night shifts. From these observations, we can infer relevant policies for taxi drivers based on the shift that they work in.

The paper is structured as follows. In Section II, we do data analysis on the New York Taxi dataset. This provides input for our MDP, which is explained in Section III. We assess the performance of the MDP in Section IV, where we conduct numerical experiments. Finally, the paper is concluded in Section V.

II. Dataset and Methodology

In our research, we use 14,776,615 taxi rides collected in New York City over a period of one month (January 2013) [1]. From each ride record, we use the following fields: taxi

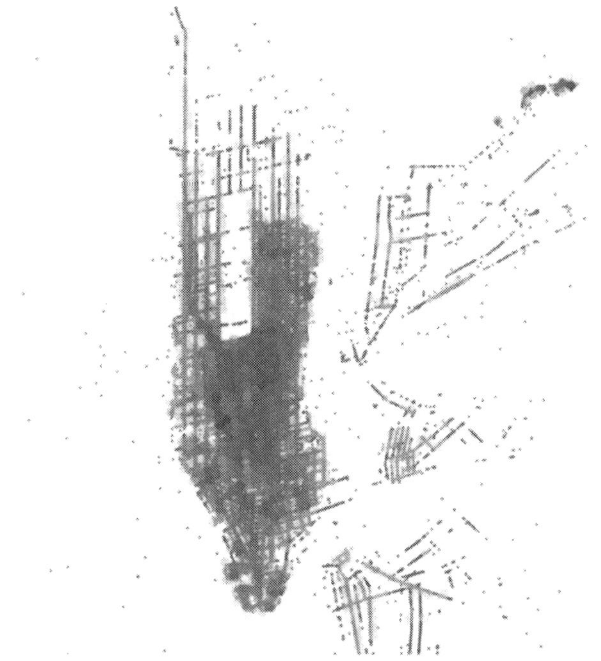

Figure 1. Rotated Manhattan with the total revenue for NYC Taxi by pick-up location in Jan 2013.

Figure 2. Rotated Manhattan with the total revenue for NYC Taxi by drop-off location in Jan 2013.

ID, pick-up time, pick-up longitude, pick-up latitude, drop-off time, drop-off longitude, drop-off latitude, the number of passengers per ride, average velocity, trip distance, traveling time, and fare amount. We omit the records containing missing or erroneous GPS coordinates. Records that represent rides that started or ended outside Manhattan, as well as trip durations longer than 1 hour and trip distances greater than 50 kilometers are omitted as well. Furthermore, we collect the drivers who drive for six to nine hours consistently to yield a clean dataset containing approximately 13.5 millions taxi rides. We observe that most of the pick-up locations are in the Manhattan area.

We concentrate on the island of Manhattan area in NY. This area imposes a rectangular grid of avenues and streets. However, the citys avenues are not parallel to the true north and south. For that reason, we tilted the map by 28.899 degrees according to Petzold et al. [16]. This creates blocks with the same grid system in most areas. We discretize the grid into a 50×50 grid, making each block in the grid approximately 300 meters $\times$ 300 meters. The choice for a block size of 300 meters is based on the assumption that a taxi can traverse this distance within 1 minute. Figure 1 shows the total revenue for the taxis by the pick-up location with the rotated map. Figure 2 indicates the total revenues of the drop-off location, and it shows that Lower Manhattan, along with the airport are the largest revenue generators and the drop-off location has spread to the mid-Manhattan area and also Brooklyn area.

The state of a taxi can be described by two parameters: the current location $L = \{(1,1), \ldots, (50,50)\}$ grid and the current time, $T = \{1, \ldots, 60\}$. We will denote the system state in our MDP model as $s = (x, y, t)$, which we will elaborate on in Section III.

A. Performance indicators

In this section, we present performance indicators of the taxi drivers. This will be used in the MDP to optimize the routing decision of each taxi driver. Hence, the performance indicators will be dependent on the routing policy that is being applied by the taxi drivers. To improve readability, we drop the dependency on the policy in the notation and use it only in cases where it benefits clarity.

We calculate the total business time of each taxi driver per shift. The total business time (denoted as T_{bus}) is equal to the sum of the total occupancy time (T_{occupy}) and the total seeking time (T_{seek}):

$$T_{\text{bus}} = T_{\text{occupy}} + T_{\text{seek}}. \tag{1}$$

The total occupancy time, T_{occupy} is the sum of all the trip durations with passengers of a taxi per day. And the total seeking time (T_{seek}) is the time between each trip. Figure 3 depicts the overall T_{seek} and the graphs in which we distinguish between the weekday, weekend, day shift, and the night shift. Based on the data, we consider 90% of the seeking time is less than 20 minutes for the day shift and less than 25 minutes for the night shift. Therefore, we discount any seeking time that is over 30 minutes as we assume those are the breaks for the drivers.

Logically, the T_{bus} is approximately the same for each taxi driver. To increase the revenue, the taxi drivers aim to have the maximal T_{occupy} and the minimal of T_{seek}. We define the revenue efficiency (E_{rev}) metric as the revenue earned divided by the total taxi drivers business time. This is expressed as follows:

$$E_{\text{rev}} = \frac{M}{T_{\text{bus}}} = \frac{M}{T_{\text{occupy}} + T_{\text{seek}}}, \tag{2}$$

Table I. REVENUE EFFICIENCY E_{REV}.

	Weekday dayshift	Weekday nightshift	Weekend dayshift	Weekend nightshift	Overall
Top 10%	0.59203	0.62408	0.60111	0.64646	0.60869
Mean	0.49985	0.52232	0.50252	0.54871	0.50565
Standard Deviation	0.07253	0.08011	0.07787	0.07799	0.08088
Bottom 10%	0.41028	0.42174	0.40426	0.44978	0.40572

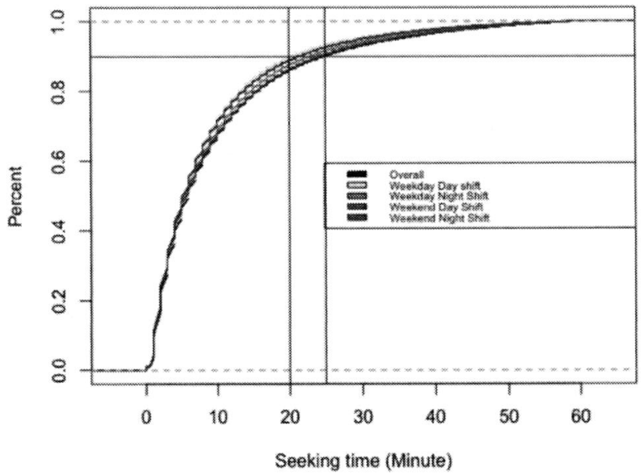

Figure 3. Seeking time for the models.

where M denotes the total money earned by the taxi driver during that period.

To illustrate the consistency of the taxi driver, we concentrate on the drivers who work between six hours to nine hours during the month of January. From that data, we generate the data of P_{find}, P_{dest}, T_{drive}, r (parameters of our MDP to be described in the next section) of each model and identify the top 10% and bottom 10% drivers in each model.

Table I indicates the revenue efficiency of the top 10% and bottom 10% distinguished by weekday, weekend, day shift, night shift, and the overall efficiency. Based on the table, there is approximately 20% difference between the performance of the top 10% and bottom 10% drivers. The previous studies that were mentioned above (see, e.g., [4], [8], [11], [13], [14]) attribute the difference between the performance by the top and bottom 10% drivers to the seeking time of the taxi drivers. This warrants research to determine if our model can provide a better solution for the taxi drivers for seeking passengers.

III. MARKOV DECISION PROCESS

In order to model the taxi service in New York City, we adopt the framework of MDPs. This framework allows us to deal with the uncertain demand over the different periods in the grid, and to model them explicitly. The MDP is a stochastic decision process with a set of states (S) and a set of possible actions (A) that transition the states from one to another. Each action will correspond to the process of the current state to the new state with a probability transition function and a reward function. The collection of optimal actions for each state is called the policy, which maximizes the total reward over several numbers of steps. The objective of our model is to minimize the seeking time for the taxi to maximize the expected revenues.

A. System States

The state for a taxi is described by its current locations and the current time. The details are explained as follows.

Location $(x, y) \in L = \{1, \ldots, 50 \times 1, \ldots, 50\}$: the area is divided into grid 50×50 grid cells;

Time $t \in T = \{1, \ldots, 60\}$: we use minutes as the interval of a time slot, and a total of 1 hour as time horizon.

Each pick-up and drop-off location is assigned to a grid cell. We remove the records that contain 1) incomplete data information, 2) trip distance over 100 kilometers, 3) trip durations over 60 minutes, 4) pick-up and drop-off locations with the same coordinates, 5) pick-up and drop-off locations outside the grid, and 6) shifts that are shorter than six hours and longer than nine hours.

We denote the system state of our MDP model as $s = (x, y, t)$, and the collection of all admissible states is denoted by S.

B. Actions

The admissible actions from a given state s have nine possibilities to choose from. We use numbers $1, \ldots, 9$ to index the directions. We express them formally as:

$$A = \begin{array}{|c|c|c|} \hline 7 & 8 & 9 \\ \hline 4 & 5 & 6 \\ \hline 1 & 2 & 3 \\ \hline \end{array},$$

where, e.g., action 9 moves the taxi to the neighboring north-east location.

C. Parameters of the MDP model

In this subsection, we state the parameters used in the rest of MDP model.

The probability parameters are defined as:

- $P_{\text{find}}(x, y)$ describes the probability of successfully picking up a passenger in grid cell (x, y). We can calculate the probability of picking up a passenger in the cell by dividing the number of successful pick-ups in the cell ($n_{\text{find}}(x, y)$) by the total number of times this cell is visited by a vacant taxi. The vacant taxi includes the taxis that drop off passengers in grid cell (x, y) ($n_{\text{drop-off}}(x, y)$) and also the taxis that are seeking for passengers ($n_{\text{OSRM}}(x, y)$). To locate the vacant taxi every minute during the seeking trip, we use the API provided by Open Source Routing Machine [17], to estimate the coordinates. We use one hour time slots between 12:00 to 13:00 for the day shift model and 0:00 to 1:00 for the night shift model. In our overall model, we took the average of the day time and night time models to estimate the number of vacant taxis at each grid during the month of January in 2013. Thus,

$$P_{\text{find}} = \frac{n_{\text{find}}(x, y)}{n_{\text{find}}(x, y) + n_{\text{drop-off}}(x, y) + n_{\text{OSRM}}(x, y)}.$$

- $P_{\text{dest}}(x, y, x', y')$ describes the probability of a passenger travelling from grid cell (x, y) to the grid cell (x', y'). To estimate the destination probability for a time slot, we calculate the number of trips between each pair of source and destination locations in that time slot and get a 50×50 matrix. The value is divided by the sum of the entire number of trips of the grid cells. Therefore, P_{dest} has the empirical probability distribution of a passenger choosing destination location (x', y') when he is picked up at location (x, y).

The time parameters are defined as:

- $T_{\text{seek}}(a)$: The required time to travel from one location to a neighboring location based on action $a \in A$. We assume that the average speed of seeking trips is approximately 300 meters per minute. Thus, a taxi can traverse on cell when $a = 2, 4, 5, 6, 8$, and hence $T_{\text{seek}}(a) = 1$ in this case. In case $a = 1, 3, 7, 9$, then we set $T_{\text{seek}}(a)$ equal to 2, due to the diagonal movement.
- $T_{\text{drive}}(x, y, x', y')$: The driving time from (x, y) to (x', y'). We can calculate the total driving time from grid cell (x, y) to grid cell (x', y') and then divide by the number of trips from grid cell (x, y) to grid cell (x', y'). We calculate T_{drive} individually for all models. From the calculation, there is approximately +15.67% driving time difference between the day shift model and the night shift model, and there is a +4.14% difference between the weekend and the weekday.
- We assume there is no waiting time for passengers to get in and out of the vehicle.

The reward is defined as:

- $r(x, y, x', y')$: The expected reward from grid cell (x, y) to grid cell (x', y'). Similar to T_{drive}, we calculate the average fare of the number of trips between each pair of source and destinations as the expected fare. Note that due to this definition, we reward does not depend on the action of the taxi driver. We calculate r separately for all models. Similarly to T_{drive}, there is approximately +6.21% reward difference between the day shift model and the night shift model, and there is a +1.21% difference between the weekend and the weekday.

D. State transition function

The state transition function is a function that describes the probability that one moves from state (x, y, t) after taking decision a moves to state (x', y', t'). Assuming the current state is $S = (x, y, t)$ and action a is taken, there are two possible outcomes of the transition:

1) The taxi successfully finds a passenger in grid (x, y) within $T_{\text{seek}}(a)$ minutes. The taxi with the passenger goes to destination (x', y') with probability $P_{\text{dest}}(x, y, x', y')$. The taxi arrives at location (x', y') with $T_{\text{drive}}(x, y, x', y')$ as the total time used to travel from (x, y) to (x', y'). The taxi driver receives $r(x, y, x', y')$ as the expected reward. Then the taxi will start seeking for a passenger from grid cell (x', y'). In this case, the new state becomes $s' = (x', y', t + T_{\text{seek}}(a) + T_{\text{drive}}(x, y, x'y'))$.
2) The taxi does not find a passenger after $T_{\text{seek}}(a)$ minutes being in grid (x, y) with the probability $(1 - P_{\text{find}}(x, y))$. The taxi driver does not receive a reward and saves the driving time T_{drive}. The taxi driver starts to make the next action at grid cell (x', y'). Hence, the state of the taxi driver becomes $s' = (x', y', t + T_{\text{seek}}(a))$.

E. The objective function

The objective function of the MDP model is to maximize the total expected rewards starting from an initial state. The terminal states are the states with $t = 60$. No more actions can be taken once the system reaches the terminal states. The maximal expected reward for an action a in state $s = (x, y, t)$ is expressed as $V(s, a)$ shown in (3).

$$\begin{aligned} V(s,a) &= (1 - P_{\text{find}}(x, y)) \times \\ &\max_{a' \in A} V(x, y, t + T_{\text{seek}}(a), a') + \\ &\sum_{(x',y') \in L} P_{\text{find}}(x, y) \times P_{\text{dest}}(x, y, x', y') \times \\ &\big[r(x, y, x', y') + \\ &\max_{a' \in A} V(x', y', t + T_{\text{seek}}(a) + T_{\text{drive}}(x, y, x', y'), a')\big]. \end{aligned} \tag{3}$$

The optimal policy π^* is defined as:

$$\pi^*(s) = \arg\max \{V(s, a)\}, \tag{4}$$

and the optimal value function is given by

$$V^*(s) = V(s, \pi^*(s)). \tag{5}$$

F. Markov Decision Process Solution

In order to solve the Markov decision problem to derive the optimal policy, we employ dynamic programming to maximize the expected rewards. The algorithm starts from time $t = 60$ and then traces backward to time $t = 1$. The algorithm is listed in Algoritm 1.

Table II. REVENUE EFFICIENCY E_{REV}.

	Weekday dayshift	Weekday nightshift	Weekend dayshift	Weekend nightshift	Overall
Top 10%	0.59203	0.62408	0.60111	0.64646	0.60869
$P_{\text{find}}(x, y)$	0.52267	0.50915	0.51463	0.45475	0.50030
Bottom 10%	0.41028	0.42174	0.40426	0.44978	0.40572

Algorithm 1 Solving MDP using Dynamic Programming

Input: $L, A, T, P_{\text{find}}, P_{\text{dest}}, r, T_{\text{drive}}, T_{\text{seek}}$
Output: The best policy π^*

V is a $\mid L \mid \times \mid T \mid$ matrix; $V \leftarrow 0$
for $t = \mid T \mid$ to 1 do
    for all $(x, y) \in L$ do $\triangleright s = (x, y, t)$
        $a_{max} \leftarrow a$ that maximizes $V(s, a)$
$\pi^*(s) \leftarrow a_{max}$
$V^*(s) \leftarrow V(s, a_{max})$
return π^*

IV. CASE STUDY

In this section, we present our case study on the New York Taxi dataset. We evaluate the MDP for the expected reward based on the dataset from January 2013. We assume that the NYC taxis have two shifts per day and each shift is a 12-hour period. We analyze the taxi's expected reward in 1) the day-time shift within six to nine hours of its operating time, 5 am to 5 pm and 2) the night-time shift, 5 pm to 5 am and 3) the weekdays from Monday to Friday, and 4) the weekend from Friday to Sunday. After filtering the data, we have approximately 170,000, 205,000, 145,000, and 193,000 shifts, respectively, for the Weekday day-time shift, Weekday night-time shift, Weekend day-time shift, and Weekend night-time shift. Although the weekend has a fewer number of days in January, the total number of shifts of the weekend night time is almost the same as for the weekday night time.

The results of the case study (see also Table II) shows that in our model

- $P_{\text{find}}(x, y)$ is 0.52267 which is 27.58% better than the bottom 10%, and it is 11.65% less effective than the top 10% for the Weekday day-time model.
- For the weekday night-time model, $P_{\text{find}}(x, y)$ is 0.50915 which is 27.52% better than the bottom 10%. It is 16.74% less effective than the top 10%.
- For the weekend day-time model, $P_{\text{find}}(x, y)$ is 0.51463 which is 20.16% better than the bottom 10%. It is 18.57% less effective than top 10%.
- For the weekend nighttime model, $P_{\text{find}}(x, y)$ is 0.45475 which is almost the same as the bottom 10% and it is 29.14% less effective than the top 10%.
- The overall model, $P_{\text{find}}(x, y)$ is 0.50030 which is 23.41% better than the bottom 10% and it is 17.79% less effective than top 10%.

The results of the case study show that our model is capable of reducing the time to find a passenger for a taxi driver significantly. Consequently, the end result is that the earnings of the taxi drivers increases. This benefit is expressed as approximately a 10% improvement in efficiency.

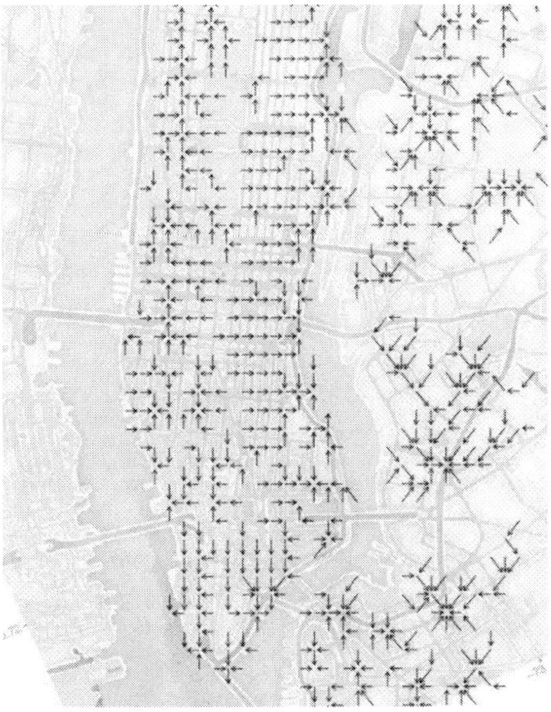

Figure 4. Recommended movements by the MDP model.

V. CONCLUSION AND FUTURE DISCUSSION

In this paper, we use MDP to model the taxi service strategy and determine the optimal policy for taxi drivers with a daytime and nighttime model during the weekdays and the weekend. This paper proposed to model the passenger-seeking process to receive the best move for a taxi that is seeking for the next passenger. Figure 4 shows the recommended movement by the MDP Model.

From the results of the case study, we observe that the weekend night time draws an interesting discussion. It has a similar number of shifts as compared to the weekday night time model, but the revenue efficiency did not improve compared to the bottom 10% drivers. A possible explanation might be that the experienced drivers would use their experience to look for the best location to seek customers. Consequently, the data may not have provided enough evidence to improve the bottom 10% drivers.

In our data analysis, we found cases where there are pick-up and drop-off locations in the Hudson River. We can assume that this is an error in the GPS system. Similar to this issue,

P_{dest} was estimated from a small number of trips from one location to another. This could sometimes result in a high probability, for instance, 1 of 3, would have created a 33% of probability going from one location to another. Further research is needed to develop methods to get a more accurate estimate.

REFERENCES

[1] N. Taxi, L. Commission et al., "2014 taxicab fact book," 2014.

[2] Y. Ge et al., "An energy-efficient mobile recommender system," in Proceedings of the 16th ACM SIGKDD international conference on Knowledge discovery and data mining - KDD '10. New York, New York, USA: ACM Press, 2010, p. 899. [Online]. Available: http://dl.acm.org/citation.cfm?doid=1835804.1835918

[3] H. Rong, X. Zhou, C. Yang, Z. Shafiq, and A. Liu, "The rich and the poor: A markov decision process approach to optimizing taxi driver revenue efficiency," in Proceedings of the 25th ACM International on Conference on Information and Knowledge Management. ACM, 2016, pp. 2329–2334.

[4] J. Yuan, Y. Zheng, L. Zhang, X. Xie, and G. Sun, "Where to find my next passenger," in Proceedings of the 13th international conference on Ubiquitous computing. ACM, 2011, pp. 109–118.

[5] Y. Zheng, J. Yuan, W. Xie, X. Xie, and G. Sun, "Drive Smartly as a Taxi Driver," in 2010 7th International Conference on Ubiquitous Intelligence & Computing and 7th International Conference on Autonomic & Trusted Computing. IEEE, oct 2010, pp. 484–486. [Online]. Available: http://ieeexplore.ieee.org/document/5667121/

[6] M. Qu, H. Zhu, J. Liu, G. Liu, and H. Xiong, "A cost-effective recommender system for taxi drivers," in Proceedings of the 20th ACM SIGKDD international conference on Knowledge discovery and data mining - KDD '14. New York, New York, USA: ACM Press, 2014, pp. 45–54. [Online]. Available: http://dl.acm.org/citation.cfm?doid=2623330.2623668

[7] D. Zhang et al., "Understanding Taxi Service Strategies From Taxi GPS Traces," IEEE Transactions on Intelligent Transportation Systems, vol. 16, no. 1, feb 2015, pp. 123–135. [Online]. Available: http://ieeexplore.ieee.org/lpdocs/epic03/wrapper.htm?arnumber=6841047

[8] P. Castro, D. Zhang, and S. Li, "Urban traffic modelling and prediction using large scale taxi gps traces," Pervasive Computing, 2012, pp. 57–72.

[9] Y. Ge, C. Liu, H. Xiong, and J. Chen, "A taxi business intelligence system," in Proceedings of the 17th ACM SIGKDD international conference on Knowledge discovery and data mining - KDD '11. New York, New York, USA: ACM Press, 2011, p. 735. [Online]. Available: http://dl.acm.org/citation.cfm?doid=2020408.2020523

[10] B. D. Ziebart, A. L. Maas, A. K. Dey, and J. A. Bagnell, "Navigate like a cabbie: Probabilistic reasoning from observed context-aware behavior," in Proceedings of the 10th international conference on Ubiquitous computing. ACM, 2008, pp. 322–331.

[11] C.-M. Tseng and C.-K. Chau, "Viability analysis of electric taxis using new york city dataset," in Proceedings of the Eighth International Conference on Future Energy Systems. ACM, 2017, pp. 328–333.

[12] T. Altshuler, R. Katoshevski, and Y. Shiftan, "Ride sharing and dynamic networks analysis," arXiv preprint arXiv:1706.00581, 2017.

[13] S. Chawla, Y. Zheng, and J. Hu, "Inferring the Root Cause in Road Traffic Anomalies," in 2012 IEEE 12th International Conference on Data Mining. IEEE, dec 2012, pp. 141–150. [Online]. Available: http://ieeexplore.ieee.org/document/6413908/

[14] Y. Huang, F. Bastani, R. Jin, and X. S. Wang, "Large scale real-time ridesharing with service guarantee on road networks," Proceedings of the VLDB Endowment, vol. 7, no. 14, 2014, pp. 2017–2028.

[15] S. Qian, J. Cao, F. L. Mouël, I. Sahel, and M. Li, "Scram: a sharing considered route assignment mechanism for fair taxi route recommendations," in Proceedings of the 21th ACM SIGKDD International Conference on Knowledge Discovery and Data Mining. ACM, 2015, pp. 955–964.

[16] C. Petzold. How far from true north are the avenues of manhattan? [Online]. Available: http://www.charlespetzold.com/etc/AvenuesOfManhattan/ (2015)

[17] D. Luxen and C. Vetter, "Real-time routing with openstreetmap data," in Proceedings of the 19th ACM SIGSPATIAL international conference on advances in geographic information systems. ACM, 2011, pp. 513–516.

Japanese Kanji Characters are Small-World Connected Through Shared Components

Mark Jeronimus[*], Sil Westerveld[†], Cees van Leeuwen[‡], Sandjai Bhulai[§] and Daan van den Berg[¶]

[*] Airsupplies Nederland BV, The Netherlands, Email: mark.jeronimus@gmail.com
[†] Nishino, Amsterdam, The Netherlands, Email: research@silwesterveld.com
[‡] Laboratory for Perceptual Dynamics, KU Leuven, Leuven, Belgium, Email: Cees.vanLeeuwen@kuleuven.be
[‡] Center for Cognitive Science, TU Kaiserslautern, Kaiserslautern, Germany
[§] Faculty of Science, Vrije Universiteit Amsterdam, Amsterdam, The Netherlands, Email: s.bhulai@vu.nl
[¶] Docentengroep IvI, Faculty of Science, University of Amsterdam, Amsterdam, The Netherlands, Email: d.vandenberg@uva.nl

***Abstract*—We investigate the connectivity within different incremental sets of Japanese Kanji characters. Individual characters constitute the vertices in the network, components shared between them provide their edges. We find the resulting networks to have a high clustering coefficient and a low average path length, characterizing them as *small worlds*. We examine the statistical significance of these findings and the role of the degree distributions. We review the evidence that the small-world topologies of these networks are due to the successive elimination of components in the writing system and discuss the implications of the results for language evolution.**

Keywords*–Japanese characters; Kanji; components; radicals; small-world networks; phase transition; Zipf's law; Gelb's hypothesis

I. Introduction

Small-world networks are sparsely connected networks that have a high cluster coefficient (CC) in combination with a low average path length (APL) [1]. The CC on a vertex A which is adjacent to vertices $B_1, \ldots, B_n$, is the number of edges between nodes $B_1, \ldots, B_n$ divided by the maximum of $n(n-1)/2$. As such, the CC on A expresses A's local interconnectivity; the CC of a network is the average of all its vertices. The APL is defined as the average number of edges in the shortest path between all pairs of vertices in the network, and as such expresses its global connectivity.

In real-life, small-world networks have been found in a broad variety of fields: power grids [1], neuronal networks in nematode worms [2], the primate brain [3] [4], the World Wide Web [5], and networks of social relationships [6]. Some evidence suggests that small-world topologies are an emergent property resulting from self-organization in a population of communicating agents [7]–[11]. Small worlds have also been found in language networks of co-occurring words [12], and even more specifically, in far eastern writing systems. An investigation in Chinese characters sharing 'radicals' [13] appears to be closest to ours. These authors investigated the network topology of modern-day Chinese characters and found small-world properties, as well as a non-Poisson degree distribution. Even though Chinese and Japanese characters differ considerably nowadays, computational results of these authors are comparable to ours and others in the field. On a slightly higher level, various research teams constructed networks of co-occurring characters [14], words [14]–[16] and phrases [17] in Chinese. Like [13], these authors find small-world properties, possibly indicating that the same self-organizing forces shaping logographic languages at character level are also shaping writing systems on a larger scale.

Interestingly enough, a similar word level investigation was conducted in Japanese two-Kanji words as well [18] [19]. Despite the difference in characters and methods, these authors also find small-world networks, affirming consistent sharing of characters between words in logographic languages. But as it turns out, an investigation of network topologies in Japanese at character level is still missing. It is this gap that our investigation hopes to fill, conjoining all aforementioned investigations, and as such interconnecting the field of research on network structures in Japanese and Chinese writing systems at both word and character level.

The structure of the paper is as follows. We discuss the Japanese writing system in Section II. We then proceed to show that Kanji is a small-world network in Section III. In Section IV we state our conclusions, provide a discussion on the results, and discuss possible extensions of our work.

II. The Japanese Writing System

A writing system reflects the history of the civilization in which it emerged, and some writing systems have developed a striking level of complexity. The Japanese language, notably, employs four character sets: Hiragana, a 46-piece syllabic script; Katakana, also 46 characters, is similar to Hiragana though mainly used for foreign words, expressions and emphases; Kanji, a logographic symbol script related to the Chinese characters, and finally Romaji, the Roman alphabet, used mostly for numbers, advertisements and in pop culture. All four character sets are represented in the following sentence:

マークは明日、月曜１０時にあの寺で待っています。

Tomorrow, Monday, at 10 o'clock, Mark
will be waiting near that temple

Table I. THREE TIMES THE CHARACTER FOR 'FUN' OR 'ENTERTAINING'. NOTICE THE DIFFERENCE IN COMPOSITIONAL STRUCTURE, ESPECIALLY REGARDING THE 'THREAD'-COMPONENT (THE 'LITTLE SIDEBURNS' IN THE TRADITIONAL CHARACTER).

乐	simplified (modern day) Chinese
樂	traditional Chinese, Cantonese, Taiwanese
楽	Japanese

The first three characters: マーク, 'Mark', are Katakana; the number 10 is written in Romaji. The characters: は, に, あ, の, で, っ, て, い, ま, and す are Hiragana. The remaining characters: 明, 日, 月, 曜, 時, 寺, and 待 are Kanji. Japanese words are usually comprised of Katakana only (マーク), Hiragana only (あの), Kanji only (月曜, 時, 寺) or a combination of Kanji and Hiragana (待って). In Kanji-only words, combinatorial deployment of characters shows close correspondence to word compounds in other languages. For instance, the single character word for 'gold' (金) and the single character word for 'fish' (魚) are commonly combined into a single two-Kanji word 金魚, meaning 'goldfish'. Fishing (釣) and stick (竿) make 'fishing rod' (釣竿). Estimations for the total number of existing Kanji characters range from 40,000–100,000 and new characters could theoretically still be added today [20], but the vast majority of these characters are rarely used. Although all far eastern logographic languages are thought to stem from the same source, there are considerable differences between Japanese Kanji, Chinese characters, and the writing systems in Taiwan and Hong Kong nowadays. Japan has some unique Kanji and a post-war simplification effort in China resulted in a substantial difference between the sets (see Table I). Japanese, Cantonese (from Hong Kong) and Taiwanese characters did not undergo such simplification, but nonetheless diverged over time, and are different from Japanese Kanji too.

Many complex Kanji characters can be seen as compounds of elementary building blocks. We will call these building blocks *components*, and a clear distinction should be made from a Kanji's *radical*, which is traditionally the Kanji's component used for dictionary indexing. As an example, the single-component character 日 (meaning 'day' or 'sun') and the single-component character 月 (meaning 'moon') are combined into a two-component character 明, which means 'bright'. Only the sun-component, however, is considered to be its radical. Both Japanese and Chinese dictionaries traditionally recognize 214 radicals, but many modern electronic Kanji dictionaries employ a 252-piece component file, from which any and every combination of components can be selected for character lookup. It is this 252-piece set, which has considerable overlap with but is not identical to the traditional 214-piece radical set, that was used for this investigation. The exact specification of the 252-component KRADFILE can be found on [21].

Japanese Kanji is organized into several cumulative sets. The KyouIku ("education") is a 1,006-piece set of commonly used Kanji maintained by the Japanese ministry of education. It covers roughly 90% of the Kanji used in the Japanese corpus and is used to determine which characters should be learned by Japanese children in each year of elementary school. The JouYou (lit.: "commonly used") is a set of 1,945 Kanji characters and has also been maintained by the Japanese ministry of education, since 1981. It is a superset of KyouIku, extending it by 939 characters learned in secondary school, covering 98.66% of the Kanji used in the Japanese corpus and contains all Kanji allowable in governmental documents. Finally, the JIS X.0208 is a Japanese Industrial Standard defining a 6,355-piece character set, which extends the JouYou by another 4,410 characters, covering 99.98% of all Kanji characters used. Our focus will be on these three character sets, in particular with their intrinsic structures. These structures, as we will show, share characteristic properties with other spontaneously evolved self-organized complex systems.

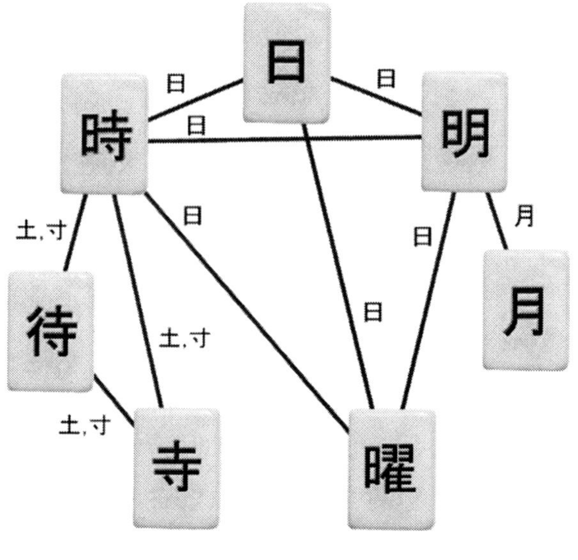

Figure 1. Graph of the Kanji from the example sentence mentioned in the introduction. Vertices represent individual Kanji characters, connected if they share at least one component as identified by the label.

III. KANJI IS A SMALL-WORLD NETWORK THROUGH SHARED COMPONENTS

We may envisage the cumulative sets of Kanji characters as networks, in which the vertices are characters connected by an edge if they share at least one component (see Figure 1).

An undirected network of n vertices can have a maximum of $n(n-1)/2$ edges; all three networks have a small fraction of this, classifying them as sparse. Omitting disconnected vertices, the KyouIku network has 1,004 nodes and 73,173 edges (density 14.53%), the JouYou network has 1,943 nodes and 292,234 edges (density 15.49%), the JIS.X.0208 has 6,355 nodes and 3,354,225 edges (density 16.61%).

In literature, values for CC and APL in real-life small-world networks have mostly been compared to theoretical values of CC and APL in Erdös-Rényi (ER) random networks [22] and to those of actually randomized networks [1] of similar numbers of vertices and edges. A stricter comparison can be made by randomly cross-wiring pairs of edges, a procedure known as the Maslov-Sneppen (MS) algorithm [23]. This algorithm randomly selects two pairs of connected vertices (v_1, v_2) and (v_3, v_4) such that all four vertices are different and then rewires them to (v_1, v_4) and (v_3, v_2). Repeating this operation

Table II. FROM EACH KANJI NETWORK, WE CONSTRUCTED 1,000 ERDÖS-RÉNYI RANDOM NETWORKS AND 1,000 MASLOV-SNEPPEN RANDOM NETWORKS BY 10^6 ITERATIONS OF THE RESPECTIVE ALGORITHM. BOTH ER-RANDOMIZATIONS AND MS-RANDOMIZATIONS WERE USED AS DIFFERENT NULL HYPOTHESES TO TEST THE STATISTICAL SIGNIFICANCE OF THE VALUES FOR CC AND APL FOUND IN THE KANJI NETWORKS.

		ER-randomized			MS-randomized		
	actual	mean (μ)	std.dev. (σ)	z-score	mean (μ)	std.dev. (σ)	z-score
KyouIku CC	0.629	0.145	$2.178 \cdot 10^{-4}$	$2.218 \cdot 10^{3}$	0.330	$1.377 \cdot 10^{-3}$	$2.169 \cdot 10^{2}$
KyouIku APL	1.962	1.855	$3.129 \cdot 10^{-11}$	$3.440 \cdot 10^{12}$	1.900	$7.620 \cdot 10^{-4}$	$8.196 \cdot 10^{1}$
Jouyou CC	0.604	0.155	$6.072 \cdot 10^{-5}$	$7.395 \cdot 10^{3}$	0.321	$5.198 \cdot 10^{-4}$	$5.446 \cdot 10^{2}$
Jouyou APL	1.888	1.845	$0.437 \cdot 10^{-14}$	$9.760 \cdot 10^{11}$	1.858	$2.724 \cdot 10^{-4}$	$1.089 \cdot 10^{2}$
JIS.X.0208 CC	0.582	0.166	$3.203 \cdot 10^{-5}$	$1.298 \cdot 10^{3}$	0.321	$1.200 \cdot 10^{-4}$	$2.174 \cdot 10^{3}$
JIS.X.0208 APL	1.843	1.834	0	∞	1.836	$5.165 \cdot 10^{-5}$	$1.360 \cdot 10^{2}$

for a large number of iterations effectively randomizes the network, but preserves the exact degree distribution.

For assessing the statistical significance of the actual CC and APL of the three Kanji networks, we generated 1,000 ER-randomized networks and 1,000 MS-randomized networks from each of the three Kanji networks by rewiring the original networks 10^6 iterations with the respective methods. The CC of all three Kanji networks is far larger than that of either an ER-random network or a MS-random network making them highly clustered (Table II). It should be noted that the significant difference between CC for MS-random networks and ER-random networks also suggests that the exact degree distribution might play a crucial role in facilitating the high clustering coefficient of these networks (Figure 2). The APL-values of the networks are relatively low, making the networks globally well-coupled despite their low edge density.

The KyouIku network has two vertices with degree zero (面, meaning 'surface' and 飛, meaning 'to fly'). As disconnected vertices lead to undefined path lengths, these two vertices were excluded from the experiments. The network's best-connected Kanji vertex is 速, meaning 'fast', which has 450 edges, connecting almost half the network. The characters in KyouIku contain a total of 219 different components of which 30 are used only once. The most common component is the enclosure component 口 which is shared by 181 characters in the set. The JouYou network, like the KyouIku network, also had two isolated vertices removed from calculations (again 面 and 飛). In this network, the Kanji vertex with the highest degree is 籍, meaning 'one's family register', which has 922 connections, connecting almost half the JouYou network. In this set of characters, there are 237 different components of which 13 are used for one character only. The enclosure component 口 is again the most common component, being present in 345 different characters. The JIS.X.0208-network is a connected network; there is a path from every vertex to every other vertex. Only one Kanji vertex in the network (飛, meaning 'to fly') has exactly degree one (being adjacent only to 飜, meaning 'to turn over'). In this network, the most edges on a single vertex is 3,001, for 檜 (meaning 'cedar'), which is thereby connected to almost half the network. Again, the enclosure 口 is the most occurring component, which is shared by 1,325 Kanji vertices in this network. The rarest components are 鬯 and 鼎 both appearing only once. Plotted vertex degree histograms show irregular distributions for all three networks, meaning that they do not qualify for the characteristic of being scale-free [24] (Figure 2).

IV. DISCUSSION AND FUTURE WORK

The clusters in the Japanese Kanji sets are an immediate result of the distribution of components among characters. Any single component completely interconnects all characters having that component, effectively creating an integrated module, often increasing the network's CC significantly. However, this has possibly not always been the case; the 2nd century A.D. dictionary *Shuōwén Jiězì* ("Explaining Simple and Analyzing Compound Characters"), describes 9,353 characters indexed by 540 radicals and possibly containing an even larger number of components. None of the far eastern logographic languages has nearly that many components nowadays, signifying the number must have dropped dramatically through time.

This considerable reduction in visual complexity might have been symbiotically accompanied by another interesting development. Research has shown that the pronunciation of a modern-day Kanji closely corresponds to the components it contains [25]–[27]. For instance, the single-component Kanji 中, meaning 'middle' is pronounced as *chuu*, but so are very different compound Kanji containing the same component: 忠 ('loyal'), 沖 ('shore'), 仲 ('relation'), 虫 ('insect'), 狆 ('Japanese Spaniel'). It might be somewhat problematic to understand how these five Kanji would actually share a quantity of meaning (in this case the concept of 'middle') but clearly, they do share their pronunciation.

Together, these observations may be interpreted as support for *Gelb's hypothesis*. In his influential study, Ignace Gelb hypothesized that characters in human written languages tend to evolve from picture-based logographic symbols to sound-based alphabetic symbols through time, with the "degree of abstractness serving as the main index of sophistication" [28], [29]. Interestingly enough, the statistical footprint of both Kanji characters and their components seems to provide further support for this theory. Although words in Japanese are distributed very much like words in non-logographic languages (Russian, Arabic, Spanish), following Zipf's law [30]–[33], the frequency distribution of individual Kanji characters more closely resembles those of alphabetic letters in Cyrillic, Arabic, and Roman scripts (Figure 3) but perhaps more surprisingly – so does the set of individual components. So, even if Kanji and Kanji components would be pure logographic symbols and word-like carriers of meaning, their statistical behavior tells a different story, classifying them as letters like б, л, ш, И, m, u, ñ, d, ة, ك, ب, ش. more than anything else.

The composition of Kanji characters is often primarily explained through its combined meanings of their components (e.g., in textbooks [34], [35]) but these explanations might be of mnemonical or folkloristic nature more than historically

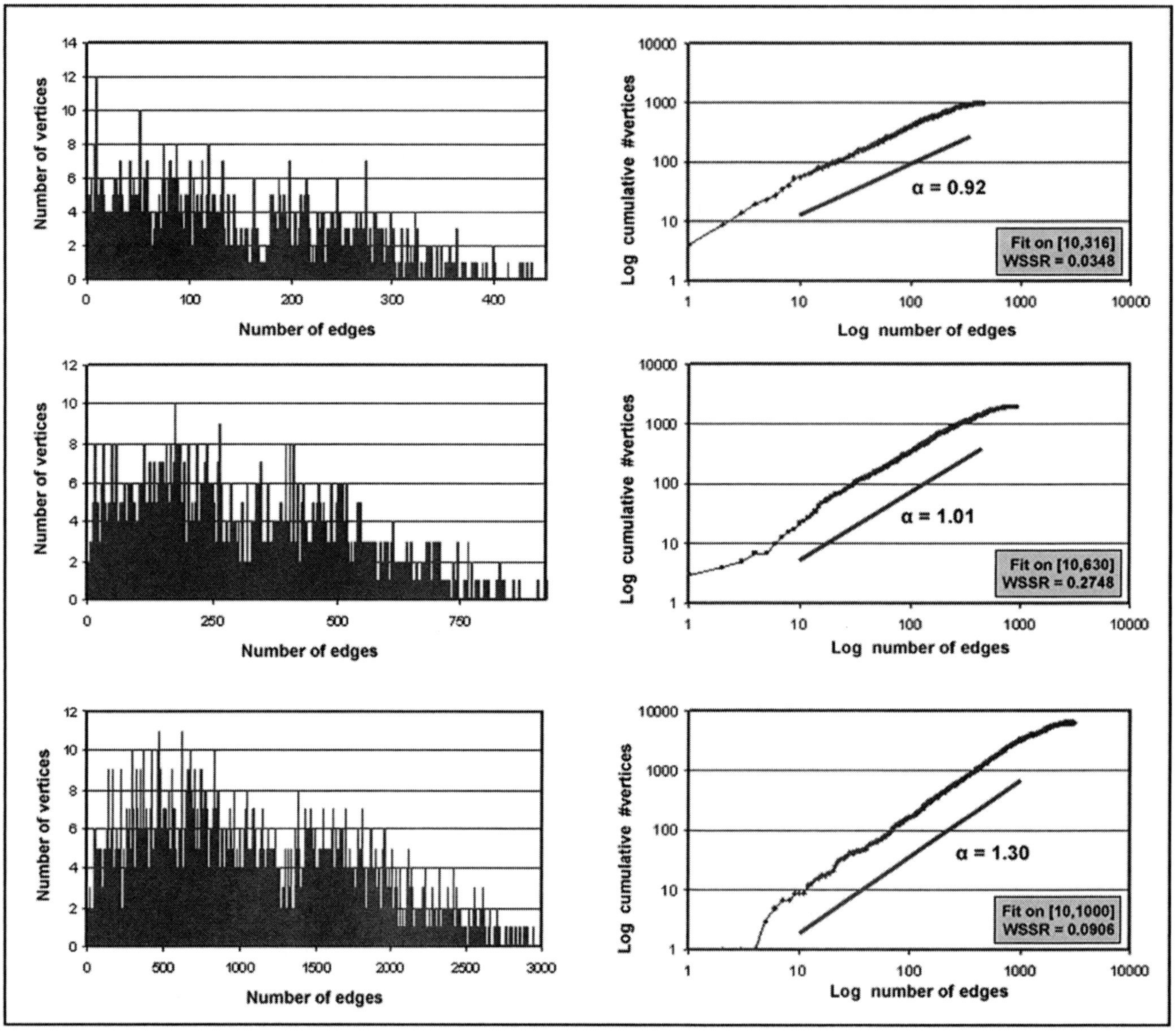

Figure 2. Degree distributions (left) of Kanji networks (top: KyouIku, middle: JouYou, bottom: JIS X.02.08) show apparent featureless patterns. However, log-log plots of the cumulative networks of the same plots (right-hand side) show largely linear tendencies on the central part. The red line corresponds to both the exponent and the interval used for the specific network, the text directly below is the value of its exponent. The values in the inset boxes are fitting intervals and fitting errors. All fits were done with Fityk on Linux by the Levenberg-Marquardt method from random initial conditions.

accurate accounts of Kanji construction. If the interpretation of our findings is correct, modern-day Kanji, at least to some extent, behave more like alphabetic letters than like logographic pictures. From this perspective, clustering (or small-worldness) in a network of Japanese (or Chinese) characters might just be a side effect of a much larger process: that of a language being in the midst of a phase transition from being picture-based to being alphabet-based.

ACKNOWLEDGMENTS

The starting point for this investigation was sparked by JWPCE, a freely available Japanese word processor for Windows OS written by Glenn Rosenthal (http://www.physics.ucla.edu/ grosenth/japanese.html). Sergei Sharoff from Leeds University maintains a broad multitude of freely available language corpora. We are grateful to both Glenn and Sergei for disclosing these resources. Our thanks go out to and to Charles Adamson for many helpful remarks and comments, to anonymous reviewers of both Entropy and NDPLS for their high-quality work and constructive comments. The support from Ramon Ferrer-i-Cancho from Llenguatges i Sistemes Informàtics (LSI) of Universitat Politècnica de Catalunya has been indispensable – thanks, Ramon. Finally, a recognition to Hans Dekkers, Guus Delen, Betty Bijl and Cristine Cabi from IvI/UvA who have freed some of my (Daan) time to do some research, which I have used to produce this paper.

REFERENCES

[1] D. Watts and S. Strogatz, "Collective dynamics of small-world networks." Nature, vol. 393, no. 6684, 1998, pp. 440–442.

[2] T. Achacoso and W. Yamamoto, AY's Neuroanatomy of C. elegans for Computation. CRC Press, 1992.

[3] K. Stephan et al., "Computational analysis of functional connectivity between areas of primate cerebral cortex," Phil. Trans. R. Soc. B., vol. 355, no. 1393, 2000, pp. 111–126.

[4] O. Sporns and J. Zwi, "The small world of the cerebral cortex," Neuroinformatics, vol. 2, no. 2, 2004, pp. 145–162.

[5] L. Adamic, The Small World Web. Springer, 1999.

[6] S. Wasserman and K. Faust, Social Network Analysis: Methods and Applications. Cambridge University Press, 1994.

[7] P. Gong and C. van Leeuwen, "Emergence of scale-free network with chaotic units," Phys. A, vol. 321, no. 3-4, 2003, pp. 679–688.

[8] ——, "Evolution to a small-world network with chaotic units," Europhys. Lett., vol. 67, no. 2, 2004, pp. 328–333.

[9] M. Rubinov, O. Sporns, C. van Leeuwen, and M. Breakspear, "Symbiotic relationship between brain structure and dynamics," BMC Neurosci., vol. 10, 2009, p. 55.

[10] D. Van den Berg and C. van Leeuwen, "Adaptive rewiring in chaotic networks renders small-world connectivity with consistent clusters," Europhys. Lett., vol. 65, no. 4, 2004, pp. 459–464.

[11] D. van den Berg, P. Gong, M. Breakspear, and C. van Leeuwen, "Fragmentation: loss of global coherence or breakdown of modularity in functional brain architecture?" Frontiers in systems neuroscience, vol. 6, 2012.

[12] R. Ferrer-i-Cancho and R. Sole, "The small world of human language," Proc. R. Soc. B., vol. 268, no. 1482, 2001, pp. 2261–2265.

[13] J. Li and J. Zhou, "Chinese character structure analysis based on complex networks," Phys A, vol. 380, 2007, pp. 629–638.

[14] Y. Shi, W. Liang, J. Liu, and C. K. Tse, "Structural equivalence between co-occurrences of characters and words in the chinese language," in International symposium on nonlinear theory and its applications, 2008, pp. 94–97.

[15] Z. Liu and M. Sun, "Chinese word co-occurrence network: its small-world effect and scale-free property," Journal of Chinese Information Processing, vol. 21, no. 6, 2007, pp. 52–58.

[16] S. Zhou, G. Hu, Z. Zhang, and J. Guan, "An empirical study of chinese language networks," Physica A: Statistical Mechanics and its Applications, vol. 387, no. 12, 2008, pp. 3039–3047.

[17] Y. Li, L. Wei, Y. Niu, and J. Yin, "Structural organization and scale-free properties in chinese phrase networks," Chinese Science Bulletin, vol. 50, no. 13, 2005, pp. 1305–1309.

[18] K. Yamamoto and Y. Yamazaki, "A network of two-Chinese-character compound words in the Japanese language," Physica A: Statistical Mechanics and its Applications, vol. 388, no. 12, 2009, pp. 2555–2560.

[19] ——, "Structure and modeling of the network of two-Chinese-character compound words in the Japanese language," Physica A: Statistical Mechanics and its Applications, vol. 412, 2014, pp. 84–91.

[20] Y.-M. Chou, S.-K. Hsieh, and C.-R. Huang, Lecture Notes in Computer Science, State-of-the-Art Survey. Springer-Verlag, 2007, pp. 133–145.

[21] "Kradfile," http://nihongo.monash.edu//kradinf.html, last access date: 31 October, 2017.

[22] A. Fronczak, P. Fronczak, and J. A. Hołyst, "Average path length in random networks," Phys Rev E, vol. 70, no. 5, 2004, pp. 1–4.

[23] S. Maslov and K. Sneppen, "Specificity and stability in topology of protein networks," Science, vol. 296, no. 5569, 2002, pp. 910–913.

[24] A. Barabasi and R. Albert, "Emergence of scaling in random networks," Science, vol. 286, no. 5439, 1999, pp. 509–512.

[25] H. Townsend, "Phonetic components in japanese characters," Master's thesis, San Diego Status University, 2011.

[26] E. Toyoda, A. Firdaus, and C. Kano, "Identifying useful phonetic components of kanji for learners of japanese," Japanse Language and Literature, 2013, pp. 235–272.

[27] K. Tamaoka, "Psycholonguistic nature of the japanese orthography," Studies in Language and Literature, vol. 11, no. 1, 1991, pp. 49–82.

[28] T. Miyamoto, "The evolution of writing systems: against the gelbian hypothesis," New Frontiers in Artificial Intelligence, 2007, pp. 345–356.

[29] I. Gelb, A study of writing: the foundations of grammatology. The University of Chicago, 1952.

[30] G. Zipf, Human Behavior and the Principle of Least Effort. Addison-Wesley Press, 1949.

[31] ——, The Psycho-Biology of Language. MIT Press, 1935.

[32] R. Ferrer-i-Cancho and R. Sole, "Least effort and the origins of scaling in human language," in Proc. of the National Academy of Sciences, vol. 100, no. 3, 2003, pp. 788–791.

[33] R. Ferrer-i Cancho, "Optimization models of natural communication," Journal of Quantitative Linguistics, 2017, pp. 1–31.

[34] J. Heisig, Remembering the Kanji, Volume 1: a complete course on how not to forget the meaning and writing of Japanese characters. University of Hawaii Press, 2007.

[35] Y. Watanabe, Learning Kanji Through Stories. Kurosio Publs., 2008.

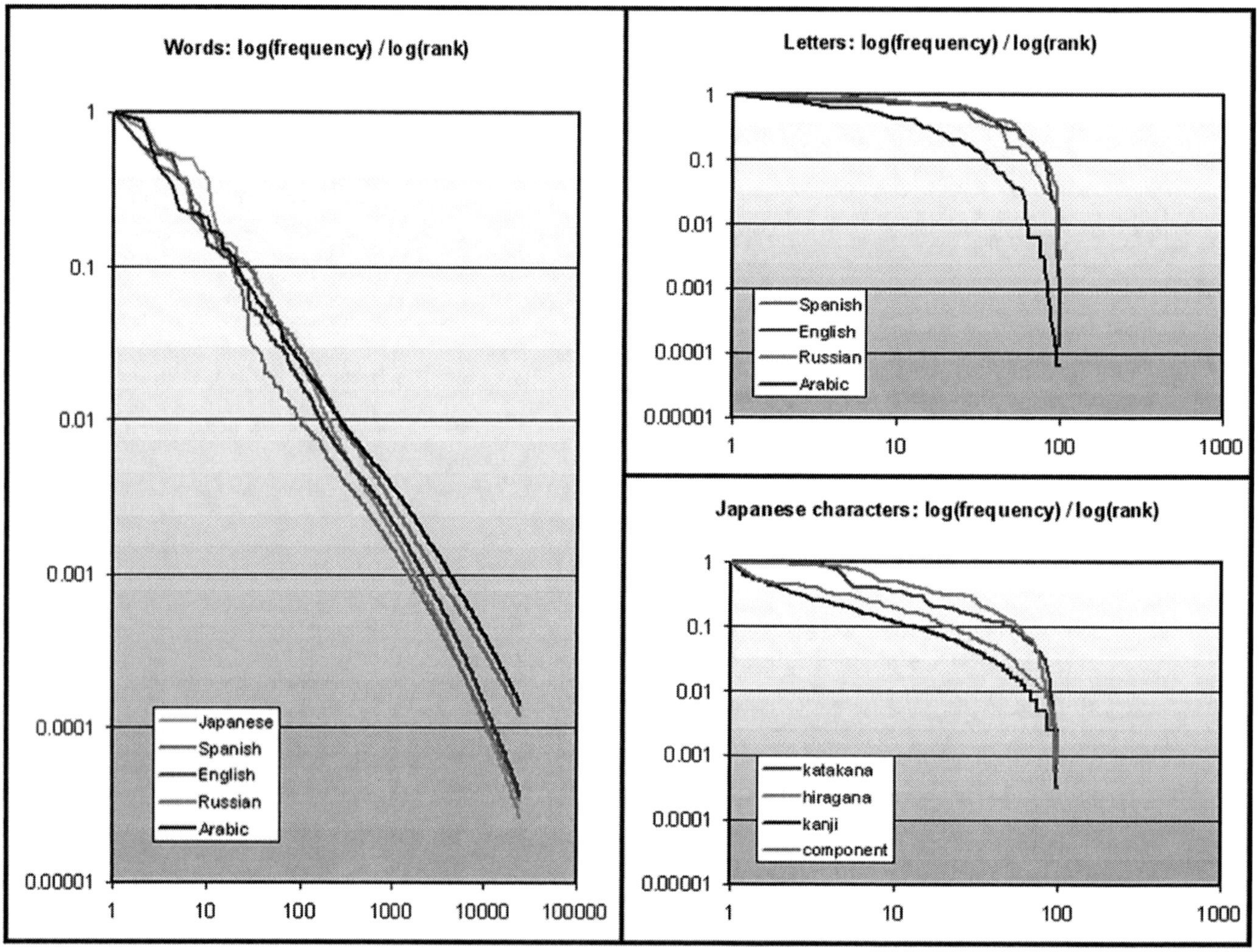

Figure 3. Written words in Japanese, as in most other languages, closely follow a power law distribution known as Zipf's law in linguistics (left). But even though single Kanji characters are often interpreted as carriers of meaning, their statistical behaviour more closely resembles that of letters in non-logographic writing systems (top right), and the same goes for its components.

Spatio-Temporal Modeling for Residential Burglary

Maria Mahfoud
CWI,
Stochastics,
Amsterdam, The Netherlands
Email: M.Mahfoud@cwi.nl

Sandjai Bhulai
Vrije Universiteit Amsterdam,
Faculty of Science,
Amsterdam, The Netherlands
Email: s.bhulai@vu.nl

Rob van der Mei
CWI,
Stochastics,
Amsterdam, The Netherlands
Email: R.D.van.der.Mei@cwi.nl

***Abstract*—Spatio-temporal modeling is widely recognized as a promising means for predicting crime patterns. Despite their enormous potential, the available methods are still in their infancy. A lot of research focuses on crime hotspot detection and geographic crime clusters, while a systematic approach to include the temporal component of the underlying crime distributions is still under-researched. In this paper, we gain further insight in predictive crime modeling by including a spatio-temporal interaction component in the prediction of residential burglaries. Based on an extensive dataset, we show that including additive space-time interactions leads to significantly better predictions.**

Keywords–Predictive analytics; forecasting; spatio-temporal modeling; residential burglary

I. Introduction

How the police should respond to crime is a constant source of discussion and debate among scholars and practitioners. Over time, new strategies have been developed that use data to influence decision making and direct crime control. This data was first used to indicate the underlying problems within a community by identifying clusters of repeating crime incidents. This was followed by using data to map crime to allow for rapid response to emerging crime problems and hotspots. The most recent development is intelligence-led policing, an objective method for formulating strategic policing priorities by using data analysis and crime intelligence for strategic planning and resource allocation in order to reduce, disrupt and prevent crime. The better integration of the available information systems allows the police to create a picture of the criminal environment and to predict the emerging areas of criminality [1].

Within an intelligence-led framework, proactive policing corresponds with an initial response of the law enforcement agencies to prevent crimes before being committed rather than reacting to criminal acts. Proactive policing requires the ability to predict crime hotspots and concentrations to identify likely targets for police intervention. The identification of these targets is one of the main goals of predictive policing [2].

Although the use of statistical analysis for predicting crimes has been around for decades, the Geographical Information System (GIS) revolution, in the recent years, has led to a surge of analytical techniques to identify likely targets in order to prevent criminal activities. Perry [2] organizes these techniques around six analytic categories: hot spot analysis, regression methods, data mining techniques, near-repeat methods, spatio-temporal analysis and risk terrain analysis. As stated by [3], "the most under-researched area of spatial criminology is that of spatio-temporal crime patterns". The same point has been made by Law et al. [4] who discusses spatio-temporal approaches in past crime research proposing a Bayesian spatio-temporal approach for modeling crime trends. Bernasco and Elffers [5] also address this issue of integrating the spatial and the temporal dimension of crime in order to advance the analysis of crime data. They mentioned that crime varies spatio-temporally illustrating this by an example from [6] on residential burglaries. Especially for residential burglaries, a body of research has shown the repeat and the near-repeat victimization effects [7]–[10]. Therefore, modeling the space-time interactions of residential burglaries are important to capture these effects.

Displaying statistical information on a map allows for conveying information in a format which is ideal for operational decision making. Spatio-temporal information can ideally be understood when displayed on a map, however, there are a number of issues related to the mapping of information in the policing domain. Among these is the use of choropleth maps. As noted by [3], "one particular problem among crime analysis is the incorrect tendency to map real values with choropleth (thematic) maps, resulting in the misleading impression that is often given by larger or unequal areas (Harries, 1999)". Chainey et al. [11] also mention the need of a threshold specification to identify hotspots. In their paper, they indicate also the influence of the parameter setting on the ability to predict future crimes using hotspot maps. The same problem was discussed by [12] who addresses the problem of hotspot identification and the variation of maps that can be obtained using the same data. They state that the choice of a thematic range represents a problem in itself.

An additional problem related to crime mapping is the varying sizes and shapes of geographic administrative boundary areas. Eck et al. [12] propose the use of small uniform grids as a solution to this problem. This results in a high-resolution model. This type of models provides a more realistic forecast in terms of structure and spatial variability [13]. However, it does not necessarily improve the forecast accuracy [14]. Roberts [15] highlights the necessity of evaluating the spatial and temporal variation in the skill of the model in order to define the scales at which the model forecast should be believed.

This research focuses on residential burglaries and attempts to provide more clarity in predictive crime modeling and mapping by addressing the limitations discussed above. The major aims of this study are to find an accurate probability distribution of residential burglaries taking account of the space-time interactions, and to identify a cut-off value to classify areas as high-risk areas. Wang and Brown [16] model criminal incidents in Charlottesville using a spatio-temporal generalized additive model (ST-GAM) and extend it to a local spatio-temporal generalized additive model (LST-GAM). They applied the ST-GAM to predict the probability distribution of criminal incidents. In the ST-GAM, the temporal information of previous criminal incidents is modeled as a dummy variable indicating the time of the last committed criminal incident. They show that the ST-GAM and the LST-GAM outperform their previous spatial generalized linear model (GLM) and the hot spot model. This research extends the model proposed by [16] by allowing for more complicated space-time interactions.

Inspired by [17], we propose a generalized additive model (GAM) for modeling the probability distribution of residential burglaries in one district of Amsterdam based on regular lattice data (grid boxes of 125×125 meters). The model extends the base model similar to the one discussed in [16] by allowing for additive space-time interactions. We show that the model provides a useful forecast from a radius of 312.5 meters from the centroid of the grid. However, a clear improvement in the forecast accuracy is observed from the first neighborhood (187.5 meters from the centroid of the grid).

The remainder of this paper is organized as follows. Section II describes the used data set and the data analysis. Section III provides the methodological framework underlying this research. Section IV illustrates the results of the analysis. Section V concludes this research.

II. Data

A. Data description

The data used for this research was provided by the Dutch Police. It contains all recorded incidents of residential burglaries that happened in one district of Amsterdam, with the highest burglary rate, between January 1, 2008 and April 30, 2014. The data was recorded at a monthly level and grouped into grids of 125×125 meters. The data is thus regular lattice data. Only the grids that correspond to urban areas were selected resulting in 1,812 grid locations. In total, there were 115,968 records with a total number of 11,450 incidents.

In addition, each crime incident recorded contained the latitude/longitude coordinates on the grid level, the time of occurrence (month, year) and different covariates that correspond to the demographic factors and the socio-economic factors that are associated with this grid. Next, to these covariates, the Dutch police also use some spatio-temporal indicators that specify when the last incident happened in a specific grid or combination of grids (neighborhood) using different time intervals. These spatio-temporal indicators are crime specific, for example, the number of residential burglaries in a specific grid one month before the reference date. The covariates that correspond to the demographic and the socio-economic factors are location-specific covariates and are constant over time. These covariates count 44 attributes, including population, average values of houses in the postal code area of the corresponding grid, percentage low incomes in the postal code area of the corresponding grid, and so on. Next, to these covariates, we also used some covariates that correspond with the geographic information of the city, such as the distance to the nearest highway access. In total, there were 61 covariates.

B. Data exploration

A first analysis of the recorded incidents shows that only 1.2% of the total records had a higher number of residential burglaries than 1, while 91.61% of the records was equal to 0. For this reason, the occurrence of residential burglaries (binary) was considered as the response variable.

1) Missing values: The first problem encountered using the above-described data was a large number of missing values. The response variable contains no missing values. However, 113,408 of the 115,968 records contain at least one missing value. It is clear that removing every row that contains a missing value is not the best option as it will reduce the sample size by 97.8%.

Further analysis of the missing values shows that all missing values were observed for the location-specific covariates. Moreover, when a covariate contains missing values, at least 23% of the data was missing. Due to a large number of covariates and the high percentage of missing values we decided to remove the corresponding covariates. This concerns 18 of the 44 location-specific covariates.

A deeper analysis of the covariates shows that the covariates that correspond to age categories were not complete (they did not sum up to 100%) and at least 25% of the observed values for each variable was equal to zero, which is not likely. For these reasons, these variables were also removed from the data set. Furthermore, the variable TSLI (the number of months since the last incident in the grid) was not always consistent with the corresponding spatio-temporal indicators and based on common sense, this variable is expected to be highly correlated with the other spatio-temporal indicators. For this reason, this variable was also removed from the data set.

2) Near zero-variance covariates: Further analysis of the data shows that many covariates have only some unique values with low frequencies. These variables, also called near zero-variance variables, can cause numerical problems. Kuhn [18] considered a variable as a near zero-variance variable if two conditions were approved. The first one is that the percentage of unique values should be less than 20%. The second one is that the ratio of the most frequent to the second most frequent value should be greater than 20. The analysis of the near zero-variance covariates in our data set was performed using the `nearZeroVar` function from the caret package [19]. This analysis reveals that 16 covariates have a near zero-variance, which were removed from the data set.

The final data exploration was, mainly, performed following the protocol described in [20].

3) Outliers: First, a Cleveland dotplot was drawn for each covariate to identify potential outliers. The plots show that some covariates have potential outliers indicated by the isolated points. These outliers were replaced by the maximum values observed after removing the outliers from the data set. Moreover, the covariates CB (number of cafes and bars in the

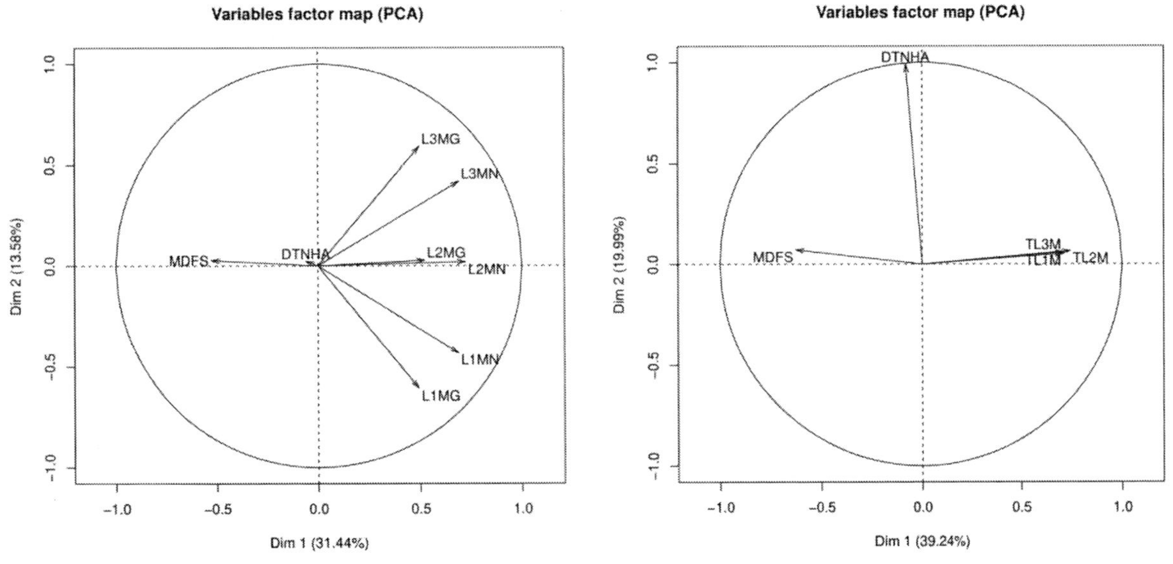

(a) (b)

Figure 1. PCA biplot of the covariates. The left panel indicates higher correlation between the number of residential burglaries observed in the grid and its direct neighborhood within the same time unit. The right panel shows the PCA biplot after aggregating the spatio-temporal indicators that correspond to the same time-unit. As can be seen from this panel, TL1M, TL2M and TL3M are highly correlated.

grid), REST (number of restaurants in the grid), and SHOP (number of shops in the grid) are highly unbalanced. To avoid problems due to a large number of zeros and to reduce the dimensionality of the data, these covariates were grouped into one covariate called public places (PP). This covariate has 19 unique values but is highly unbalanced. PP was divided into three categories. The first category is when no public places were observed in the grid. The second category is when there are at most five public places in the grid, and the last category is when there are more than five public places. This to distinguish between the grids in terms of crowdedness. Furthermore, EI (the number of educational institutions in the grid) is also highly unbalanced and has only three unique values, this covariate was used as a binary covariate (fPP).

4) Collinearity: Ignoring collinearity increases type II errors and leads to serious problems with forward and backward selection procedures [21]. As we are, among others, interested in the covariates that drive residential burglaries, we should be very careful about collinear covariates. To assess collinearity between the covariates, the variance inflation factor (VIF) was used. The VIF measures the amount by which the variance of a parameter estimator is increased due to collinearity with other covariates rather than being orthogonal [22]. First, the VIF was calculated using all covariates. The covariate with the highest VIF was removed and the VIFs have calculated again. This process was repeated until all VIF values were smaller than two. Note that the use of this threshold is subjective as there is no true VIF threshold. In the literature, different VIF values were suggested. Kennedy [23], among other authors, recommends a threshold of ten. A threshold of five was recommended by [24]. However, as mentioned in [21], the use of a VIF threshold of ten or even five is too high [25]. By using a threshold of two, we aim to be more conservative about collinearity. The VIF analysis shows that L6MN (number of incidents in the direct neighborhood in the sixth month and earlier before the reference time), L6MG (number of incidents in the grid in the sixth month and earlier before the reference time), and ADFS (average distance from the centroids of the grid to the nearest known 10 burglars) are collinear with other covariates and were removed from the data set.

Residential burglaries are known to have the repeat and near-repeat victimization effect where residential burglaries cluster over time and space [7] [26] [9]. Due to this effect, collinearity is expected between the spatio-temporal indicators. To provide more insight into the relationships between these covariates, the principal component analysis (PCA) biplot was used. The left panel of Figure 1 shows higher correlations between the number of incidents observed in the grid and in its direct neighborhood within the same time unit. The spatio-temporal indicators that correspond to the same time unit were aggregated resulting in three covariates TL1M, TL2M, and TL3M where TLxM is the total number of incidents observed in the grid and its direct neighborhood x months before the reference time. A PCA biplot was drawn using these covariates. As can be seen from the right panel of Figure 1, higher collinearity is observed between TL1M, TL2M, and TL3M. Again, to avoid loss of information, these covariates were grouped together into a new covariate, TL3, which is the total observed incidents in the grid and its direct neighborhood in the last three months. To check for outliers in TL3, a Cleveland dotplot was drawn and this plot shows no extreme observations. A PCA biplot was drawn again using TL3, MDFS (distance from the center of the grid to the nearest known burglar) and DTNHA (distance from the center of the

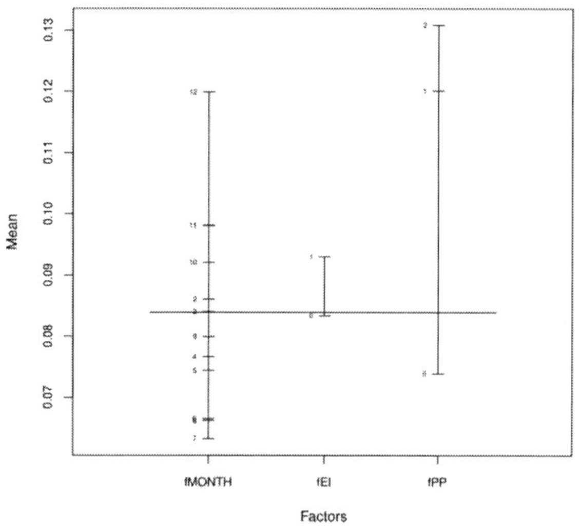

Figure 2. Design plot showing the average incidents per class for each factor variable.

grid to the nearest highway access), which shows that MDFS is negatively correlated with TL3 (this plot is not shown here but the same result can be concluded from Figure 1). We decided to use TL3 and leave MDFS out of the analysis.

Furthermore, conditional boxplots were used to assess collinearity between continuous and categorical covariates. This reveals that collinearity between SD and DTNHA exists. The covariate sub-district (SD) also shows some collinearity with TL3. To avoid problems due to collinearity, SD was omitted from the analysis.

The final set of covariates includes eight covariates, namely the space covariates X and Y; the temporal covariates YEAR and MONTH; the categorical covariates public places (fPP) and educational institutions (fEI); the total observed incidents in the grid and its direct neighborhood in the last three months (TL3) and finally, the distance to the nearest highway access (DTNHA).

5) Relationships between the response and the covariates: The relationship between the response variable and the nominal variables was assessed graphically by a design plot (Figure 2). As illustrated in Figure 2, higher mean values of the residential burglaries were observed between October and February, with the highest mean in December. This period is characterized by a short daylight period, while occupancy times of the residents remain the same. Due to the cover of darkness and the absence of the residents, burglars have a lower risk of being spotted. The highest value observed in December can be explained by the Christmas days and New Years Eve that are attractive days for burglars. Furthermore, a higher mean was observed in grids containing educational institutions (fEI) or public places (fPP). Moreover, crowded areas have a higher mean compared to quiet areas.

Finally, histograms of the TL3 and DTNHA for areas with residential burglary were plotted. A deeper analysis on TL3 shows that 93.14% of the incidents has occurred within grids with TL3 higher than zero. For this reason, the histogram of TL3 was drawn considering only TL3 values that are higher than zero. This shows a highly skewed distribution with peaks for TL3 values between two and four. Moreover, the distribution of DTNHA reveals a high peak of residential burglaries for distances between 875 and 1,000 meters.

In the next section, we introduce our generalized additive model (GAM) for modeling the probability distribution of residential burglaries. The model extends a base model by allowing for additive space-time interactions.

III. METHODOLOGY

Given the covariates discussed in Section II, the occurrence of residential burglaries in a certain grid i, and in a certain month t, was modeled using a GAM using the binomial distribution and the logistic link function (see, e.g., [27], [28]). To be more precise, the model is not a GAM with the binomial distribution but rather one with a Bernoulli distribution. The use of the logit link is to ensure that the fitted values are bounded in $(0, 1)$.

The choice of GAM is based on the expected non-linear relationships between the covariates and the response. A non-linear relationship is expected between the response and the distance to the nearest highway access (DTNHA). This can be explained by the two types of burglars identified by [29], the first being the opportunity burglar that prefers to operate within its own neighborhood and the second being the professional burglar who selects its targets based on the highest expected loot and operates mostly in suburban areas and areas that are near highways, because they are unaware of the local situation and escape routes. A non-linear relationship is also expected for TL3 due to the repeat and near-repeat victimization effects. The covariate MONTH is also expected to have a non-linear effect on the residential burglaries. This is due to the repeat victimization effect and the daylight-darkness effect [30]. For these reasons, smoothers will be used to model these covariates.

We use a GAM model that allows for space-time interactions as follows:

$$\begin{aligned}\text{logit}(\mu_{i,t}) = \text{fEI}_i + \text{fPP}_i + \text{YEAR}_t + f_1(\text{TL3}_{i,t}) + \\ f_2(\text{DTNHA}_{i,t}) + f_3(\text{MONTH}_t) + f_4(\text{X}_i, \text{Y}_i),\end{aligned} \quad (1)$$

where $\mu_{i,t} = \mathbb{E}(y_{i,t})$, $y_{i,t}$ follows a Bernouilli distribution, $i \in \{1, \ldots, 1812\}$, $t \in \{1, \ldots, 60\}$. The functions f_1 and f_2 are one-dimensional smoother functions of the covariates represented by a cubic regression spline (CRS). f_3 is a one-dimensional smoother represented by a cyclic cubic regression spline (CCRS). This is to avoid big jumps between the January and the December value of the smoother [31]. The function f_4 is a two-dimensional isotropic smoother for space represented by thin plate regression splines (TPRS). The TPRS was used for smoothing the spatial co-ordinates because they are measured on the same unit [28].

The model was fitted using the penalized iteratively re-weighted least squares ($\text{P} - \text{IRLS}$), while the optimal amount of smoothing was estimated using the UnBiased Risk Estimator (UBRE) [28]. All analyses were conducted using the `mgcv` package [28] from the R statistical and programming environment [32].

IV. RESULTS

Now that we can generate the probability function of residential burglaries through the GAM model, which cut-off value θ should be used to classify high-risk areas and which spatial scale provides a useful forecast? In practice, the choice of the cut-off value is mostly left to law enforcement agencies who choose a cut-off value based on the available resources and their risk preferences. Some of them choose a cut-off value of 0.8, others select areas based on the top 3% or the top 5% percentiles to classify areas as high-risk areas. However, the use of a hard cut-off value as 0.8 strongly depends on the estimated probabilities. In our case, this will result in a clear under-estimation of risk areas. If one decided to use a fraction of top percentiles, then this should be at least equal to the expected percentage of incidents. Elsewhere, the risk areas will be undoubtedly under-estimated.

Considering our training set, the average incidents (binary) over the five years, ranging between 2008 and 2012, was about 8.3%. This means that on average 151 grids, from the total grids of 1,812, should be considered as risky grids. Using the 97% percentile results in considering only 55 grids as high-risk areas. Doing this, we know apriori that we are under-estimating the risk areas. Some people will argue that the given resources do not allow to cover this high number of grids. In our point of view, from a safety perspective, the grids that should be flagged as high-risk areas should at least match the expected grids with incidents and should be independent of the available resources. After classifying the areas as high-risk areas, smart allocation methods can be used to cover the risk areas using the available resources.

Given the estimated probability distribution, the optimal cut-off (the average) considering the different neighborhoods ($\theta_1 = 0.171$) and the optimal cut-off at the grid level ($\theta_2 = 0.126$) were further used to classify areas as high-risk areas. The reason of using both cut-off values is because the optimal cut-off on grid level was quite different from the optimal cut-offs that correspond to the other neighborhoods.

The generated heat maps of January and April are given in Figure 3. From this figure, a clear difference is observed in the number of grids that are flagged as high-risk grids. In fact, more incidents are expected in January compared to April. Therefore, the predicted high-risk area in January is larger compared to the one in April. The heat maps also show that most realizations were located within the high-risk area or within their lower bounds.

In January, more incidents are expected compared to April, this is in agreement with historical data (see Figure 2). The heat maps also show that most realizations are located within the high-risk area or within its lower bound.

V. CONCLUSION

In this research, we developed a GAM model to predict the probability distribution of residential burglaries. The results show that the covariate TL3, the total incidents in the grid and its neighborhood in the last three months, has a dominant effect in the model. Apparently, this covariate captures a large part of the spatio-temporal effect in residential burglaries. Moreover, a small part of the variation in the data was captured by the model. The low power of the model may be due to the high resolution of the data used.

Finally, θ_1 and θ_2 were used to assess the performance of the model and these cut-offs were compared with the cut-off obtained for the maximum performance. Results show that both values provide similar results to the maximum performance observed, while the cut-offs that correspond to the maximum performance considering the different metrics cover a wide range, which can be difficult to interpret from a decision-making point of view.

REFERENCES

[1] J. H. Ratcliffe, Intelligence-Led Policing. Willan publishing, 2008.

[2] W. L. Perry, Predictive policing: The role of crime forecasting in law enforcement operations. Rand Corporation, 2013.

[3] J. H. Ratcliffe, "Crime mapping: spatial and temporal challenges," in Handbook of quantitative criminology. Springer, 2010, pp. 5–24.

[4] J. Law, M. Quick, and P. Chan, "Bayesian spatio-temporal modeling for analysing local patterns of crime over time at the small-area level," Journal of quantitative criminology, vol. 30, no. 1, 2014, pp. 57–78.

[5] W. Bernasco and H. Elffers, "Statistical analysis of spatial crime data," in Handbook of quantitative criminology. Springer, 2010, pp. 699–724.

[6] J. H. Ratcliffe, "Residential burglars ad urban barriers: a quantitative spatial study of the impact of canberra's unique geography on residential burglary offenders," http://crg.aic.gov.au/reports/ratcliffe.html, 2001, last access date: 31 October, 2017.

[7] W. Bernasco and P. Nieuwbeerta, "How do residential burglars select target areas? a new approach to the analysis of criminal location choice," British Journal of Criminology, vol. 45, no. 3, 2005, pp. 296–315.

[8] S. D. Johnson et al., "Space–time patterns of risk: a cross national assessment of residential burglary victimization," Journal of Quantitative Criminology, vol. 23, no. 3, 2007, pp. 201–219.

[9] M. Short, M. D'Orsogna, P. Brantingham, and G. Tita, "Measuring and modeling repeat and near-repeat burglary effects," Journal of Quantitative Criminology, vol. 25, no. 3, 2009, pp. 325–339.

[10] W. Bernasco, S. D. Johnson, and S. Ruiter, "Learning where to offend: Effects of past on future burglary locations," Applied Geography, vol. 60, 2015, pp. 120–129.

[11] S. Chainey, L. Tompson, and S. Uhlig, "The utility of hotspot mapping for predicting spatial patterns of crime," Security Journal, vol. 21, no. 1, 2008, pp. 4–28.

[12] J. Eck, S. Chainey, J. Cameron, and R. Wilson, "Mapping crime: Understanding hotspots," http://discovery.ucl.ac.uk/11291/, 2005, last access date: 31 October, 2017.

[13] E. E. Ebert, "Neighborhood verification: A strategy for rewarding close forecasts," Weather and Forecasting, vol. 24, no. 6, 2009, pp. 1498–1510.

[14] C. F. Mass, D. Ovens, K. Westrick, and B. A. Colle, "Does increasing horizontal resolution produce more skillful forecasts?" Bulletin of the American Meteorological Society, vol. 83, no. 3, 2002, pp. 407–430.

[15] N. Roberts, "Assessing the spatial and temporal variation in the skill of precipitation forecasts from an nwp model," Meteorological Applications, vol. 15, no. 1, 2008, pp. 163–169.

[16] X. Wang and D. E. Brown, "The spatio-temporal generalized additive model for criminal incidents," in Intelligence and Security Informatics (ISI), 2011 IEEE International Conference on. IEEE, 2011, pp. 42–47.

[17] N. H. Augustin, V. M. Trenkel, S. N. Wood, and P. Lorance, "Space-time modelling of blue ling for fisheries stock management," Environmetrics, vol. 24, no. 2, 2013, pp. 109–119.

[18] M. Kuhn, "Building predictive models in r using the caret package," Journal of Statistical Software, vol. 28, no. 5, 2008, pp. 1–26.

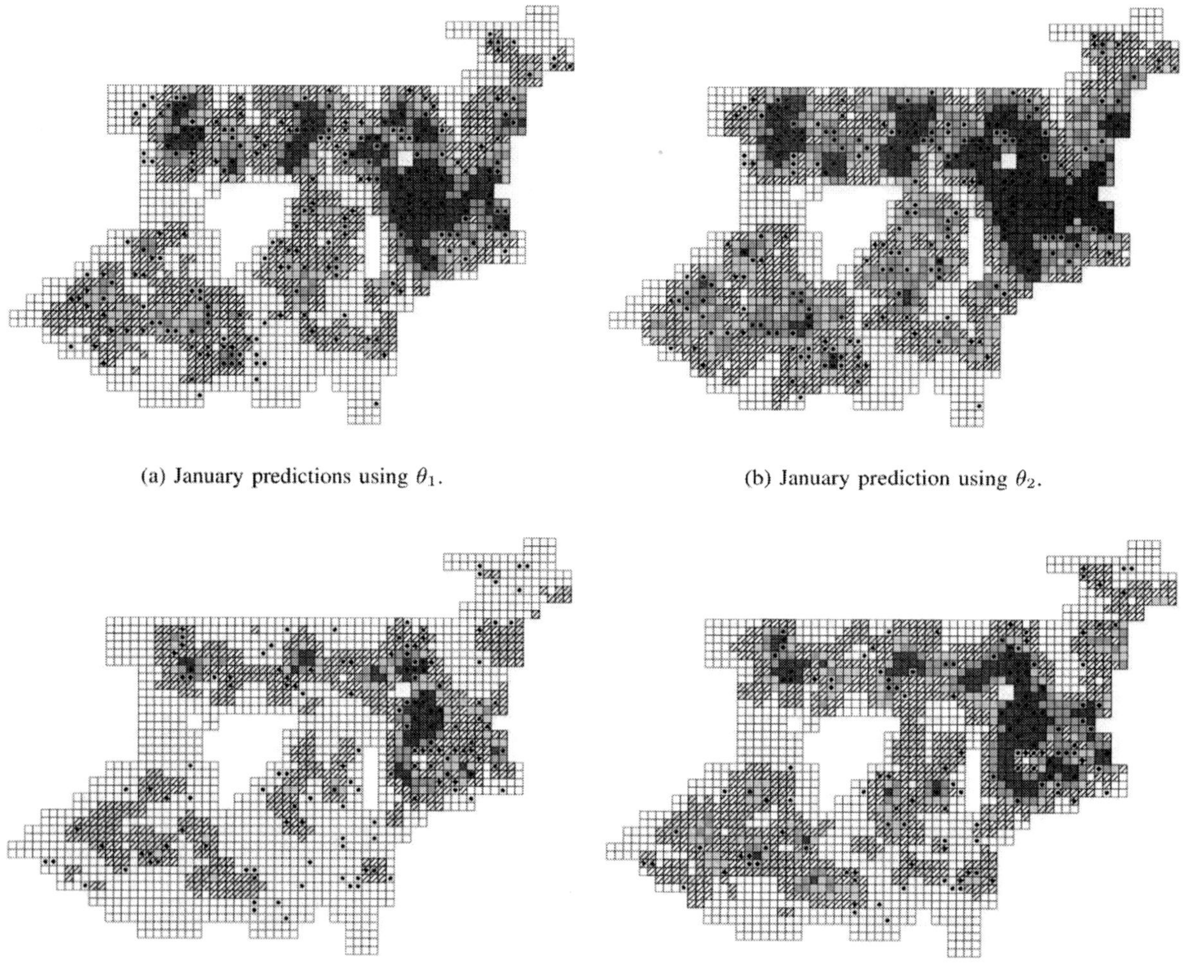

(a) January predictions using θ_1.

(b) January prediction using θ_2.

(c) April predictions using θ_1.

(d) April predictions using θ_2.

Figure 3. Heat maps of January and April using θ_1 and θ_2 and including the estimated lower bounds. The heat maps show that almost all incidents are located within the estimated high-risk area or within their lower bounds. It can also be seen that the estimated high-risk area of January is larger than the one of April. The maps obtained using θ_1 show that almost all incidents are located within the high-risk area or within their lower bound. However, the total high-risk area is smaller compared to a high-risk area obtained using θ_2. This result is very appealing for the resource allocation.

[19] M. Kuhn et al., the R Core Team, and M. Benesty., caret: Classification and Regression Training, 2014, R package version 6.0-37, Last access date: 31 October, 2017. [Online]. Available: http://CRAN.R-project.org/package=caret

[20] A. F. Zuur, E. N. Ieno, and C. S. Elphick, "A protocol for data exploration to avoid common statistical problems," Methods in Ecology and Evolution, vol. 1, no. 1, 2010, pp. 3–14.

[21] A. F. Zuur, E. N. Ieno, and G. M. Smith, Analysing ecological data. Springer New York, 2007, vol. 680.

[22] D. Liao and R. Valliant, "Variance inflation factors in the analysis of complex survey data," Survey Methodology, vol. 38, no. 1, 2012, pp. 53–62.

[23] P. Kennedy, A guide to econometrics, 6th ed. Willey-Blackwell, 2008.

[24] P. Rogerson, Statistical methods for geography. Sage, 2001.

[25] D. C. Montgomery, E. A. Peck, and G. G. Vining, Introduction to linear regression analysis. Wiley, 1992.

[26] S. D. Johnson, "Repeat burglary victimisation: a tale of two theories," Journal of Experimental Criminology, vol. 4, no. 3, 2008, pp. 215–240.

[27] T. J. Hastie and R. J. Tibshirani, Generalized additive models. CRC Press, 1990, vol. 43.

[28] S. Wood, Generalized additive models: an introduction with R. CRC press, 2006.

[29] C. van den Handel, O. Nauta, P. van Soomeren, and P. van Amersfoort, "Hoe doen ze het toch? modus operandi woningin-braak," https://hetccv.nl/onderwerpen/woninginbraak/documenten/hoe-doen-ze-het-toch-modus-operandi-woninginbraak/, 2009, last access date: 31 October, 2017.

[30] T. Coupe and L. Blake, "Daylight and darkness targeting strategies and the risks of being seen at residential burglaries," Criminology, vol. 44, no. 2, 2006, pp. 431–464.

[31] A. Zuur, E. N. Ieno, N. Walker, A. A. Saveliev, and G. M. Smith, Mixed effects models and extensions in ecology with R. Springer, 2009.

[32] R Core Team, R: A Language and Environment for Statistical Computing, 2013, last access date: 31 October, 2017. [Online]. Available: http://www.R-project.org/

Detecting Fake Reviews through Sentiment Analysis Using Machine Learning Techniques

Elshrif Elmurngi, Abdelouahed Gherbi
Department of Software and IT Engineering
École de Technologie Supérieure
Montreal, Canada
Email: elshrif.elmurngi.1@ens.etsmtl.ca, abdelouahed.gherbi@etsmtl.ca

Abstract— **Recently, Sentiment Analysis (SA) has become one of the most interesting topics in text analysis, due to its promising commercial benefits. One of the main issues facing SA is how to extract emotions inside the opinion, and how to detect fake positive reviews and fake negative reviews from opinion reviews. Moreover, the opinion reviews obtained from users can be classified into positive or negative reviews, which can be used by a consumer to select a product. This paper aims to classify movie reviews into groups of positive or negative polarity by using machine learning algorithms. In this study, we analyse online movie reviews using SA methods in order to detect fake reviews. SA and text classification methods are applied to a dataset of movie reviews. More specifically, we compare five supervised machine learning algorithms: Naïve Bayes (NB), Support Vector Machine (SVM), K-Nearest Neighbors (KNN-IBK), KStar (K*) and Decision Tree (DT-J48) for sentiment classification of reviews using two different datasets, including movie review dataset V2.0 and movie reviews dataset V1.0. The measured results of our experiments show that the SVM algorithm outperforms other algorithms, and that it reaches the highest accuracy not only in text classification, but also in detecting fake reviews.**

Keywords- Sentiment Analysis; Fake Reviews; Naïve Bayes; Support Vector Machine; k-Nearest Neighbor; KStar; Decision Tree -J48.

I. INTRODUCTION

Opinion Mining (OM), also known as Sentiment Analysis (SA), is the domain of study that analyzes people's opinions, evaluations, sentiments, attitudes, appraisals, and emotions towards entities such as services, individuals, issues, topics, and their attributes [1]. "The sentiment is usually formulated as a two-class classification problem, positive and negative" [1]. Sometimes, time is more precious than money, therefore instead of spending time in reading and figuring out the positivity or negativity of a review, we can use automated techniques for Sentiment Analysis.

The basis of SA is determining the polarity of a given text at the document, sentence or aspect level, whether the expressed opinion in a document, a sentence or an entity aspect is positive or negative. More specifically, the goals of SA are to find opinions from reviews and then classify these opinions based upon polarity. According to [2], there are three major classifications in SA, namely: document level, sentence level, and aspect level. Hence, it is important to distinguish between the document level, sentence level, and the aspect level of an analysis process that will determine the different tasks of SA. The document level considers that a document is an opinion on its aspect, and it aims to classify an opinion document as a negative or positive opinion. The sentence level using SA aims to setup opinion stated in every sentence. The aspect level is based on the idea that an opinion consists of a sentiment (positive or negative), and its SA aims to categorize the sentiment based on specific aspects of entities.

The documents used in this work are obtained from a dataset of movie reviews that have been collected by [3] and [9]. Then, an SA technique is applied to classify the documents as real positive and real negative reviews or fake positive and fake negative reviews. Fake negative and fake positive reviews by fraudsters who try to play their competitors existing systems can lead to financial gains for them. This, unfortunately, gives strong incentives to write fake reviews that attempt to intentionally mislead readers by providing unfair reviews to several products for the purpose of damaging their reputation. Detecting such fake reviews is a significant challenge. For example, fake consumer reviews in an e-commerce sector are not only affecting individual consumers but also corrupt purchaser's confidence in online shopping [4]. Our work is mainly directed to SA at the document level, more specifically, on movie reviews dataset. Machine learning techniques and SA methods are expected to have a major positive effect, especially for the detection processes of fake reviews in movie reviews, e-commerce, social commerce environments, and other domains.

In machine learning-based techniques, algorithms such as SVM, NB, and DT-J48 are applied for the classification purposes [5]. SVM is a type of learning algorithm that represents supervised machine learning approaches [6], and it is an excellent successful prediction approach. The SVM is also a robust classification approach [7]. A recent research presented in [2] introduces a survey on different applications and algorithms for SA, but it is only focused on algorithms used in various languages, and the researchers did not focus on detecting fake reviews [8]-[12]. This paper presents five supervised machine learning approaches to classify the sentiment of our dataset which is compared with two different datasets. We also detect fake positive reviews and fake negative reviews by using these methods. The main goal of our study is to classify movie reviews as a real reviews or fake reviews using SA algorithms with supervised learning techniques.

The conducted experiments have shown the accuracy of results through sentiment classification algorithms. In both cases (movie reviews dataset V2.0 and movie reviews dataset V1.0), we have found that SVM is more accurate than other methods such as NB, KNN-IBK, KStar, and DT-J48.

The main contributions of this study are summarized as follows:

- Using the Weka tool [29], we compare different sentiment classification algorithms which are used to classify the movie reviews dataset into fake and real reviews.
- We apply the sentiment classification algorithms using two different datasets with stopwords. We realized that using the stopwords method is more efficient than without stopwords not only in text categorization, but also to detection of fake reviews.
- We perform several analysis and tests to find the learning algorithm in terms of accuracy.

The rest of this paper is organized as follows. Section II presents the related works. Section III shows the methodology. Section IV explains the experiment results, and finally, Section V presents the conclusion and future works.

II. RELATED WORKS

Our study employs statistical methods to evaluate the performance of detection mechanism for fake reviews and evaluate the accuracy of this detection. Hence, we present our literature review on studies that applied statistical methods.

A. *Sentiment analysis issues*

There are several issues to consider when conducting SA [13]. In this section, two major issues are addressed. First, the viewpoint (or opinion) observed as negative in a situation might be considered positive in another situation. Second, people do not always express opinions in the same way. Most common text processing techniques employ the fact that minor changes between the two text fragments are unlikely to change the actual meaning [13].

B. *Textual reviews*

Most of the available reputation models depend on numeric data available in different fields; an example is ratings in e-commerce. Also, most of the reputation models focus only on the overall ratings of products without considering the reviews which are provided by customers [14]. On the other hand, most websites allow consumers to add textual reviews to provide a detailed opinion about the product [15] [16]. These reviews are available for customers to read. Also, customers are increasingly depending on reviews rather than on ratings. Reputation models can use SA methods to extract users' opinions and use this data in the Reputation system. This information may include consumers' opinions about different features [17] and [18].

C. *Detecting Fake Reviews Using Machine Learning*

Filter and identification of fake reviews have substantial significance [19]. Moraes et al. [20] proposed a technique for categorizing a single topic textual review. A sentiment classified document level is applied for stating a negative or positive sentiment. Supervised learning methods are composed of two phases, namely selection and extraction of reviews utilizing learning models such as SVM.

Extracting the best and most accurate approach and simultaneously categorizing the customers written reviews text into negative or positive opinions has attracted attention as a major research field. Although it is still in an introductory phase, there has been a lot of work related to several languages [21]-[23]. Our work used several supervised learning algorithms such as SVM, NB, KNN-IBK, K* and DT-J48 for Sentiment Classification of text to detect fake reviews.

D. *A Comparative Study of different Classification algorithms*

Table I shows comparative studies on classification algorithms to verify the best method for detecting fake reviews using different datasets such as News Group dataset, text documents, and movie reviews dataset. It alsoproves that NB and distributed keyword vectors (DKV) are accurate without detecting fake reviews [11] and [12]. While [10] finds that NB is accurate and a better choice, but it is not oriented for detecting fake reviews. Using the same datasets, [8] finds that SVM is accurate with stopwords method, but it does not focus on detecting fake reviews, while [9] finds that SVM is only accurate without using stopwords method, and also without detecting fake reviews. However, in our empirical study, results in both cases with movie reviews dataset V2.0 and with movie reviews dataset V1.0 prove that SVM is robust and accurate for detecting fake reviews.

TABLE I. A COMPARATIVE STUDY OF DIFFERENT CLASSIFICATION ALGORITHMS.

Reference	Year	Data Source	Size of dataset	Using Supervised Learning	Using Unsupervised learning	Language	Classification algorithms	Detecting Fake Review	Using stopwords	The best method
[8]	2013	Movie Reviews dataset	2000 Movie Reviews	yes	no	English	NB,SVM,IBK,DT	no	yes	SVM
[9]	2004	Movie Reviews dataset	2000 Movie Reviews	yes	no	English	NB, SVM	no	no	SVM
[10]	2011	News Group dataset	20 categories with 1000 documents	yes	no	English	NB, SVM	no	yes	NB
[11]	2016	Movie Reviews dataset	4000 movie reviews	yes	no	Chinese	NB, SVM, K-NN LLR, Delta TFIDF, LDA-SVM, TFIDF, DKV	no	no	DKV
[12]	2013	Movie Reviews dataset	1400 Movie Reviews, 2000 Movie Reviews	yes	no	English	NB, SVM	no	no	NB
This work	2017	Movie Reviews dataset	1400 Movie Reviews, 2000 Movie Reviews	Yes	no	English	NB,SVM,IBK,DT-J48	yes	yes	SVM

III. METHODOLOGY

To accomplish our goal, we analyze a dataset of movie reviews using the Weka tool for text classification. In the proposed methodology, as shown in Figure 1, we follow some steps that are involved in SA using the approaches described below.

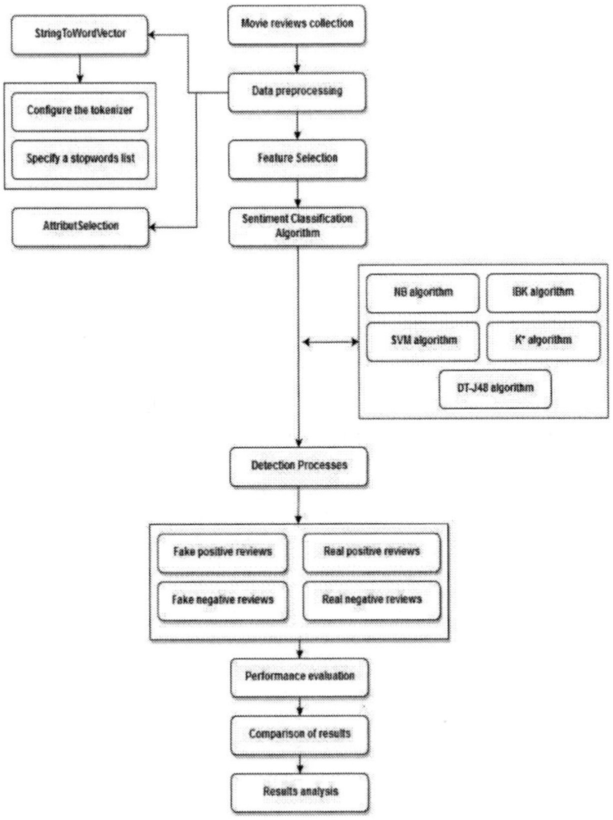

Figure 1. Steps and Techniques used in Sentiment Analysis

Step 1: Movie reviews collection

To provide an exhaustive study of machine learning algorithms, the experiment is based on analyzing the sentiment value of the standard dataset. We have used the original dataset of the movie reviews to test our methods of reviews classification. The dataset is available and has been used in [12], which is frequently conceded as the standard gold dataset for the researchers working in the field of the Sentiment Analysis. The first dataset is known as movie reviews dataset V2.0 which consists of 2000 movie reviews out of which 1000 reviews are positive, and 1000 reviews are negative. The second dataset is known as movie reviews dataset V1.0, which consists of total 1400 movie reviews, 700 of which are positive and 700 of which are negative. A summary of the two datasets collected is described in Table II.

TABLE II. DESCRIPTION OF DATASET

Dataset	Content of the Dataset
Movie Reviews Dataset V2.0	2000 Movie Reviews (1000+ & 1000-)
Movie Reviews Dataset V1.0	1400 Movie Reviews (700+ & 700-)

Step 2: Data preprocessing

The preprocessing phase includes two preliminary operations, shown in Figure 1, that help in transforming the data before the actual SA task. Data preprocessing plays a significant role in many supervised learning algorithms. We divided data preprocessing as follows:

1) StringToWordVector

To prepare the dataset for learning involves transforming the data by using the StringToWordVector filter, which is the main tool for text analysis in Weka. The StringToWordVector filter makes the attribute value in the transformed datasets Positive or Negative for all single-words, depending on whether the word appears in the document or not. This filtration process is used for configuring the different steps of the term extraction. The filtration process comprises the following two sub-processes:

• Configure the tokenizer

This sub-process makes the provided document classifiable by converting the content into a set of features using machine learning.

• Specify a stopwords list

The stopwords are the words we want to filter out, eliminate, before training the classifier. Some of those words are commonly used (e.g., "a," "the," "of," "I," "you," "it," "and") but do not give any substantial information to our labeling scheme, but instead they introduce confusion to our classifier. In this study, we used a 630 English stopwords list with movie reviews dataset V2.0. Stopwords removal helps to reduce the memory requirements while classifying the reviews.

2) Attribute Selection

Removing the poorly describing attributes can significantly increase the classification accuracy, in order to maintain a better classification accuracy, because not all attributes are relevant to the classification work, and the irrelevant attributes can decrease the performance of the used analysis algorithms, an attribute selection scheme was used for training the classifier.

Step 3: Feature Selection

Feature selection is an approach which is used to identify a subset of features which are mostly related to the target model, and the goal of feature selection is to increase the level of accuracy. In this study, we implemented five feature selection methods widely used for the classification task of SA with Stopwords methods. The results differ from one method to the other. For example, in our analysis of Movie

Review datasets, we found that the use of SVM algorithm is proved to be more accurate in the classification task.

Step 4: Sentiment Classification algorithms

In this step, we will use sentiment classification algorithms, and they have been applied in many domains such as commerce, medicine, media, biology, etc. There are many different techniques in classification method like NB, DT-J48, SVM, K-NN, Neural Networks, and Genetic Algorithm. In this study, we will use five popular supervised classifiers: NB, DT-J48, SVM, K-NN, KStar algorithms.

1) Naïve Bayes(NB)

The NB classifier is a basic probabilistic classifier based on applying Bayes' theorem. The NB calculates a set of probabilities by combinations of values in a given dataset. Also, the NB classifier has fast decision-making process.

2) Support Vector Machine (SVM)

SVM in machine learning is a supervised learning model with the related learning algorithm, which examines data and identifies patterns, which is used for regression and classification analysis [24]. Recently, many classification algorithms have been proposed, but SVM is still one of the most widely and most popular used classifiers.

3) K-Nearest Neighbor (K-NN)

K-NN is a type of lazy learning algorithm and is a non-parametric approach for categorizing objects based on closest training. The K-NN algorithm is a very simple algorithm for all machine learning. The performance of the K-NN algorithm depends on several different key factors, such as a suitable distance measure, a similarity measure for voting, and, k parameter [25]- [28].

A set of vectors and class labels which are related to each vector constitute each of the training data. In the simplest way; it will be either positive or negative class. In this study, we are using a single number ''k'' with values of k=3. This number decides how many neighbors influence the classification.

4) KStar (K)*

K-star (K*) is an instance-based classifier. The class of a test instance is established in the class of those training instances similar to it, as decided by some similarity function. K* algorithm is usually slower to evaluate the result.

5) Decision Tree (DT-J48)

The DT-J48 approach is useful in the classification problem. In the testing option, we are using percentage split as the preferred method.

Step 5: Detection Processes

After training, the next step is to predict the output of the model on the testing dataset, and then a confusion matrix is generated which classifies the reviews as positive or negative. The results involve the following attributes:

- True Positive: Real Positive Reviews in the testing data, which are correctly classified by the model as Positive (P).
- False Positive: Fake Positive Reviews in the testing data, which are incorrectly classified by the model as Positive (P).
- True Negative: Real Negative Reviews in the testing data, which are correctly classified by the model as Negative (N).
- False Negative: Fake Negative Reviews in the testing data, which are incorrectly classified by the model as Negative (N).

True negative (TN) are events which are real and are effectively labeled as real, True Positive (TP) are events which are fake and are effectively labeled as fake. Respectively, False Positives (FP) refer to Real events being classified as fakes; False Negatives (FN) are fake events incorrectly classified as Real events. The confusion matrix, (1)-(6) shows numerical parameters that could be applied following measures to evaluate the Detection Process (DP) performance. In Table III, the confusion matrix shows the counts of real and fake predictions obtained with known data, and for each algorithm used in this study there is a different performance evaluation and confusion matrix.

TABLE III. THE CONFUSION MATRIX

	Real	**Fake**
Real	True Negative Reviews (TN)	False Positive Reviews (FP)
Fake	False Negative Reviews (FN)	True Positive Reviews (TP)

Fake Positive Reviews Rate = FP/FP+TN (1)
Fake Negative Reviews Rate = FN/TP+FN (2)
Real Positive Reviews Rate = TP/TP+FN (3)
Real Negative Reviews Rate = TN/TN+FP (4)
Accuracy = TP+TN/TP+TN+FN+FP (5)
Precision = TP/TP+FP (6)

The confusion matrix is a very important part of our study because we can classify the reviews from datasets whether they are fake or real reviews. The confusion matrix is applied to each of the five algorithms discussed in Step 4.

Step 6: Comparison of results

In this step, we compared the different accuracy provided by the dataset of movie reviews with various classification algorithms and identified the most significant classification algorithm for detecting Fake positive and negative Reviews.

IV. EXPERIMENTS AND RESULT ANALYSIS

In this section, we present experimental results from five different supervised machine learning approaches to classifying sentiment of our datasets which is compared with movie review dataset V2.0 and Movie Review dataset V1.0. Also, we have used the same methods at the same time to detect fake reviews.

A. *Experimental result on dataset V2.0*

1) *Confusion matrix for all methods*

The number of real and fake predictions made by the classification model compared with the actual results in the test data is shown in the confusion matrix. The confusion matrix is obtained after implementing NB, SVM, K-NN, K*, DT-J48 algorithms. Table IV displays the results for confusion matrix for V2.0 dataset. The columns represent the number of predicted classifications made by the model.
The rows display the number of real classifications in the test data.

TABLE IV. CONFUSION MATRIX FOR ALL METHODS

Classification algorithms	SA	Real	Fake
NB	Real	781	219
	Fake	187	813
KNN-IBK (K=3)	Real	804	196
	Fake	387	613
K*	Real	760	240
	Fake	337	663
SVM	Real	**809**	**191**
	Fake	**182**	**818**
DT-J48	Real	762	238
	Fake	330	670

2) *Evaluation parameters and accuracy for all methods*

Five main performance evaluation measures have been introduced for Classification algorithms. These include Fake Positive Reviews predictive value, Fake Negative Reviews predictive value, Real Positive Reviews predictive value, Real Negative Reviews predictive value, accuracy and Precision. Table V shows the results of evaluation parameters for all methods and provides a summary of recordings obtained from the experiment. SVM surpasses as the best accuracy among the other classification algorithms with 81.35%. The tabulated observations list the readings as well as accuracies obtained for a specific supervised learning algorithm on a dataset of a movie review.

TABLE V. EVALUATION PARAMETERS AND ACCURACY FOR ALL METHODS.

Classification algorithms	Fake Positive Reviews %	Fake Negative Reviews %	Real Positive Reviews %	Real Negative Reviews %	Precision %	Accuracy %
NB	21.9	18.7	81.3	78.1	78.8	79.7
K-NN-IBK (K=3)	19.6	38.7	61.3	80.4	75.8	70.85
K*	24	33.7	66.3	76	73.4	71.15
SVM	19.1	18.2	81.8	80.9	81.1	**81.35**
DT-J48	23.8	33	67	76.2	73.8	71.6

The graph in Figure 2 shows a rate of Fake Positive Reviews, Fake Negative Reviews, Real Positive Reviews, Real Negative Reviews, Accuracy, and Precision for comparative analysis of all different algorithms.

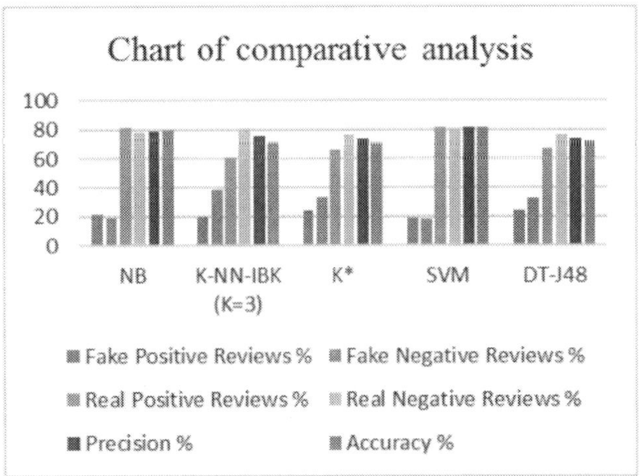

Figure 2. Comparative analysis of all methods

The comparison in Table VI indicates that the classification accuracy of SVM algorithm was better than NB, KNN-IBK, K*, and DT-J48 algorithms.

TABLE VI. COMPARISON OF ACCURACY OF CLASSIFIERS

Classification algorithms	Accuracy %
NB	79.7
KNN-IBK (K=3)	70.85
K*	71.15
SVM	**81.35**
DT-J48	71.6

The graph in Figure 3 shows accuracy rate of NB, SVM, (K-NN, k=3), and DT-J48 algorithms. We obtained a higher accuracy in SVM algorithm than in the other algorithms.

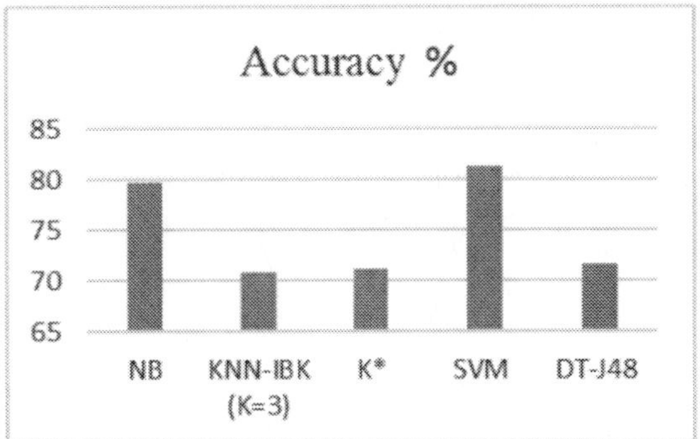

Figure 3. Graph showing the accuracy of different algorithms

Table VII shows the time taken by each algorithm to build prediction model. As it is evident from the table, K-star takes the shortest amount of time of 0 seconds to create a model and SVM takes the longest amount of time of **14840** seconds to build a model.

TABLE VII. TIME TAKEN TO BUILD MODEL

Classification algorithms	Time taken to build model (milliseconds)
NB	110
KNN-IBK (K=3)	10
K*	0
SVM	**14840**
DT-J48	340

B. Experimental results on dataset v1.0

1. Confusion matrix for all methods

The previous section compared different algorithms with different datasets. In this section, the algorithms are applied to perform a sentiment analysis on another dataset. From the results presented in Table VIII, the confusion matrix displays results for movie reviews dataset v1.0.

TABLE VIII. CONFUSION MATRIX FOR ALL METHODS

Classification algorithms	SA	Real	Fake
NB	Real	455	245
	Fake	162	538
KNN-IBK (K=3)	Real	480	220
	Fake	193	507
K*	Real	491	209
	Fake	219	481
SVM	Real	**516**	**184**
	Fake	**152**	**548**
DT-J48	Real	498	202
	Fake	219	481

2. Evaluation parameters and accuracy for all methods

Five main performance evaluation measures have been introduced for Classification algorithms. These include Fake Positive Reviews predictive value, Fake Negative Reviews predictive value, Real Positive Reviews predictive value, Real Negative Reviews predictive value, accuracy and Precision. Table IX displays the results of evaluation parameters for all methods and provides a summary of recordings obtained from the experiment. As a result, SVM surpasses for best accuracy among the other classification algorithms with 76%.

TABLE IX. EVALUATION PARAMETERS AND ACCURACY FOR ALL METHODS

Classification algorithms	Fake Positive Reviews %	Fake Negative Reviews %	Real Positive Reviews %	Real Negative Reviews %	Precision %	Accuracy %
NB	35	23.1	76.9	65	68.7	70.9
K-NN-IBK (K=3)	31.4	27.6	72.4	68.6	69.7	70.5
K*	29.9	31.3	68.7	70.1	69.7	69.4
SVM	26.3	21.7	78.3	73.7	74.9	**76**
DT-J48	28.9	31.3	68.7	71.1	70.4	69.9

The graph in Figure 4 displays a rate of Fake Positive Reviews, Fake Negative Reviews, Real Positive Reviews, Real Negative Reviews, Accuracy, and Precision for comparative analysis of all different algorithms.

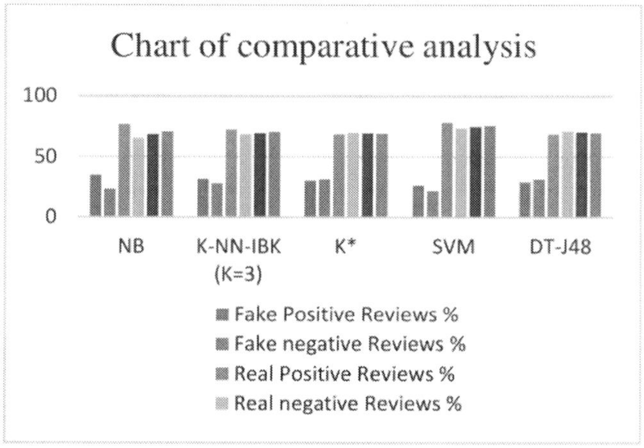

Figure 4. Comparative analysis of all methods

The comparison in Table X indicates that the classification accuracy of SVM algorithm was better than NB, KNN-IBK, and DT-J48 algorithms.

TABLE X. COMPARISON OF ACCURACY OF CLASSIFIERS

Classification algorithms	Accuracy %
NB	70.9
KNN-IBK (K=3)	70.5
K*	69.4
SVM	**76**
DT-J48	69.9

The graph in Figure 5 displays accuracy rate of NB, SVM, (K-NN, k=3), DT-J48 algorithms. We obtained a higher accuracy of SVM algorithm than other algorithms.

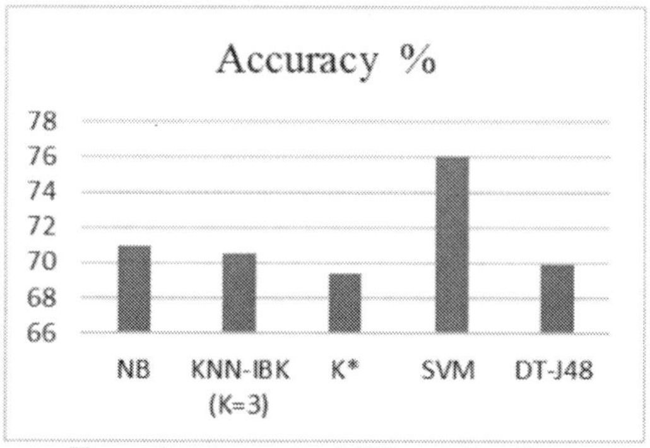

Figure 5. Accuracy of different algorithms

TABLE XI. TIME TAKEN TO BUILD MODEL

Classification algorithms	Time taken to build model (milliseconds)
NB	90
KNN-IBK (K=3)	0
K*	10
SVM	**4240**
DT-J48	330

Table XI displays the time taken by each algorithm to build prediction model. As it is evident from the table, K-NN takes the shortest amount of time of 0 seconds to create a model and SVM takes the longest amount of time of 4.24 seconds to build a model.

C. *Discussion*

Table XII and Figure 6 present the summary of the experiments. Five supervised machine learning algorithms: NB, SVM, K-NN, K*, DT-J48 have been applied to the online movie reviews. We observed that well-trained machine learning algorithms could perform very useful classifications on the sentiment polarities of reviews. In terms of accuracy, SVM is the best algorithm for all tests since it correctly classified 81.35% of the reviews in dataset V2.0 and 76% of the reviews in dataset V1.0. SVM tends to be more accurate than other methods.

TABLE XII. THE BEST RESULT OF OUR EXPERIMENTS

Experiments	Fake Positive Reviews of SVM %	Fake Negative Reviews of SVM %	Precision of SVM %	Accuracy of SVM %
Results on dataset V2.0	**19.1**	**18.2**	81.1	**81.35**
Results on dataset V1.0	**26.3**	**21.7**	74.9	**76**

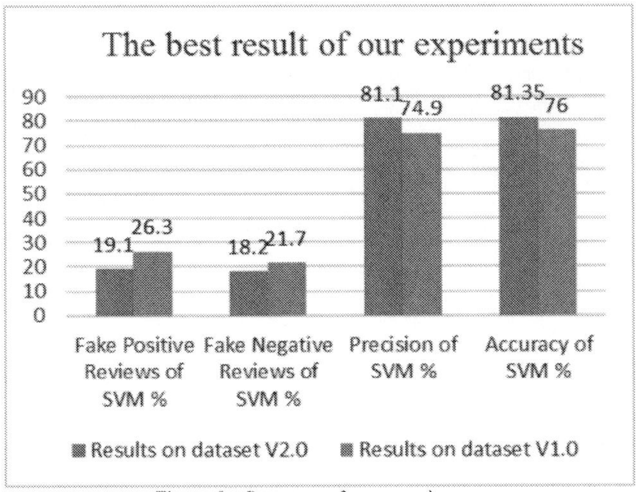

Figure 6. Summary of our experiments

The presented study emphasizes that the accuracy of SVM is higher for Movie Review dataset V2.0. However, the detection process of Fake Positive Reviews and Fake Negative Reviews offers less promising results for Movie Review dataset V2.0 in comparison to Movie Review dataset V1.0 as evident from table XII.

V. CONCLUSION AND FUTURE WORK

In this paper, we proposed several methods to analyze a dataset of movie reviews. We also presented sentiment classification algorithms to apply a supervised learning of the movie reviews located in two different datasets. Our experimental approaches studied the accuracy of all sentiment classification algorithms, and how to determine which algorithm is more accurate. Furthermore, we were able to detect fake positive reviews and fake negative reviews through detection processes.

Five supervised learning algorithms to classifying sentiment of our datasets have been compared in this paper: NB, K-NN, K*, SVM, and DT-J48. Using the accuracy analysis for these five techniques, we found that SVM algorithm is the most accurate for correctly classifying the reviews in movie reviews datasets, i.e., V2.0 and V1.0. Also, detection processes for fake positive reviews and fake negative reviews depend on the best method that is used in this study.

For future work, we would like to extend this study to use other datasets such as Amazon dataset or eBay dataset and use different feature selection methods. Furthermore, we may apply sentiment classification algorithms to detect fake reviews using various tools such as Python and R or R studio, Statistical Analysis System (SAS), and Stata; then we will evaluate the performance of our work with some of these tools.

ACKNOWLEDGMENT

Mr. Elshrif Elmurngi would like to thank the Ministry of Education in Libya and Canadian Bureau for International Education (CBIE) for their support to his Ph.D. research work.

REFERENCES

[1] B. Liu, "Sentiment analysis and opinion mining," Synthesis lectures onhuman language technologies, vol. 5, no. 1, 2012, pp. 1–167.

[2] W. Medhat, A. Hassan, and H. Korashy, "Sentiment analysis algorithmsand applications: A survey," Ain Shams Engineering Journal, vol. 5,no. 4, 2014, pp. 1093–1113.

[3] B. Pang, L. Lee, and S. Vaithyanathan, "Thumbs up? sentiment classi-fication using machine learning techniques," in Proceedings of EMNLP,2002, pp. 79–86. [Online]. Available :http://www.cs.cornell.edu/People/pabo/movie%2Dreview%2Ddata/

[4] J. Malbon, "Taking fake online consumer reviews seriously," Journal ofConsumer Policy, vol. 36, no. 2, 2013, pp. 139–157.

[5] R. Xia, C. Zong, and S. Li, "Ensemble of feature sets and classificationalgorithms for sentiment classification," Information Sciences, vol. 181,no. 6, 2011, pp. 1138–1152.

[6] T. Barbu, "Svm-based human cell detection technique using histogramsof oriented gradients," cell, vol. 4, 2012, p. 11.

[7] G. Esposito, LP-type methods for Optimal Transductive Support VectorMachines. Gennaro Esposito, PhD, 2014, vol. 3.

[8] P. Kalaivani and K. L. Shunmuganathan, "Sentiment classification of movie reviews by supervised machine learning approaches," Indian Journal of Computer Science and Engineering, vol. 4, no. 4, pp. 285-292, 2013.

[9] B. Pang and L. Lee, "A sentimental education: Sentiment analysis usingsubjectivity summarization based on minimum cuts," in Proceedings ofthe 42nd annual meeting on Association for Computational Linguistics.Association for Computational Linguistics, 2004, p. 271. [Online]. Available from: http://www.cs.cornell.edu/People/pabo/movie%2Dreview%2Ddata/

[10] S. Hassan, M. Rafi, and M. S. Shaikh, "Comparing svm and naive bayesclassifiers for text categorization with wikitology as knowledge enrich-ment," in Multitopic Conference (INMIC), 2011 IEEE 14th International.IEEE, 2011, pp. 31–34..

[11] C.-H. Chu, C.-A. Wang, Y.-C. Chang, Y.-W. Wu, Y.-L. Hsieh, and W.-L. Hsu, "Sentiment analysis on chinese movie review with distributedkeyword vector representation," in Technologies and Applications ofArtificial Intelligence (TAAI), 2016 Conference on.IEEE, 2016, pp.84–89

[12] V. Singh, R. Piryani, A. Uddin, and P. Waila, "Sentiment analysis ofmovie reviews and blog posts," in Advance Computing Conference(IACC), 2013 IEEE 3rd International. IEEE, 2013, pp. 893–898.

[13] G. Vinodhini and R. Chandrasekaran, "Sentiment analysis and opinionmining: a survey," International Journal, vol. 2, no. 6, 2012, pp. 282–292.

[14] G. Xu, Y. Cao, Y. Zhang, G. Zhang, X. Li, and Z. Feng, "Trm: Computingreputation score by mining reviews." in AAAI Workshop: Incentives andTrust in Electronic Communities, 2016.

[15] N. Tian, Y. Xu, Y. Li, A. Abdel-Hafez, and A. Josang, "Generating prod-uct feature hierarchy from product reviews," in International Conferenceon Web Information Systems and Technologies.Springer, 2014, pp.264–278.

[16] N. Tian, Y. Xu, Y. Li, A. Abdel-Hafez, and A. Jøsang, "Product featuretaxonomy learning based on user reviews." in WEBIST (2), 2014, pp.184–192.

[17] A. Abdel-Hafez and Y. Xu, "A survey of user modelling in social mediawebsites," Computer and Information Science, vol. 6, no. 4, 2013, p. 59.

[18] A. Abdel-Hafez, Y. Xu, and D. Tjondronegoro, "Product reputationmodel: an opinion mining based approach," in SDAD 2012 The 1stInternational Workshop on Sentiment Discovery from Affective Data,2012, p. 16.

[19] N. Jindal and B. Liu, "Opinion spam and analysis," in Proceedings of the2008 International Conference on Web Search and Data Mining. ACM,2008, pp. 219–230.

[20] R. Moraes, J. F. Valiati, and W. P. G. Neto, "Document-level sentimentclassification: An empirical comparison between svm and ann," ExpertSystems with Applications, vol. 40, no. 2, 2013, pp. 621–633.

[21] B. Liu, M. Hu, and J. Cheng, "Opinion observer: analyzing and com-paring opinions on the web," in Proceedings of the 14th internationalconference on World Wide Web. ACM, 2005, pp. 342–351.

[22] A. Fujii and T. Ishikawa, "A system for summarizing and visualizingarguments in subjective documents: Toward supporting decision making,"in Proceedings of the Workshop on Sentiment and Subjectivity in Text.Association for Computational Linguistics, 2006, pp. 15–22.

[23] L.-W. Ku, Y.-T. Liang, and H.-H. Chen, "Opinion extraction, summariza-tion and tracking in news and blog corpora," in Proceedings of AAAI,2006, pp. 100–107.

[24] C. Cortes and V. Vapnik, "Support-Vector Networks," Machine Learning, vol. 20, 1995.

[25] Y. Song, J. Huang, D. Zhou, H. Zha, and C. L. Giles, "Iknn: Informativek-nearest neighbor pattern classification," in PKDD. Springer, 2007, pp.248–264.

[26] G. Bhattacharya, K. Ghosh, and A. S. Chowdhury, "An affinity-basednew local distance function and similarity measure for knn algorithm,"Pattern Recognition Letters, vol. 33, no. 3, 2012, pp. 356–363.

[27] M. Latourrette, "Toward an explanatory similarity measure for nearest-neighbor classification," Machine Learning: ECML 2000, 2000, pp. 238–245.

[28] S. Zhang, "Knn-cf approach: Incorporating certainty factor to knnclassification." IEEE Intelligent Informatics Bulletin, vol. 11, no. 1, 2010,pp. 24–33.

[29] M. Hall, E. Frank, G. Holmes, B. Pfahringer, P. Reutemann, and I. H.Witten, "The weka data mining software: an update," ACM SIGKDDexplorations newsletter, vol. 11, no. 1, 2009, pp. 10–18.

Aspect Term Extraction from Customer Reviews using Conditional Random Fields

Hardik Dalal
e-mail: hardik.dalal@dal.ca

Qigang Gao
e-mail: qggao@cs.dal.ca

Faculty of Computer Science
Dalhousie University
Halifax, NS Canada

Abstract — E-commerce customers generate a vast amount of information about services and products using comments and blogs. Customer reviews serve as one source of this information and they are a critical aspect of e-Business. Reviews are a vital source of feedback and they also help businesses to determine market trends, demographics, and develop knowledge about their competition. Collecting reviews from customers is only half of the challenge. The other half includes mining these reviews to gain insights. Sentiment Analysis techniques help to extract sentiments and determine the perceived product quality or level of customer satisfaction. Our work is focused on detecting product features from customer reviews which, is a part of Aspect Level Sentiment Analysis research. We address the task by expressing it as a sequence-labeling problem in which features are required to be labeled from sentences. The process is similar to that of Named Entity Extraction (NER). However, we are now targeting a different type of entity, i.e., product features. In comparison to NER, Aspect Term Extraction (ATE) poses unique challenges and we address them using Conditional Random Field (CRF), a conditional probability based model. Using dependency parsing, we have engineered a set of optimum features that allow for promising results.

Keywords – Aspect-based Sentiment Analysis; Aspect-term Extraction; Data Analytics; Conditional Random Fields

I. Introduction

The term 'Social Media' was coined in 1997 but it did not gain much traction in the real world until the Web 2.0 Summit in 2004. During the summit, Tim O'Reilly talked about the commercialization of Web 2.0 and he emphasized user-generated content and its usage. His speech was focused on creating platforms for users with the help of the Internet. Today, customer-generated review websites like Yelp and Amazon have also made major contributions in driving Social Media. Review websites are driven by users who post comments and share their experience about products and services. The content is rich in customer opinions and if used right, it can aid consumers and producers in many ways. However, to make informed decisions based on reviews, consumers have to read thousands of reviews. The overwhelming number of reviews will likely turn down the consumer from reading them. Based on these facts, we realized that the hidden value of customer reviews is never completely appreciated.

The rest of the paper is organized as follows. The remaining subsections of this section describes the research question we asked ourselves to address the problem and challenges faced in solving the problem. Section II talks about the major contributions in the field. Section III describes the data we used by our model. It also explains how we processed the data into feature vector which was fed to our model. Section IV depicts our model of choice and feature selection. Experiment plan, results and evaluation of our model are shown in Section V. Lastly, the paper concludes with the lesson learned and potential future enhancements.

A. *Research Question*

The research question that we ask ourselves in this paper focus on finding meaningful information from a large set of reviews. We intend to answer the following question: how can we extract product aspects from reviews? The answer to the question points to the core technique that is responsible for extracting aspects from reviews.

B. *Challenges*

ATE brings a very unique set of challenges when compared to NER. This is because ATE is different from NER on some fundamental levels. First, aspect terms are describing properties of a product. These aspect terms vary from product to product, e.g. a camera will have 'photo quality' as one of the many aspects, and, similarly 'screen size' for a laptop. An entity on the other hand, falls into one of the following categories: organization, person, location, or miscellaneous [1]. NER systems can detect percentages, ages of people, and dates [2].

Second, an entity usually follows certain characteristics throughout corpus such as capitalized first word, starting with 'the', membership to a group of words, etc. NER also tend to have explicit rules to detect certain type of entities, e.g. a date as an entity has a month and a value less than 32. ATE do not follow such traits because they are mostly nouns. In order to detect aspect terms, other linguistic features are important.

II. Survey on Related Works

There are several key techniques that have been proposed by researchers to solve ATE. For a better understanding, we divide the techniques into four major categories based on the properties of reviews that they exploit. The categories are:

1. Frequency-based
2. Relation-based
3. Supervised learning-based
4. Model-based

In the remaining part of this section, we will discuss notable work that is done in these categories.

A. Frequency-based methods

Frequency-based methods are based on the statistic that most of the aspects are nouns and noun phrases. According to a study by Liu et al. [3], around 60 to 70% of aspects are nouns. This fact is used to find frequent aspects from reviews. There are several techniques proposed, such as Hu et al. [4], which extract aspects by finding frequent nouns. Noun and noun phrases are determined from Part-Of-Speech (POS) tags and a threshold is decided experimentally. It is interesting to note that implicit features only account for 15-20% of the total aspects.

A method proposed by [5] uses a Web-based information retrieval system that used a Pointwise Mutual Information (PMI) score to evaluate the associations between phrases. A score that was estimated from Web search hit counts and the most frequent aspects after applying a threshold was retained.

[6] uses one of the few methods under the frequency-based category that do not rely on external sources like a Web search. The authors devised an unsupervised aspect-related term learning method using linguistic and statistical information. Their method is theoretically domain independent.

B. Relation-based methods

Relation-based approaches exploit syntactic relations among sentences to extract aspects and sentiments. One of these milestones is proposed in [3] and it explores opportunities in Pros, Cons and Review-type formats. The extraction is carried out using a supervise rule discovery, which involves labeling the dataset manually and feeding it to the association rule mining algorithm. The labelled dataset is used to derive an association rule in the form of X->Y with some confidence percentage. One of the key aspects of this work was that they could extract implicit aspects, those that are not specific and possess a hidden reference to an aspect.

[7] proposed a very interesting method to extract aspects by detecting sentiment-laden sentences in reviews and they used only those sentences to extract aspects. The motivation here is that most sentences that express some opinion are likely to target an aspect of products. [8] and [9] used a dependency parser to identify aspects and the sentiments that are associated with them. In [10], the authors developed a better technique to detect aspects and opinions, which was called Double-Propagation. The idea here lies in iteratively going through the syntactic relationships between aspects and sentiment words. Each iteration generates an aspect or sentiment word, which is added to the respective list and it is used in next iteration. This goes on until there are no additions to the list. The sentiment words are mostly adjectives, while the aspect words are nouns or noun phrases.

C. Supervised Learning-based methods

The current state-of-the-art techniques for aspect-based sentiment analysis, under the supervised learning category, are based on the Hidden Markov Model (HMM) and Conditional Random Field (CRF).

In [11], the authors have proposed a supervised learning technique that naturally integrates HMM with linguistic features to extract product feature-opinion pairs. The technique is partially adapted from a very common problem in Information Retrieval (IR), called Named Entity Recognition (NER). The problem of NER is to detect the names of people, places and organizations from text using POS tags. The proposed technique uses POS tags to identify product features and categorize them under components, functions, features and opinions. Based on the position of entities (beginning, middle or end) and the respective category, two tag sets are defined: a basic and pattern tag set. A basic tag set determines the category and a pattern tag set determines the position of the entity. These two sets together form a hybrid tag set that is integrated in HMM to determine the sequence of hybrid tags with higher probability.

A benchmark work using CRF is [12], which allows the extraction of opinion targets (aspects) from a cross-domain scenario. The authors proposed 5 features for their CFR-based approach namely token, POS, short dependency path, word distance and opinion sentence.

D. Model-based methods

Topic modeling in Machine Learning is to learn abstract concepts about available topics from large textual corpuses. There are mainly two models under this category that are used by researchers to detect aspects from product features, Latent Dirichlet Allocation (LDA) and Probabilistic Latent Semantic Indexing (PLSI). The authors in [13] used the extended probabilistic model to extract 'topic-sentiment' pairs from Web logs. The basic assumption was that every blog post is generated from sampling words from a model, which is a combination of a background language model, topic language model, positive sentiment model and negative sentiment model. The authors could extract topics/subtopics, correlations between the topics and relate the sentiments to their respective topics/subtopics.

Our contribution is based on a supervised learning algorithm/model which is independent of Web or outside source. Our model uses a combination of syntactic relations in sentences and probability theory to extract aspect terms. It strikes a good balance between the available techniques in Relation, Supervised Learning and Model-based approaches.

III. Dataset Description and Preparation

We used two datasets from the same source. One of them is freely available dataset from [14] consists of reviews of nine products and most of them are electronic products. Another dataset consisting of three products is also available on the same source. We merged the 12 dataset files into 6 based on the type of product. For example, the Canon PowerShot SD500 and Canon S100 dataset files are merged into Cameras file. The following table represents the number of reviews and aspects in merged files:

TABLE I. NUMBER OF REVIEWS AND ASPECTS IN EACH DATASET

Dataset	# of reviews	# of aspects
Antivirus (A)	380	250
Audio devices (B)	1220	632
Cameras (C)	530	387
Computers (D)	531	354
Mobile phones (E)	554	473
Routers (F)	1191	585

A. *Dataset Description*

Reviews used in this project are of the Free Format type. This format gives freedom to users to express their views and hence the name. This type offers the most challenging research problems as it has the most unstructured information compared to formats that, for example, include a pros and cons part.

A. *Data Preparation*

A text dataset is an unstructured form of information with knowledge that is hidden in a formed relationship among the occurrences of word, order, grammatical relations, etc., We need the data to be in a structured format that can be consumed by the model. The intrinsic relationships are converted to a vector (aka feature vector) that is fed to a model to learn those relationships. The features are chosen closely to address the problem of aspect extraction. Tagging schemes are adopted to encode this information. This is described in detail later in this section.

1) *Tokenization*

We have used the Stanford Tokenizer using Spark to ensure parallel processing. It uses Penn Treebank and a deterministic approach to tokenize a sentence [15].

2) *Tagging*

We used two types of tagging:

a) POS Tagging: We used the Stanford POS Tagger, a part of the Stanford CoreNLP Suite, to tag each review [16].

b) IO Tagging: IO (Inside, Outside) tagging is a very simple yet effective way to encode information to tokens. Each token is either labeled as 'I' if the token is a named entity under consideration and 'O' otherwise.

3) *Dependency Parsing*

We have used the Stanford Dependency Parser to extract relations and we have used head and dependent tokens.

IV. Aspect Term Extraction using Conditional Random Fields

CRF is a generative sequence labelling model. According to Lafferty et al. [17], CRF specifies the probabilities of a sequence based on an observed sequence. The observed sequence, known as features, serves as an input to the model. CRF builds conditional probabilities based on these features. Possibility that a label will occur in a sequence is dependent on the current, previous and future sequence. Lafferty et al. [17], defines CRF as follows:
Let $G = (V, E)$ be a graph such that

$$\boldsymbol{Y} = (\boldsymbol{Y}_v)_{v \in V}$$

Then (X, Y) is a conditional random field in case, when conditioned on $\boldsymbol{X}$, the random variables $\boldsymbol{Y}_v$ obey the following property:

$$p(\boldsymbol{Y}_v|\boldsymbol{X}, \boldsymbol{Y}_w, w \neq v) = p(\boldsymbol{Y}_v|\boldsymbol{X}, \boldsymbol{Y}_w, w \sim v)$$

where $w{\sim}v$ means that w and v are neighbors in G.

Our aim was to handpick the features $\boldsymbol{X}$ so we can construct most accurate probability distribution for a given sequence of tokens. To achieve this aim, we planned to model the features that are capable of providing most accurate information.

A. *Feature Selection*

The selection of features is based on the observation that a word is an aspect not just because of itself but due to the neighboring words and the relationship it shares with those words. These relationships are based on lexical features aka grammar, which are semantic rules of any language. The goal is to learn these relationships using the conditional model. We model CRF so it can identify an aspect based on its POS tag, relative location and relationship to neighboring words and their POS tags.

The features that are chosen for this problem are commonly used in traditional NER systems that use features available from the text itself (also known as closed features) [18]. We are not using any external source to generate a feature vector. The following is the list of features that we use:

1) *Word:* Current (the phrase itself), previous and next word string in lowercase

2) *POS:* POS tag of current, previous and next word. POS tags provide important information about lexical category of words
3) *Head Word:* Syntactic head word of current word according to grammatical structure ('null' if current word does not have a head word)
4) *Head Word POS:* POS tag of head word ('null' if current word does not have a head word)
5) *Dependency Relations:* The dependency relation is identified from a dependency parsing of the review. The Stanford CoreNLP tool contains about 50 grammatical relations between two words [19]. This relationship is binary, meaning that a relation holds between a head (or governor) and a dependent. We derived two features: the relation that the current word shares as a dependent and governor. In other words, we derived the following two features:
    a. the relation when the current word as a governor, and
    b. the relation when the current word is a dependent.
6) *IO tag:* We are interested in modeling CRF so it correctly classifies each aspect as 'I' according to the IO tagging explained in the data preparation step.

Thus, a feature vector for a given sentence will be as follows:

$$x_i = C_i, POS_i, C_{i-1}, C_{i+1}, POS_h, Dep_g, Dep_d, IO_i$$

For example, the feature vector for review "This camera is amazing" is shown below:

x_1 = This, DT, NULL, camera, NULL, det, NULL, O
x_2 = camera, NN, This, is, This, DT, nsubj, det, I
x_3 = is VBZ, camera, amazing, NULL, NULL, amazing, NULL, O
x_4 = amazing, JJ, amazing, NULL, Camera, NN, NULL, nsubj, O

B. *Training and Test the Model*

We used the Apache Spark based implementation of CRF available on GitHub by Intel Big Data group [20]. It is licensed under Apache 2.0 allowing free usage for everyone. We forked from the main branch on GitHub to create our own implementation around it. We preferred not to alter the library and used it as is for the purpose of comparison consistency.

We trained the model on each dataset individually. We used 5-fold cross validation to determine the accuracy of the model.

V. EXPERIMENT AND EVALUATION

The results of ATE are evaluated using following three metrics

$$Precision = \frac{Extracted\ Aspects \cap Gold\ Standard\ Aspects}{Extracted\ Aspects}$$

$$Recall = \frac{Extracted\ Aspects \cap Gold\ Standard\ Aspects}{Gold\ Standard\ Aspects}$$

$$F\text{-}measure = \frac{2 \times Recall \times Precision}{Recall + Precision}$$

The Gold Standard Aspects parameter is the number of aspects originally found in the dataset and the Extracted Aspect parameter represents the number of aspects detected by the model.

A. *Experiment Plan*

In our approach, we used hidden linguistic features that we extracted in the pre-processing step. These features contain a lot of information about the aspects and instead of leaning towards Web sources, we trained our model to use implicit features only. Our plan involves starting out with the bare minimum number of features and progressively adding more and recording the change in performance. This approach seems like trial-and-error, but, compared to NER problem, this problem is unique, and hence handcrafted features usually work best. We also believe that adding too much information might lead to over fitting the model so we wanted to keep the feature vector small.

As said, we are using features we can find from within the data. We found a total of 10 features that we could use to train our model. These features are:

- Current token and its POS, 2 features
- Previous and next token and their POS, 4 features
- Head token and its POS, 2 features
- Dependency relation the current token shares as governor and as dependent, 2 features. Each one is itself a varying size array of values. We also handpicked some of the dependency to improve the performance. These relations are named "selected dependency relations".

The next section shows the results that we recorded during the experiments in condensed tables. The sub columns A, B, C, etc. represents the merged dataset mentioned in Table I.

B. *Experiment Results*

The bare minimum number of features including current, previous and next token and their POS tags resulted in an F-measure of 0.41.

TABLE II. F-MEASURE OBSERVED ON EACH DATASET FROM CURRENT, PREVIOUS AND NEXT TOKEN AND POS TAG

F-measure						Avg
A	*B*	*C*	*D*	*E*	*F*	
0.437	0.572	0.471	0.414	0.414	0.576	0.411

The next major result was observed with similar features but replacing POS tags with selected dependency relations. The average F-measure improved to 0.57 (+0.16).

Table III. F-MEASURE OBSERVED ON EACH DATASET FROM CURRENT, PREVIOUS AND NEXT TOKEN AND SELECTED DEPENDENCY RELATION

F-measure						Avg
A	*B*	*C*	*D*	*E*	*F*	
0.526	0.648	0.548	0.516	0.529	0.689	0.576

A minor increase in F-measure (+0.01) was obtained when we added head token POS instead of selected dependency relationships.

TABLE IV. F-MEASURE OBSERVED ON EACH DATASET FROM CURRENT, PREVIOUS AND NEXT TOKEN AND HEAD TOKEN POS TAG

F-measure						Avg
A	*B*	*C*	*D*	*E*	*F*	
0.535	0.661	0.538	0.548	0.533	0.69	0.584

The best result was observed with head token POS and selected dependency relations. The observed F-measure with such features was 0.58 (+0.18).

TABLE V. F-MEASURE OBSERVED ON EACH DATASET FROM CURRENT, PREVIOUS AND NEXT TOKEN AND HEAD TOKEN POS TAG AND SELECTED DEPENDENCY RELATION

F-measure						Avg
A	*B*	*C*	*D*	*E*	*F*	
0.537	0.657	0.564	0.511	0.556	0.695	0.586

1) Optimal Feature Set

After the experiments shown before, we found the optimal set of features and they are as follows:

- Current token
- Head token POS
- The dependency relation that the current token shares with another token as governor and as dependent

We narrowed down the relationships that the current token shares as governor to only adjectival modifier (amod), nominal subject (nsubj) and dependent (dep) [10]. This is based on the study by Hu et al. [4] indicating that about 60 to 70% of aspects are nouns. So, instead of feeding the model all of the relations, we handpicked a few of them to increase the likelihood of extracting correct aspects. Similarly, we determined the three relations namely nsubj, direct object (dobj), and dep are useful when the current token is dependent as it suggests that the dependent word is likely a noun phrase and hence a potential aspect.

2) SemEval-2014 ABSA Dataset

We also tested our model against datasets provided in Aspect-Based Sentiment Analysis task in the International Workshop on Semantic Evaluation (SemEval-2014) [21]. The conference focuses on evaluating computational semantic analysis systems and falls under the Special Interest Group of the Association for Computational Linguistics. The conference has several tasks and Aspect Based Sentiment Analysis is one of them. The results are shown in Table VI below.

TABLE VI. RESULT OBSERVED ON SEMEVAL DATASET FROM CURRENT, PREVIOUS AND NEXT TOKEN AND HEAD TOKEN POS TAG AND SELECTED DEPENDENCY RELATION

	F-measure	
	Laptop Dataset	*Restaurant Dataset*
SemEval-Baseline	0.356	0.471
Our model	0.507	0.522
SemEval-Best	0.744	0.84

Some of the best works at the conference used SVM like [22] and [23] and CRF like [18] and [24]. [25] shows a very unique contribution by using a combination of SVM and HMM.

C. Experiment Observations

It was interesting to see that certain features like token's POS tags and neighboring token's POS tags proved to be bad for our model. After investigating, we found that this happened due to the tagging scheme that we used. IO tagging shares very limited knowledge of current tokens' neighboring words, meaning that it does not indicate what the next and previous tokens (and its POS tag) are. This also caused issues when tagging multi-word aspects. Multi-word aspects require more information about current tokens such as whether the previous token and current token together represent an aspect or the current token and the next one together represent an aspect. Since our tagging scheme was unable to generate such information, our experiments only tagged one-word aspects during training, which ultimately affected the results.

The head token did not help the model to predict the current token but the head tokens' POS tag did help the model. This is because the head token for aspects varies between train and test data but the POS tag is usually consistent.

We also noticed that some datasets contain words along with symbols that Stanford Tokenizer cannot tokenize. For example, we found "-LRB-" and "-RRB-" in Computer reviews. Such phrases caused the Stanford CoreNLP toolkit to misinterpret relationships and the structure of the sentence. In other words, POS tag and dependency relations associated to tokens were incorrect and the result was a faulty feature vector.

We compared our model with some of the best works submitted in SemEval-2014 ABSA task and found that our features were very limiting. For example, [18] used WordNet, name list and word clusters. When comparing with other type of models such as SVM, we found that results of NER system were fed into the model as a feature like in [23]. The authors of [25] used only lexical features to detect aspects like we did. The difference between our and their feature set was that their feature set included all the features we used and a few more, such as prefixes, suffixes, and POS bigrams and trigrams. In [26], the authors used frequency based information such as PMI and Term Frequency – Inverse Document Frequency (TF-IDF) as features. These features helped them identify commonly occurring aspect terms. Our model did miss some of the commonly occurring aspects because of the lack of frequency based information. They also used NER-based information to identify whether a token is person, place or organization, which we did not.

We did not find any significant work carried our using LDA or other topic-based algorithms. The reason participants did not use LDA for this problem was because of the lack of data available to train the model. LDA suffers from a very common problem called cold start problem. LDA requires substantial amount of information to achieve decent results. A breakthrough research to address the cold start problem using Factorized LDA was published in [27]. The authors modelled reviewers rating along with the reviews to achieve impressive results. Unfortunately, SemEval dataset did not contain reviewers' information.

VI. Conclusion

CRF has its pitfalls, such as the fact that it requires highly accurate labelled training data. However, it is a very good candidate for a sequence labeling problem such as ATE. We recommend using advanced tagging scheme like Before-Inside-Outside (BIO) for labeling tokens. BIO is also advantageous for multi-word aspects. According to [28], there are about 27% aspects in restaurant domain are multi-word aspects, 44% aspects in laptop reviews. BIO is used in many state-of-the-art NER systems and it has proven to be better at tagging schemes then IO. That is because BIO has the potential to carry more informational value then IO.

Feature selection-wise, we strongly believe that a single source of information such as lexical information, is not enough to train high accuracy model. Combination of frequency-based information (e.g. TF-IDF) and open features such as word clusters can definitely help achieve better results. WordNet is an excellent source to form word clusters. Another good option is word2vec. It carries a lot of information in the form of a high dimensional vector. Moreover, the open feature makes the model portable on different datasets.

Computational wise, with the advent of Big Data frameworks like Spark and Hadoop, it is possible to optimize the algorithm. Our implementation is capable of running on a Spark cluster. However, for future work, we recommend bringing Cloud and Big Data Framework together for large scale data processing and effective resource utilization.

References

[1] E. F. T. K. Sang and F. D. Meulder, "Introduction to the CoNLL-2003 Shared Task: Language-Independent Named Entity Recognition," *Proceeding CONLL '03 Proceedings of the seventh conference on Natural language learning at HLT-NAACL 2003 - Volume 4*, vol. 4, pp. 142-147, 2003.

[2] D. M. Bikel, M. Scott, S. Richard, and W. Ralph, "Nymble: a high-performance learning name-finder," *Proceedings of the fifth conference on Applied natural language processing*, pp. 194-201, 1997.

[3] B. Liu, M. Hu, and J. Cheng, "Opinion observer: analyzing and comparing opinions on the Web," *Proceedings of the 14th International conference on World Wide Web - WWW '05*, pp. 342-351, 2005.

[4] M. Hu and B. Liu, "Mining and summarizing customer reviews," *KDD '04 Proceedings of the tenth ACM SIGKDD international conference on Knowledge discovery and data mining*, pp. 168-177, 2004.

[5] O. Etzioni et al. "Web-scale information extraction in knowitall," *WWW '04 Proceedings of the 13th international conference on World Wide Web*, pp. 100-110, 2004.

[6] J. Zhu, H. Wang, B. K. Tsou, and M. Zhu, "Multi-aspect opinion polling from textual reviews," *CIKM '09 Proceedings of the 18th ACM conference on Information and knowledge management*, pp. 1799-1802, 2009.

[7] S. Blair-Goldensohn, K. Hannan, R. McDonald, T. Neylon, G. Reis and J. Reynar, "Building a sentiment summarizer for local service reviews," *Proceedings of the WWW2008 Workshop: NLP in the Information Explosion Era (NLPIX 2008)*, vol. 14, pp. 339-348, April 2008.

[8] N. Kobayashi, R. Iida, K. Inui, and Y. Matsumoto, "Opinion Mining on the Web by Extracting Subject-Aspect-Evaluation Relations," *AAAI Spring Symposium: Computational Approaches to Analyzing Weblogs*, pp. 86-91, 2006.

[9] S. Somasundaran, G. Namata, L. Getoor, and J. Weibe, "Opinion graphs for polarity and discourse classification," *TextGraphs-4 Proceedings of the 2009 Workshop on Graph-based Methods for Natural Language Processing*, pp. 66-74, 2009.

[10] G. Qiu, B. Liu, J. Bu, and C. Chen, "Opinion word expansion and target extraction through double propagation," *Computational Linguistics*, vol. 37, no. 1, pp. 9-27, 2011.

[11] W. Jin and H. H. Ho, "A novel lexicalized HMM-based learning framework for web opinion mining," *ICML '09 Proceedings of the 26th Annual International Conference on Machine Learning*, pp. 465-472, 2009.

[12] N. Jakob and I. Gurevych, "Extracting opinion targets in a single-and cross-domain setting with conditional random fields," *EMNLP '10 Proceedings of the 2010 Conference on Empirical Methods in Natural Language Processing*, pp. 1035-1045, 2010.

[13] Q. Mei, X. Ling, M. Wondra, H. Su, and C. Zhai, "Topic sentiment mixture: modeling facets and opinions in weblogs," *WWW '07 Proceedings of the 16th International conference on World Wide Web*, pp. 171-180, 2007.

[14] B. Liu and M. Hu, "Opinion Mining, Sentiment Analysis, and Opinion Spam Detection Dataset," University of Illinois at Chicago (UIC), [Online]. Available: https://www.cs.uic.edu/~liub/FBS/sentiment-analysis.html#datasets. [Accessed 1 November 2017].

[15] C. D. Manning, P. Raghavan and H. Schutze, Introduction to Information Retrieval, Cambridge University Press, 2008.

[16] D. Jurafsky and J. H. Martin, "Chapter 8 - Word Classes and Part-of-Speech Tagging," in *Speech and Language Processing*, Prentice-Hall Inc., 2000, pp. 310-319.

[17] J. Lafferty, M. Andrew, and P. Fernando CN, "Conditional random fields: Probabilistic models for segmenting and labeling sequence data," *Proceedings of the 18th International Conference on Machine Learning 2001 (ICML 2001)*, pp. 282-289, June 2001.

[18] Z. Toh and W. Wang, "DLIREC: Aspect Term Extraction and Term Polarity Classification System," *Proceedings of the 8th International Workshop on Semantic Evaluation (SemEval 2014)*, pp. 235-240, August 2014.

[19] d. M. Marie-Catherine and C. D. Manning, "Stanford typed dependencies manual," ResearchGate, 2008.

[20] P. Meng, H. Cheng, and Q. Huang, "CRF-Spark," Intel, 14 November 2016. [Online]. Available: https://github.com/Intel-bigdata/CRF-Spark. [Accessed 1 November 2017].

[21] M. Pontiki et al. "SemEval-2014 Task 4: Aspect Based Sentiment Analysis," *Proceedings of the 8th International Workshop on Semantic Evaluation (SemEval 2014)*, pp. 27-35, 5 December 2014.

[22] J. Wagner et al. "DCU: Aspect-based Polarity Classification for SemEval Task 4," *Proceedings of the 8th International Workshop on Semantic Evaluation (SemEval 2014)*, pp. 223–229, 23-24 August 2014.

[23] S. Kiritchenko, X. Zhu, C. Cherry, and S. M. Mohammad, "NRC-Canada-2014: Detecting Aspects and Sentiment in Customer Reviews," *The 8th International Workshop on Semantic Evaluation (SemEval 2014)*, pp. 437–442, 23024 August 2014.

[24] T. &. K. Brychcin and J. Michal & Steinberger, "UWB: Machine Learning Approach to Aspect-Based Sentiment Analysis," *The 8th International Workshop on Semantic Evaluation (SemEval 2014)*, pp. 817-822, 23-24 August 2014.

[25] G. Castellucci, S. Filice, D. Croce, and R. Basili, "UNITOR: Aspect Based Sentiment Analysis with Structured Learning," *The 8th International Workshop on Semantic Evaluation (SemEval 2014)*, pp. 761–767, 23-24 August 2014.

[26] M. Chernyshevich, "IHS R&D Belarus: Cross-domain Extraction of Product Features using Conditional Random Fields," *Proceedings of the 8th International Workshop on Semantic Evaluation (SemEval 2014)*, pp. 309-313, 23-24 August 2014.

[27] S. Moghaddam and M. Ester, "The FLDA Model for Aspect-based Opinion Mining: Addressing the Cold Start Problem," *Proceedings of the 22nd international conference on World Wide Web*, pp. 909-918, 2013.

[28] P. Blinov and E. Kotelnikov, "Blinov: Distributed Representations of Words for Aspect-Based Sentiment Analysis at SemEval 2014," *Proceedings of the 8th International Workshop on Semantic Evaluation (SemEval 2014)*, pp. 140–144, 23-24 August 2014.